The Motives of Self-Sacrifice in Korean American Culture, Family, and Marriage

The Motives of Self-Sacrifice in Korean American Culture, Family, and Marriage

From Filial Piety to Familial Integrity

Chul Woo Son

WIPF & STOCK · Eugene, Oregon

THE MOTIVES OF SELF-SACRIFICE IN KOREAN AMERICAN CULTURE, FAMILY, AND MARRIAGE
From Filial Piety to Familial Integrity

Copyright © 2013 Chul Woo Son. All rights reserved. Except for brief quotations in critical publications or reviews, no part of this book may be reproduced in any manner without prior written permission from the publisher. Write: Permissions. Wipf and Stock Publishers, 199 W. 8th Ave., Suite 3, Eugene, OR 97401.

Wipf & Stock
An Imprint of Wipf and Stock Publishers
199 W. 8th Ave., Suite 3
Eugene, OR 97401

www.wipfandstock.com

ISBN 13: 978-1-62564-160-1

Manufactured in the U.S.A.

Contents

The Paradox of Sacrifice by David Augsburger vii
Acknowledgments xiii

Introduction 1

1 Self-Sacrifice and Cultural Virtues: Yielding and Filial Piety 9
2 Self-Sacrifice and Marital Expectations: Yielding and Dominance/Submission 38
3 Self-Sacrifice and Gender Inequality: Yielding as Women's Destiny 75
4 Self-Sacrifice and Marital Violence: Yielding and Chronic Abuse 104
5 Empirical Study on Self-Sacrifice in Korean American Relationship: Reality and Motives 141
6 Toward a More Authentic Approach to Self-Sacrifice 183

Appendix 193
Bibliography 223

The Paradox of Sacrifice

What Is It about The Concept of Sacrifice that Causes Us Such Pause?

AN AUTHENTIC AND GENUINE sacrifice is offered as a gift; a coerced, seduced, inveigled sacrifice is not authentic, not genuine, because it is extorted, not freely given.

The former rises out of the generosity of spirit, the richness of experienced and expressed grace; the later out of fear, intimidation, or false pretenses and promises. We see exemplars of grace-ful sacrifice and we are awed, or humbled, or challenged to do likewise; we see instances of fearful sacrifice and are appalled at injustice, at arrogance, at inhumanity.

Exploitive sacrifice is all too common; free generous sacrifice so uncommon that it gives us pause in surprise. Voluntary loving sacrifice is a gift. But even here we must pause again to define gift. Is it a free expression of the stubborn love we know as grace, or is it an encumbered contribution made as an investment and guaranteed to payback in time? We tend to give nothing free of charge and to receive nothing free of charge. But a voluntary sacrificial 'gift' should mean an utterly free, pure, obligationless gift with absolutely no expectations. Anything else is a loan, or an investment.

If we give expecting returns, to "Pay it forward" in the confidence that another will do the same for us, we are still giving with strings attached. The beliefs that support this coming payback—"*The circle will close.—Benefits will return—*" still puts the gift into the greed, not the grace column.

What if we move from an economy of ownership, an economy of scarcity, to an economy of grace, of giving, of gifts? Then sacrifice might become a usable word

Traditionally sacrifice was a noble concept. We look to those who have given themselves for the good of others with admiration and gratitude; sacrifice however, can be a ritualized ruse for exploiting the other to gain self-serving advantage. We have seen too many persons, who demand sacrifice of others, manage to extract significant gain from that sacrifice. Since greed is the true opposite of sacrifice, then it is not hard to see how lust for power, greed for affluence, drive for high success, desire for fame and popularity all require the sacrifice of many to make possible the demands and dreams of the few. Small wonder the dominant groups of society are willing to see the non-dominate minorities make the sacrifices that result from economic decisions made in the board rooms and corner offices of sky scrapers.

Sacrifice is a central concept in Christian thought, it is one of the great words in Christian theology, but it has become a relatively unused word in the theological vocabulary of practical theology. To be sure, the obligation to sacrifice still exists in every culture, but the contemporary assumption that one should be able to assist or serve to fulfill the self, not sacrifice the self, makes us unwilling to talk about sacrifices we must make or obligations we must fulfill.

Dr Chul Woo Son has brought both the word sacrifice and the practices of sacrifice back into open conversation and reconsideration in this outstanding work. It's original occasion was his doctoral dissertation entitled, "The Motives of Self-Sacrifice in Korean-American Culture, Family and Marriage: From Filial Piety to Familial Integrity." Now he has made it available to a much wider audience. Dr Son asks searching, and for pastoral therapists, genuinely troubling questions—like when is sacrifice appropriate and morally right? Or when is sacrifice exploitive and abusive? When is a greater good so crucial that one will offer everything in its service? And when is sacrifice imposed by those who dominate? When does justice demand that the call for sacrifice be fully reviewed and perhaps refused? The questions of sacrifice are crucial not just to the issues that determine balance of give and take in gender roles, marriage relationships, parental obligations to the generation that precede and the generation that follows, they are central to all human relationships. This concern, and the assumptions that reside particularly in Korean culture, led Dr Son to not just carefully examine the literature on sacrifice but to do empirical research on motives

The Paradox of Sacrifice

in Korean married partners to identify their understanding for choosing to make sacrifices within relationships. As a marital and family counselor, Dr. Son has thought long about cultural patterns that allow and sacralize the imposition of sacrifice on women for the comfort and advantage of men. Such sacrifice poisons relationships and poisons the love that links the two persons in marriage and the multiple persons into families.

Here is where constructive theology breaks out in his work. He examines the cultural patterns that permit and make permanent the dominant—submissive pairs, the top-down hierarchies, and points to the New Testament vision of the upside down marriage—a creative adjustment in a maladjusted world.

Primary problem: throughout the world, in every culture, males claim entitlement to dominate. Son explores how this is true in Korean culture, but we all recognize as we read his analysis that it is tragically true in most cultures, and oppressively true in sub-groups within any culture.

Secondary problem: throughout the world, in every culture, females are forced to yield to this dominance. Involuntary and non-voluntary sacrifice is prescribed, demanded, enforced in destructive ways.

Revolutionary answer to this problem: In the New Testament epistles, such as Galatians chapter three and Ephesians chapter five, St Paul teaches revolutionary mutual submission, where each seeks the other's good, each cares for the other's needs in a way that turns any and every culture's male and female relationships upside down. We are free to relate in new ways of equality and loving harmony that cares for the other's needs equally as for one's own, that is free to care for one's own needs as well. Here is the new situation that we find when we are "in Christ."

> "Once we have faith in Christ, we are completely free from [all governing] authority. For now that you have faith in Christ Jesus you are all children {sons and daughters} of God." (Gal 3:25–26, J. B. Phillips translation)

Then Paul sets the ultimate goal in Christ (in the church). It is *equality before God*.

> "All of you who were baptized "into" Christ have put on the family likeness of Christ. Gone is the distinction between Jew and Greek, slave and free man, male and female—you are all one in Christ Jesus. And if you belong to Christ, you are true descendants of Abraham, you are true heirs of his promise." (Galatians 3:27–29, J. B. Phillips translation)

The Paradox of Sacrifice

This is Paul's high moment of teaching how to embody the love of Jesus. This is his manifesto of Christian harmony in equality. The church is slow in practicing this most central truth, so he is setting believers on the trajectory toward this creative harmony of "neither male nor female."

However, in the social order, in the community, and in the people gathering to become the church of Jesus Christ, there is still a) slavery, b) racial superiority, c) male entitlement and dominance in practice in the church. Paul sees this slowness to claim the freedom, equality and harmony that is embodied in Jesus, and he teaches a way to revolutionize it in a change process that will work, will last, will triumph. So to the Ephesian believers he writes,

> "Live life then, with a due sense of responsibility, not as men and women who do not know the meaning and purpose of life but as those who do. . . . .and "fit in with" each other, because of your common reverence for Christ. (Ephesians 5:15, 21. Phillips)

Then Paul follows with the revolutionary idea. Women do not have to submit or adapt, but (in covenantal solidarity) they may choose to do so voluntarily in relationship with men who choose to step down from any entitlement and take the way of the servant (in covenantal self-sacrifice and service). If men learning about authentic Jesus style love, lay down their cultural entitlement to lead or to be dominant, women in reciprocal love can adapt and come to meet them. In short form, Paul says:

"Women, you are free to choose. Any and all submission is voluntary. You have a choice, and I am suggesting that where there are differences or decisions where you differ, you learn creative ways to join with your husband in a voluntary search for harmony, and learn that it is necessary to yield a part of your wants and wishes in order to find a mutually satisfactory solution."

"Men, you are free to change. Your culture and society gives you certain male privileges that are no longer acceptable to those who follow Jesus. You must learn to sacrifice, as Jesus did; submit to the greater good, as Jesus did; serve in concern for the other's welfare, as Jesus did; even give up all that is dear to you for the safety and security of the other, as Jesus did. Turn privilege upside down, as Jesus did (see Phil 2: 1–12) You have the privilege of initiating a new harmony, new equality, a new non-toxic love that is not contaminated with dominance and power, as Jesus did."

So then men are counseled to ask: What can I sacrifice to level the field with the one I love? What can I sacrifice to respect her power to choose, think, act in full expression of her insight, gifts, abilities? How can I sacrifice to change all dominance into loving mutual cooperation and collaboration?

So then women are encouraged to ask: What can I do to freely and voluntarily come to meet a man who is seeking equality? What can I yield to adapt to a more harmonious life together? How can I be flexible and willing to give up parts of what I may want at the moment to get the whole of a mutual, just and balanced loving relationship?

Sacrifice, as voluntary, loving, self-giving in grace, becomes a normal, natural, neutral concept in relationships. It can challenge cultural patterns where sacrifice as non-voluntary, possessive, other-exploiting manipulating greed is destructive to both partners.

This brief sketch of the paradox of sacrifice may help set the stage for you, as reader, to delve into the richness of Chul Won Son's thinking and theological reflecting on marriage, culture, personalities and relationships and the deeper possibilities for their transformation in Christian practice.

David Augsburger
Fuller Theological Seminary, Pasadena, CA

Acknowledgments

I OWE A DEBT of gratitude to my mentor and spiritual father, Dr. David Augsburger for his passion, insights, valuable feedback, and direction. His loving support, encouragement, amazing erudition and direction have been crucial to completing this dissertation. In fact, I can only confess that the completion of this dissertation would not have been possible without his guidance. Also, I would like to give my special thanks to Dr. Cameron Lee who has read my yet lacking dissertation and helped the statistical analysis of its survey, and Dr. Ron Hammer who has guided me as clinical supervisor, teaching me much about actual counseling and about ways of the helping hand and heart. I would also like to thank professor Kwan Jik Lee of Chongshin University in Korea, who has never spared a good word of advice whenever necessary.

More than anything I thank my lovely wife Sun-young and my children Timothy and Rachel, who have never held back their enthusiastic support and prayer up to the very completion of this dissertation. Trusting a husband and father who leaves more to be desired, the completion of this dissertation was only possible through the sacrifice and encouragement of my family, who never spared any.

I extend my gratitude to Dr. Rev. Eung-Yeol Ryu of the Korean Central Presbyterian Church, Rev. Chang Soo Ro, the Sarang Community Church, Rev. Young-kil Kim of the Thanksgiving Church, and Rev. Jung-myung Song of the Mijoo Peace Church. I am also indebted to family and friends that have contributed in prayer and support: Father- Moo-hong Son, Mother- Mi-ja Kim, Sister-Jung-hwa Son, Brother-Chang-woo Son, Chang-yeol Jeong and his wife, Sin-ja Jeong and Seung-hwan Jeong and his wife, Hye-jin Jeong. A special thank goes to my friend Charlie Koo and Yong Jin Choe for editing some parts of this dissertation in the midst of a busy schedule.

Acknowledgments

    Lastly I confess that all of this is God's grace. The beginning of this book through its completion was the grace of God, allowing my meeting of only too great a professors and partners was also the grace of God, and all the glory I lift to God, who has always been at my side, being my strength.

    Chul Woo Son

Introduction

THE CONCEPT OF SELF-SACRIFICE is so essential to both human love and Christian life that we can no longer ignore this issue en route to becoming mature persons. We as Christians are called to love and serve each other. This is often demanded as part of the Christian life: "Love your God and your neighbor as yourselves" is what Jesus commands us to do (Matt 22:37–40). The images of love found throughout the history of Christianity have implications for a Christian view of families and for the practice of self-sacrifice in family relationships.

The book *From Culture Wars to Common Ground* presents different models of love.[1] At one extreme, some Christians have identified love as self-sacrifice on behalf of others, be that husbands, wives, children, neighbors, strangers, or enemies. This meaning of Christian love has been associated with the Greek word *agape*. In this view, love becomes largely duty, commitment, and fidelity, without thought of reciprocation from others.

At the other extreme, love is identified as individual self-fulfillment. To love another is to feel elation, enrichment, passion, and even pleasure. This form of love is associated with the Greek word *eros*. In this view, the idea of sacrifice holds dark and unhappy meanings. There may be a role for love as self-sacrifice, but at most it is a necessary evil.

A middle view defines love as mutuality. Some scholars call love *equal regard*.[2] Love as equal regard includes elements of eros and sacrificial self-giving, but it moderates the two toward an equal concern for oneself and the other. Browning et al. believe that love as equal regard also was construed as the central meaning of agape as used in the New Testament.[3] In Browning's

---

1. Browning et al., *From Culture Wars to Common Ground*, 101–28.
2. Ibid., 101.
3. Ibid.

view, and in my own, love as equal regard is the most adequate view of love for families, since love in which self-sacrifice is central can easily be misappropriated to avoid conflict or dissatisfaction within the family unit. In the case of Korean cultural conditioning, family members try to avoid any potential conflict within the family dynamics, preferring to succumb to the other members' points of view and consequently ignoring their own needs. In addition, self-sacrifice can be used as a tool to emotionally manipulate one another—this is frequently employed against (culturally) weaker members, especially women and children, as duty or obligation. It is important in a family relationship that members cultivate a mutual sense of respect and service, granting one another the necessary space to act on their own developing discretions. It would be helpful to envision sacrificial love not as a unilateral expectation, but rather as bilateral service and giving.

For the Korean American family, in all familial relationships (spousal, parental, and sibling), responsibility to the family comes above all else. For Korean Americans, sacrifice for family and others is often not only demanded but assumed. In addition, in Korean American family relationships, unilateral (one-sided) sacrifice is the most cherished virtue. It is common for parents to give up everything for their children. Korean American families place a high value on the family unit rather the individual (this especially holds true for the male members of the family). An individual's personal action reflects not only on himself but also on his immediate and extended family, as well as his ancestors. An individual is expected to function in his or her clearly defined roles and positions in the family hierarchy, based on age, gender, and social class. Moreover, Confucianism's central teaching places children's fidelity to their parents as one of the most important principles. Though there are precepts (or teachings) of how parents should relate to their child, the most important is the expected fidelity to the parent. This then sets the patriarchal family relationship as the norm. To show disobedience or disrespect to the father is akin to showing such to the king. To quote a well-known Korean proverb, "Loyalty to country, obedience to parents." This family-centered mindset, with absolute obedience to the father, created the norm in Korean American culture that children (daughters, especially) must unilaterally sacrifice for their parents, to the point that it became a virtue. It is natural that the responsibility that was once held by the parents to care for their children will pass down to children to care for their parents.

Introduction

However, the misunderstanding of, and improper motives for, self-sacrifice can be detrimental to family relationships. To view love as merely the sacrifice of oneself to another is to misunderstand love in its totality. Love and the act of sacrifice should be balanced and fair, non-exploitive, caring, strong, mutual and resourceful. A distorted view of self-sacrifice can lead to a self-demanding and addictive way of life. What seems like self-sacrifice to other people may manifest itself in negative side effects (consequences) such as anger, depression, and domestic violence. Therefore, it will take a great deal of courage to question such a fundamental belief for all Koreans. For this reason, it is an urgent task for us to define what healthy motivations are for self-sacrifice within the Korean family and church.

When choosing this topic of self-sacrifice, I expected that there would be an abundance of research and material available. However, it is surprising to say that remarkably little empirical attention has been directed toward understanding the motives and consequences of willing sacrifice in family relational dynamics. There is very little literature that focuses on the motives behind self-sacrifice. I found a few titles under self-sacrifice within cultural, historical feminine and martyr perspectives, but the extant material that delves deeply into the notion of equal regard in the family as a feature of love and self-sacrifice is very few and far between. This is indicative of a notable disinterest in the overall topic of mutuality and self-sacrifice.

This paper will deal with self-sacrifice within the context of Korean and Korean American immigrants' culture and family relationships. In the first chapter, I will seek to explore how self-sacrifice is understood and practiced in Korean culture and society. At its core, the Korean culture is Confucian. Confucian values are felt in every level of family life and are dominant in forming the moral fabric of Korean society. It is important to explore how Confucianism has influenced the concept of self-sacrifice in Korean family dynamics. The family dynamics of Korean Americans undoubtedly differ from the dynamics of native Korean families, especially for second-generation Korean American immigrants influenced by the individualistic American culture. To those Korean Americans, the concept of sacrifice taught by the Confucian teachings may be unfamiliar, even strange. However, for most first-generation Korean immigrant families, they hold onto their Korean culture as a security blanket against the foreign American culture. They essentially remain as an island in a sea of dominant culture. Many Korean Americans, as castaways on these cultural islands, are still deeply influenced by Confucian culture, whether they realize this or not.

In the first chapter, I will delve into the following questions: How has Confucianism influenced the concept of self-sacrifice in Korean family relational dynamics? How is self-sacrifice taught in the framework of Confucianism, and more importantly, how is it understood and received? How is this manifested in family and societal relationship dynamics among Koreans? Finally, how is self-sacrifice perceived by the Korean culture? The examination of the entire tradition of Confucianism, two and a half thousand years of history, is beyond the scope of this research. Instead, I will limit my focus to how the teachings of Confucianism on human relationship influence Korean family relationships.

Although Confucian filial piety is still a dominant ethos of Korean family and society, rapid modernization and Western cultural influences have reduced some of its influence. At the conclusion of the first chapter, I will discuss the major transition under way in Korean society from a traditional to a modern culture. I will also explore how Koreans look at the concept of self-sacrifice from a new perspective, incorporating the Western cultural value of individualism.

In chapter 2, I will explore self-sacrifice and marital expectations. I will provide the case study of an interracial marriage between an American man and a first-generation Korean immigrant woman. I will discuss yielding and dominance/submission within a Korean American marriage relationship. I will also explore the imbalance within Korean marriage and the dilemmas this creates, suggesting that renewal is needed and that intercultural experience can be revealing and helpful. I believe this case study will provide a revealing example of a typical interracial couple's marital problems centered around cultural differences, language barriers, and contrasting family backgrounds. Through this case study, I will discuss some underlying features of Korean American couples, utilizing Bowen family systems theory, outlining some efficiencies and deficiencies in applying this framework to the context of Korean American couples. This evaluation will be mainly focused on how to help Korean women in interracial marriage with American men, because I expect to spend most of my time dealing with the issues of Korean women in my future ministry. Finally, I will give some theological implications and practical suggestions for pastors and counselors in their ministries.

Introduction

In chapter 3, I will explore self-sacrifice and gender inequality. I will discuss Korean gender relationships and the need for a new paradigm. This chapter focuses on the negative side effects of self-sacrifice and self-denial on a woman's self-development. In addition, I will deal with the unique cultural background of Korean women, which can produce negative self-sacrifice and self-denial at home and in their faith communities. In fact, Korean society has been established upon patriarchal and Confucian thought. In a society shaped by Confucian philosophy, Korean women have been denied their full humanity and trained to serve others and to live a life of complete self-sacrifice, neglecting their own needs, wishes, and desires for the sake of family and others, especially men. In looking at cultural background, I will look at the characteristics of Confucian society and the theology of *Han*. I will also deal with how Confucian and patriarchal culture contributes to Korean women's self-denial and self-sacrifice in the context of their "*Han*-laden" life. I will ask how to release this *Han* and redirect it creatively. In exploring this issue, I understand that the behavior of self-sacrifice and self-denial occur at all socioeconomic levels and within all psychological and cultural levels. However, I will limit my focus to an analysis of how theological and cultural traditions contribute to women's self-sacrifice and self-denial. At the conclusion of this chapter, I will propose some theological and practical suggestions for how pastors and Christian counselors can help women maintain their self-esteem and self-care at home and in their community.

In chapter 4, I will explore self-sacrifice and marital violence. I will argue that in Korean marriage, dominance has excused violence. I will explore the relationship between self-sacrifice and domestic violence in the Korean family. This chapter will focus on domestic violence against spouses, wives in particular, within cultural, theological, and practical perspectives, though it must be understood that domestic violence occurs at all socioeconomic levels. I will also explore how self-sacrifice imposed on women in Korean culture is related to domestic violence. In addition, I will present some of the deficiencies in Christian teaching and theology, which fail to address the issues of domestic violence and self-sacrifice. Finally, I will propose several theological resources that can deeply and positively direct pastoral interactions with victims of domestic violence. With this understanding, we will have a broader perspective on the behavior of Korean self-sacrifice.

In chapter 5, I will turn my focus to the reality of the motives out of which Korean American immigrants choose to make self-sacrifice. I will present the way in which Korean American families experience self-sacrifice. This chapter will uncover the attitudes, beliefs, and motives of self-sacrifice for Korean Americans. In what relationships do they more often make personal self-sacrifice? With what motives do they make self-sacrifice? I hope that the findings of this research will offer data for pastors, pastoral counselors, and educators on the nature and function of attitudes in caring and interdependent relationships. By recognizing and identifying the attitudes, beliefs, and motives behind self-sacrifice, I hope to help Korean Americans shift their motives for self-sacrifice from unhealthy obligation to more voluntary care-giving that is relationally healthy and mutually beneficial. Furthermore, by providing this data, I hope to provide pastors and pastoral counselors a valuable resource in counseling Korean Americans, identifying and counseling victims of domestic violence who may be driven by misconceptions of self-sacrifice. I hope to offer a new vision of equality and mutuality for all Korean American families.

In the final chapter, I will attempt to answer a significant question that is relevant to many Korean American pastors and pastoral counselors: How will we bridge the gap between the deficiencies of Confucian understanding of self-sacrifice and mutual love as prescribed by a Christian perspective? I will follow this up with a new approach and model, with a proposal for a healthier and a more judicious understanding of self-sacrifice for Korean American family relationships.

Finally, in this dissertation I will seek to understand the practice of self-sacrifice in a theological, psychological, social, and cultural context. In fact, practical theology is an active process of reflection on the practice of ministry from the perspective of theological understanding. It includes, in the dialogical process, reflection and conversation with multiple languages—those of psychology and psychotherapy, anthropology and the study of cultures, sociology and community theory, systems theory and its application to marriage, family, community and society, political science and its understanding of the social order, as well as other parallel fields in human relations, organizational theory and the practices of care-giving. Seen in this perspective, the practice of pastoral theology is a multilevel conversation that seeks the correlation of fields of knowledge and human services, a multilingual dialogue of integration and interaction that leads to thoughtful and appropriate interventions in the lives of persons and

Introduction

groups. This conversation is not a random, eclectic process of selection of items from other disciplines, but an orderly, intentional process of correlation and ongoing discovery, modification, and clarification.

This process, mapped most clearly for us in the seminal work of Don Browning, can be seen as a series of distinct movements or phases in the correlation and discernment of values and direction for interventions.[4]

These movements are as follows:

1. ***Movement One: Definition.*** The clear statement of the practical theological problem to be addressed.

2. ***Movement Two: Introduction.*** The case, event, or situation to be addressed must be clearly presented. The defined problem does not exist in abstract form, unrelated to actual life experience.

3. ***Movement Three: Reflection in Language One—Theology.*** Theological reflection on the case or event that calls for theological understanding. Ethical, theological, biblical, doctrinal, ecclesiological questions must be raised, concerns articulated, and their meanings discerned. The language employed should arise out of the theological, ethical, doctrinal or biblical vocabulary to frame the questions as a practical theological problem to be addressed.

4. ***Movement Four: Reflection in Language Two—A Behavioral Science Discipline.*** The practical theologian turns to relevant behavioral science(s) to bring specific theories to bear on the case, event, or situation. Psychology may address the person and the interpersonal relationships; cultural anthropology or sociology may address the process of culture and community; systems theory may illuminate the dynamics of both present and past relationships. All of this contributes richly to a fully human understanding of the event undergoing examination.

5. ***Movement Five: Dialogue.*** The connections are explored, the links identified, the overlapping insights identified, and the contrasts heightened and clarified as the theological reflections of movement three and the social-psychological reflections of movement four are brought into conversation and confrontation.

6. ***Movement Six: Constructive Formulation.*** It is possible for the practical theologian to begin the construction of a working model of the case or event, and to explore alternate strategies for education,

---

4. Browning, *Fundamental Practical Theology*, 55–74.

therapeutic intervention, or systemic change. Or the appropriate response may be planned reinforcement of those drives and goals that are already moving in creative directions.

In this dissertation on self-sacrifice and Korean experience in selfhood, marriage, family, church, and community, there will be multiple issues to (1) define; (2) present in concrete case or detail; (3) be given theological analysis through thoughtful reflection; (4) be explored in reflective use of the behavioral sciences; (5) receive bilingual examination from both theology and the particular correlating field; (6) and result in recommendations for intervention.

Thus, as a case in point, the cultural expectation for a Korean woman to fulfill her role within society's hierarchy is grounded in a command that she continually make personal sacrifices. This expectation will be explored theologically, ethically, and biblically; it will be examined systemically, psychologically, and sociologically; and finally, in the light of these endeavors, it will be understood more clearly. Throughout the following four chapters I will focus on understanding suffering, its role in marriage, its impact on gender relations, and the collateral damage of excused violence. This will be followed by qualitative research that will test the basic assumption, built throughout the thesis, that sacrifice and suffering are the core requirements of classic Confucian hierarchies, as interpreted in Korean culture. Out of the model that will be constructed, interventions of pastoral education, pastoral care, and pastoral therapy will emerge. This is, as Browning has defined, the process, shape, and practice of pastoral theology. The model of the six movements, grounded in the work of Browning but nuanced by other practical theologians, will be used in the concluding chapter to sum up our findings and to provide a working model of encounter, repeated reflection, correlation, and action.

1

Self-Sacrifice and Cultural Virtues
Yielding and Filial Piety

Culture molds attitudes toward family, time, clothing, eating, money, and gender. Differences of ethnicity, family background, religion, race, gender, and class influence every aspect of a person's worldview. The Korean worldview places a high value on sacrifice as a necessary virtue, an inevitable requirement in effective relationships, and a primary mode of conflict resolution.

In this first chapter, I will explore how Confucianism has influenced the concept of self-sacrifice in Korean American family relational dynamics, how self-sacrifice is taught within the framework of Confucianism, and more importantly, how it is understood and received in personal and family practices and the relational dynamics common among Korean Americans. I also will examine how self-sacrifice is portrayed in the dominant thought paradigms of the Korean culture. Finally, I will conclude this chapter by exploring the changing Confucian values, beliefs, and ethics in Korean and Korean American[1] family dynamics.

---

1. The term Korean American is used to refer to any Korean living in America with Korean heritage.

The Motives of Self-Sacrifice in Korean American Culture, Family, & Marriage

The Teachings of Confucianism on Human Relationships

Korean culture is a sophisticated mixture of Buddhism, Confucianism, Shamanism, and multiple other religions. Exploring this rich mixture and its influences are beyond the scope of this chapter, instead the focus will be on the Confucian legacy contributed mainly during the Yi dynasty (1392–1910 CE) and its continuing influence on contemporary Korean culture.[2] In addition, it is impossible to examine all of the variants in the tradition of Confucianism, with its two and a half thousand years of history, so I must necessarily limit the focus to the issue of how the teachings of Confucianism on human relationship influence the dynamics of the Korean family.

When asked about their religion in a recent Gallup poll, only 2% of Korean Americans responded "Confucian." However, when asked whether they practice or follow Confucian teachings in their daily lives, 90% answered "yes."[3] While differing in intensity, most Koreans remain strongly influenced by Confucian values. In present times, though the rituals are becoming simplified or simply abandoned, there is clear evidence that the attitude of Korean society is still firmly rooted in the teachings laid down by Confucius, as their way of life shows. Confucian values still dominate in forming the very moral fabric of contemporary Korean family and society. The continued presence of Confucianism in Korea can be found in how

---

2. Confucianism has been a major philosophy in Korea. By the eighteenth century, Korea had become a normative Confucian society. When the Chosun Dynasty succeeded the Koryo in 1392, it adopted Confucianism as the familial and state philosophy, suppressing Buddhism. The term *Confucianism* is used to refer to the popular value system of China, Korea, and Japan. This system is derived from the synthesis of the traditional cultural values espoused by Confucius and his followers and subsequently influenced by elements of Taoism, Legalism, Mohism, Buddhism, and, in the case of Korea and Japan, Shamanism. Confucianism declares the family the fundamental unit of society, responsible for the economic functions of production and consumption, as well as education and socialization, guided by moral and ethical principles. In its teachings, Confucianism has traditionally deified ancestors, institutionalized ancestor worship, and delegated the duties of ritual master to the head of the male lineage, that is, to the father and husband. Confucianism is a familial religion. As Confucianism took hold, the ideal of male superiority within the patrilineal family became more prominent in the late Chosun dynasty than it had been during the early Chosun dynasty (1392–1650). From Insook Han Park and Lee-Jay Cho, "Confucianism and the Korean Family," 117–34.

3. My English translation adapted from Ch'oe, *Han'guk Chonggyo Munhwa ro Ilnunda*, 109. Also, the Korean National Statistical Office (2005) indicates that most Koreans have a religion (total 53.1%; non-religious, 46.5%). Among people who have a religion—Christian, 34.5%; Catholic, 20.6%; Buddhist, 43%; Confucianist, 0.4%; Shamanist, Ch'ondogyo (Religion of the Heaven Way) and others, 1.5%.

individuals respond to family, school, community, workplace, politics, and government.[4] Confucianism has established the core hierarchy of relationships in the family and so defines the essential core elements of Korean family relationships. Nam-soon Kang, a professor of Women and Religion at Methodist Theological Seminary in Seoul, Korea, states, "Confucianism probably has more influence on them [Koreans] than does any other of the traditional religions or philosophies of Asia."[5]

The teachings of Confucianism have shaped and guided the way Koreans have thought and behaved for centuries.[6] Confucianism, to Koreans, is the common worldview: it defines social ethics, political concepts, academic traditions, and the daily way of life. It is said that the blood of Confucianism flows in every Korean. Having grown up in Korea, I realized that I, too, absorbed this shared heritage of Confucian influences. Sociology of Religion professor Chun-sik Ch'oe comments on its influence:

> There is the notion for modern Koreans that they are no longer under the teaching and influences of Confucianism. In truth, ever since the Chosun Dynasty, . . . (Koreans) have never lived without the teachings of Confucianism and cannot live without it just as much as a fish cannot live without water. Much like the Goldfish that is never aware of the water surrounding it, we too are never aware of the Confucianism that surround us. We have forgotten that we are Confucians. Or, we can say that our mentality as a whole is sugarcoated. Beneath the shallow cover of Christianity or Buddhism, our thoughts, actions, and relationships are fully steeped in the teachings of Confucianism. . . . Realizing how much of our lives is influenced by Confucianism is of the utmost importance in the road to understanding oneself.[7]

As professor Ch'oe remarks, one must understand the influence of Confucianism in order to have a meaningful (or actual) understanding of the motives behind crucial values and practices such as that of self-sacrifice for Koreans. Confucian thought is one of the main factors behind

---

4. Kang, "Confucian Familism," 172.

5. Ibid.

6. However, Confucianism is still considered as religion for some Koreans. No matter how Confucianism is understood, it is obvious that Confucianism is Korean's religion and defines social ethics. My English translation adapted from Tong-sop Chong, "Yugyo ui Sujik Yulli ka Han'gukin ui Kyolhon e Mich'in Yonghyang e taehan Kidokkyojok Pyongkka."

7. Ch'oe, *Han'guk Chonggyo Munhwa ro Ilnunda*, 110.

motivations of self-sacrifice in Korean culture. Therefore it is impossible, without understanding the influence of Confucian thought in Korean culture, to understand the Korean traditional culture, its family dynamics, and how deeply, extensively, and automatically Koreans value and act in self-sacrifice on behalf of others.[8]

Confucianism has been the dominant ethical guideline for governing human relationships in Korea for more than five hundred years. The principles of Confucian ideology have served as the primary influence on the behavior and customs of the Korean family. Confucianism emphasizes the virtue of humanity (Jen 仁), a universal virtue underlying all other interpersonal relationships regarding the five moral bonds: father-son, ruler-subject, husband-wife, elder and younger brother, and between friends.[9] Jen (仁) has been translated in many different ways, but the most commonly accepted translation is "the relationship between two persons." This notes that the word is formed by the combination of the character-words human (人) and two (二).[10] With this translation in mind, Jen (仁) has been further translated as human-heartedness, benevolence, love, forgiveness, kindness, gentleness. There are certain parallels between Jen (仁) and the Christian virtue of love or charity (*agape*) and the Buddhist virtue of mercy (慈悲). Confucianism holds a strong commitment to the sanctity of a consistent social rule and an established order. The Confucian finds his joy in harmony with nature, with others, and in his own humanity. Jen (仁) is always concerned with the quality of the relationship between two people. It is associated with both loyalty (chung; 忠)—loyalty to one's own heart and conscience—and reciprocity (shu; 恕)—respect and consideration for others and forgiveness of others (Analects 4:15).[11] Jen (仁) would be interpreted as universal love, but the roots of Jen (仁) are filial piety and

---

8. Pyong Gap Min, "Korean-American Family," in *Ethnic Families in America*, ed. Mindel and Habenstein, 199.

9. Ching, *Confucianism and Christianity*, 93.

10. Ch'oe, *Han'guk Chonggyo Munhwa ro Ilnunda*, 132.

11. Ching, *Confucianism and Christianity*, 94. The *Analects* (traditional Chinese: 論語; simplified Chinese: 论语; pinyin: Lún Yǔ), also known as the *Analects of Confucius*, are a record of the words and acts of the central Chinese thinker and philosopher Confucius and his disciples, as well as the discussions they held. The Chinese title literally means "discussion over [Confucius'] words. The *Analects* is the representative work of Confucianism and continues to have a tremendous influence on Chinese and East Asian thought and values today.

brotherly respect (*Analects* 1:20).[12] Filial piety is the first of all Confucian virtues, that which comes before loyalty to the sovereign, conjugal affection, and everything else.

Confucianism, with its primary focus on human relationships, regards human society as a layered network of interpersonal relationships and the multiple ethical responsibilities resulting from such relationships.[13] Confucianism teaches that the five relationships (五倫, Oh Ryun)—ruler-subject, father-son, husband-wife, between siblings, and between friends—must be honored as the five essential moral bonds that form the core commitments of person and family. Specifically, the middle three relationships are designed for regulating interpersonal relationship within the family. The other two are for mixed ties—ruler-subject and between friends. Furthermore, except for the relationship between friends, the relationships are all vertically aligned, between superior and inferiors, with interactions following the principle of unconditional respect of the superior.[14] In Confucian society, the family is considered as the model for all social organization, including government. Thus, as Nam suggests, in the Chinese and Korean languages, there are more than one hundred terms for various family relationship, which have no equivalents in Western languages.[15]

In summary, these five interpersonal relationships form the basis of Confucian principles on the duties and obligations of each individual. Of the five relationships that mold and shape family dynamics in Korean families, the three most important are father-son (filial piety), ruler-subject (hierarchy), and husband-wife (gender roles).[16] All three relationships require obedience, subservience, and self-negation, and this offers revealing clues about the motives behind self-sacrifice in Korean families. I will now explore these three dynamics.

Sacrifice in Parent-Child Relationships in Korean Culture

One of the most important doctrines of Confucianism is the requirement that children be obedient to parents. In traditional Korean society, filial piety has been the highest moral principle of the parent-child relationship

12. Ibid., 95.
13. Ching, *Confucianism and Christianity*, 96.
14. Hwang, "Filial Piety and Loyalty," 168.
15. Kang, "Confucian Familism," 173.
16. Ch'oe, *Han'guk Chonggyo Munhwa ro Ilnunda*, 195–96.

and has greatly influenced the structure and functioning of the today's Korean family system. Professor Nam-soon Kang states, regarding the Confucian family,

> The concept of filiality is more significant for understanding the Confucian family. The term *Hsiao*, translated as "filiality or filial piety" presents one of the most basic social and religious concepts of Confucian society. . . . Confucius gave this virtue of filiality a primacy in human moral development. Filiality, as the root of familism, is praised in all the Confucian Classics. In fact, the Book of Filiality (or *Hsiao Ching*), one of the Confucian Classics, is exclusively dedicated to this topic. Filiality is described as follows: "while [the parents] are living, serve them with *li*; when they die, bury them with *li*, and sacrifice for them with *li*." Filiality is considered the virtue of all virtues and the source, measure, and forms of all the virtues and is believed to direct sons toward their ultimate end in ultimate aim of piety toward Heaven. . . . Consequently, the teaching of the filiality is mainly focused on the relationship between father and sons.[17]

In the traditional Korean family, filial piety, family ties, and obedience to one's own parents always take precedence over one's own personal needs. The rules of filial piety guide the socialization of children, enforce the moral authority of the father, and require that adult children obey and serve their elderly parents and repay their indebtedness by looking after them for the rest of their lives.

Human existence, in a traditional Korean view, is centered in filial piety. A renowned Confucian scholar, T'ae-kye Yi once said, "Filial piety is the reason behind all human behavior."[18] Yul-gok Yi, another well-known Confucian scholar, has remarked that piety provides the center of all actions and is the foundation of all stable families.[19] Both scholars, in their essential agreement, speak the commonly held truth that filial piety is the radical commitment to a father-son relationship that is unilateral and authoritative and that it is this unshakable loyalty which provides the basis for duty and obligation in all moral action. There are teachings (*Ja*, 慈) to show how parents should act toward their children and how older siblings should behave toward the younger. Confucius taught that parents

17. Kang, "Confucian Familism," 174.

18. My English translation adapted from Ch'ae, *T'oegye Yulgok Ch'olhak ui Pigyo Yon'gu*, 307–10.

19. Ibid.

Self-Sacrifice and Cultural Virtues

and children should maintain a mutual attitude of benevolence. However, more emphasis has been given to how the younger must obey and respect the elder. Confucianism, as applied to the Korean family system and social life, demands children's one-sided obedience to and respect for parents and other adult family members.[20]

The Korean family system and social life, under Confucian influence, emphasizes absolute obedience and respect for parents and other adults. Table 1.1 lists the obligations that children must fulfill to their parents.[21]

Table 1.1 Duties of children toward their parents

Duties	Examples
Obeying: Children must respect their parents' opinions and authority. This respect must be expressed through their daily behavior.	Children must consult with their parents and seek agreement or permission from them in making decisions. If parents do not approve the decisions, children must stop insisting on their own ideas (*Kuk-mong-yo-keul*). When called, children must immediately answer. If their mouths are full, they must empty their mouths first and then answer (*Myong-shim-bo-kam*).
Attending: Children must take care of their parents' every need.	When parents are ill, attending to their illnesses must be given priority by children (*Kuk-mong-yo-keul*). Children must take care of their parents' bedding before and after their sleep (*Yi-Ki*). Parents must be kept warm in winter and cool in summer, and laid down at night (for sleep) and greeted with good morning at dawn (*So-hak*). Children must constantly check if their parents are in need of anything (*So-hak*).
Supporting: Related to the attending category, teaching emphasizes more materialistic comforts for parents.	Children must make sure that parents are comfortably housed, fed, and dressed (*Dong-Mon-Seun-Sup*).

---

20. Min, 208.

21. Uichol Kim and Soo-Hyang Choi, "Individualism, Collectivism, and Child Development," in *Cross-Cultural Roots*, ed. Greenfield and Cocking, 227–57.

Duties	Examples
Comforting: Whereas categories 2 and 3 are concerned with physical comfort, category 4 focuses more on creating psychological ease and entertainment, by not worrying them.	Children must let their parents know their coming in, going out, and whereabouts (*Myong-shim-bo-kam*). Children must be careful not to expose themselves to danger (*Yi-ki*).
Honoring: Even after their parents pass away, children are encouraged to honor their parents' achievements, fulfill their intentions, complete their undertaking, and sustain their social networks.	Children must restrain themselves form dietary and sexual pleasure for 3 years after their parents' death (*So-hak*). In extreme cases, even the concubine of a father must be given good care by the children after their father's death (*So-hak*).

Korean children are obligated to support their aging parents, with the eldest son expected to live with his parents in the same household. He is expected to provide materialistic comforts and psychological care for his parents in their old age. He was also obligated to perform ceremonial duties of ancestral worship after the parent's death. Even if the children live separately, they are expected to visit their parents frequently, especially on special occasions such as birthday celebrations, ancestral worship, and national holidays like New Year's and Korean Thanksgiving.

It should be noted that filial piety is a beautiful and revered value both in name and action and has had positive effects on the foundations of Korean families. Piety is giving respect and support to young, middle-aged, and aging parents. Originally the concept addressed duties from the parents to the children, as well. However, the concept of filial piety that Koreans now possess appears to be an almost one-sided game. In playing this one-sided game, children are expected to sacrifice everything for their parents without question or objection. Mandatory self-sacrifice to the parent, seen simply as an obligated duty or blind submission—as ransom, even—is unreasonable, unacceptable, and problematic.

In this sense, the existing hierarchy of parent-child relationships may actually create barriers to children freely choosing to make sacrifices. Children may perceive pressure in a hierarchical relationship to give up their own appropriate needs and goals for the good of their parents in the name of filial piety, imposed by society's expectation. Such pressure may make it difficult for the children to truly and freely choose to sacrifice. Rather than supporting their parents out of genuine love and sacrifice, this becomes an inescapable and obligated duty. If this responsibility is continually imposed

Self-Sacrifice and Cultural Virtues

on children, as a backlash, they will choose not to sacrifice for their parents or live with them as the preceding generation may have chosen to do. Recently, for instance, rather than living with their parents in their old age, more and more Korean Americans, as well as Korean families, are choosing to send their parents to nursing homes or other senior care communities.

Kyoung-il Kim states that traditional filial piety was a result of both parents and children living and working together, sharing common goals, values, time, and space.[22] In the current state of Korean urban society, where parents and children no longer share this commonality, this is no longer the case. As noted earlier, Koreans honor piety with such devoted commitment that it functions like a religion of sorts. However, children are unable to maintain a traditional sense of filial piety in terms of time, space, or ability, financial or otherwise. Due to differences in the way the generations view the responsibility of piety, conflicts inevitably arise between the two. Parents who raised their children with the expectation that the children would fully support them in their later years are increasingly disappointed. As children grow up, they find that they are unable to care for their parents as much as their parents expected or demanded, in the amount of time or in the measure of care invested. As this conflict deepens, the impacts can be felt in ways such as parents being abused or abandoned or increasing pressures being placed upon them, such as being asked to take care of their grandchildren. Since the number of elderly will increase in coming days, Koreans must reflect deeply on the meanings and problems that emerge as forms of filial piety evolve. Otherwise, filial piety performed in name alone will only result in deepening conflict between the generations.

On the other hand, the problem also lies in parental self-sacrifice. It is common for Korean parents to give up everything for their children. They often choose to forego their own best interests for the sake of the child. In fact, in parenting, there are by necessity a great number of sacrifices which must be made for the benefit of a child. Being a good parent is inherently a selfless act and requires the renunciation of the parent's self-interest.

However, some questions remain. Do Korean parents feel satisfied and fulfilled in their own lives? Do they receive any positive rewards as a result of their sacrifices? Why do parents make these sacrifices? Although parents willingly subjugate their own desires to the needs of their children, these sacrifices may be made out of a sense of necessity rather than any clear sense of choice. When a parent labors for the child's happiness and

---

22. Kim, *Kongja ka Chugoya Nara ka Sanda*, 150–57.

welfare, it is often a costly personal sacrifice—its magnitude measured in factors of time, emotion, freedom, material resources, and other relational costs. However, when parents overstate their efforts and relentlessly remind rather than reasonably explain sacrifices to their children, the relationship may be damaged. For instance, when a mother decides to give up her career to stay home to raise her son, she makes a very personal sacrifice (status, money, freedom, etc.). However, she may also gain peace of mind, freedom from social censure, and social approval from certain quarters, and hopefully, a happier son and a more peaceful family. But if she has to reiterate her forbearance of personal freedom to her son loudly, her sacrifice can become a burden for her child, her spouse, and ultimately herself. This sacrifice is not out of self-giving but tainted by resentment, bitterness, complaint, and regret. Choices made in response to duty and obligation tend to evoke resistance in both the giver and the receiver, and as the result of mandated choices, all participants need to consider how others in relationship respond including those who benefit from this sacrifice. Because demanding self-sacrifice in the name of tradition and social mandate will often produce negative consequences in interpersonal relationships, especially in family dynamics, this pattern should not be understood as routine or normal behavior in the name of virtue or tradition. Pastors and pastoral counselors must understand the hidden cultural dynamics to deal with the underlying philosophies and core beliefs as they try to help Korean Americans.

In chapter 5, we will lay the empirical, theoretical, and theological groundwork to understand the motives directing self-sacrifice in Korean American family dynamics. I will investigate the motives and the relational dynamics behind self-sacrifice in the course of this study by conducting an empirical study of sacrifice among Korean Americans. However, as historical, philosophical, and cultural background, this chapter will address the influence of Confucianism in forming values of self-sacrifice.

The Patriarchal (Hierarchical) Korean Family System

Traditionally, the ideal family type in Korea was a patriarchal stem family in which the central familial relationship was not between husband and wife, but rather between parent and child, especially father and son. This indicates that Korean family relationship is not grounded on equality and mutuality, but on hierarchy. These relationships, characterized by authority,

Self-Sacrifice and Cultural Virtues

obedience, and one-sided benevolence, create patterns of influence flowing from the more powerful to the weaker. Authority rested with the (male) head of the household, and differences in status existed among the other family members.[23]

In a Confucian patriarchal family, the family as an entity takes precedence over its individual members, and the family group is inseparably identified with the clan. The most important function of family members is to maintain and preserve the household within the traditional Confucian system. Confucian society became organized around two core principles: that males shall dominate females and that elders shall dominate the young.[24]

In the patriarchal and hierarchical system, individual identity is closely tied to one's position held within family and society. The children must not fail to show respect to those who are older. For example, while Westerners shake hands as if the two parties of are equal standing, Koreans are expected to bow in terms of their social ranking, from lower to higher.[25] Age difference is one of the most important elements that define relationships among Koreans and Korean Americans. Ranking and hierarchy are inherent in Korean society and determine one's rank or status in this vertical Korean society, and as such, every member must accept the cost of sacrifice, and when necessary, degrade himself as a condition for belonging to this society or community.

Hierarchy Seen in Korean Language

Hierarchy is reflected linguistically in the Korean language, where there are thirty-six words for "I," each with its use dictated by its social status, honorific or derogatory, in the conversation.[26] The language used varies depending on age differentials between the speaker and the person addressed. Calling an adult by his or her first name may make the person feel offended or uncomfortable. Koreans are not accustomed to American's use of the first name as a gesture of friendliness. They would never use first

---

23. Park and Cho, "Confucianism and the Korean Family," 117–34.
24. Kim, "Transformation on Family Ideology," 71.
25. My English translation adapted from Yi, *Han'gukin ui Uisik Kujo*, 1:106.
26. Ibid., 107. E.g., there are thirty-six Korean words for the word "I," such as: 나, 저, 오(吾), 아(我), 여 (予, 余), 짐(朕), 신(臣), 본인(本人), 소인(小人), 불초(不肖), 둔마(鈍馬), 졸자(拙者).

19

names to the older, but call each other by their job titles, such as "Teacher Park," "Director Son," or "Pastor Kim." These terms reflect the fact that the traditional Korean community functions according to a rigid hierarchy based on age or status. As another example, when you hand something to an elderly person you should hold the object with both hands. Koreans bow their heads slightly as a greeting, rather than just saying "hi" or waving. These are just a few examples of how to express respect to older people. This pattern even exists in relationships between Korean family members. Children are ranked by age, with the younger required to respect the older. Rather than calling each other by first name, brothers and sisters must address one another by honorific title of elder brother or elder sister.[27]

Having grown up in a hierarchical culture, when I was accepted into a PhD program at Fuller, I was surprised by the fact that Dr. Augsburger, my mentor, referred to me as one of his colleagues. Additionally, when other students called their professors by their first names, it made me very uncomfortable. In fact, I was envious of this relationship where one was able to relate to his mentor as a friend. If this friendly atmosphere can be maintained without losing respect for the teacher-student relationship, conversations become fruitful. He can ask critical questions, offering differing thoughts and opinions. Many Korean students, including myself, resist participating in such friendly interchanges with a mentor, and find it difficult to relate equally with faculty, unsure whether to argue against or work with them. Personalities aside, this is likely due to the fact that the Korean students were raised in a culture where such friendships with persons of higher positions were unheard of.

It is interesting to note the following comparison. Koreans have a narrow definition of friendship. Friendship is limited to peers, defined by age. To Koreans, friendship refers to a close relationship within the same age group, a narrow definition when compared to the American concept of friendship. A younger person cannot give opinions freely to an older person for instance, and their communication channels are fixed and rigid. For Koreans entering Western society, when they do not encounter a parallel concept of peer-limitations in friendship, it is difficult if not impossible to know how to interact with people of different age groups. Because of such

27. Hyung (형) is the honorific title for elder brother, masculine form. Nuna (누나) is the honorific title for elder sister, masculine form. Oppa (오빠) is the honorific title for elder brother, feminine form. Unni (언니) is the honorific title for elder sister, feminine form. There are separate titles, both masculine and feminine, for younger brother and sister, as well.

culturally shaped constraints, Koreans may act out socially coerced motives of self-sacrifice rather than volunteering participation as a free choice. Direct openness of expression and assertiveness by the younger to the older, and even by children to parents in family relationships, is often seen as rude or aggressive. Free expression of feelings or needs is discouraged, even (especially) for children; much like the old English proverb goes, "Children should be seen and not heard."

Harmony: "Woori" Culture

Because Koreans emphasize harmony as a high value within community, they tend to be strongly influenced by the opinions of other members of their family or community when making decisions. If they make a decision based on their own preferences without considering others, they are likely to be labeled as selfish. We all care about our appearance to others. We all want to present ourselves positively. What that means can vary from culture to culture. In Eastern culture, presenting ourselves positively means, "I do not break the rules, I behave as I am expected to, and I can be trusted to be a good friend or a good person in my group, helping others." That is how Koreans present themselves; to be desirable, to be modest, following the rules, doing what is expected. On the other hand, for Westerners, this means acting within the validity of one's own individual feelings and emotions. However, Asians do not see individuals as isolated from society, and societal rules and norms regulate the actions of the individual. How one judges the other, especially an elder or someone in a superior position, becomes the norm to which one judges oneself. In particular, Koreans constantly compare themselves to others, and those others have a powerful effect on one's own life.

It is interesting to note here that language usage reflects subtle differences between individualism and collectivism. There is a Korean word, "*woori.*" It means "we" or "ours," instead of "*na,*" which means "I." American culture is an "I" culture, but Korean culture is a "we" culture. For instance, an American says, "This is my friend, my school, my car, my home, my country." Koreans do not have this "my." They say that "it is our country, our house, our school, our teacher, in the extreme, our wife." That is the core of collectivism in the Korean culture. It is interesting to note that this value is demonstrated in how Korean parents discipline their children versus how American parents do so. When punishing a child in the United States, that child is sent to his or her room. The child's freedom or rights are restrained, however temporarily. In contrast, the Korean child may be told to leave the house. No matter how serious (in most cases, it is not) the threat is, the underlying tone of this punishment is rejection from family and, ultimately, shame from society.

Hermit Kingdom: Hiding Is Virtue

Thanks to the rigid principles set by emphasizing their relative importance in hierarchy, age, and harmony, hiding one's inner thoughts and feelings has become a virtue to Korean Americans. Self-sacrifice, the motivation to internalize one's opinions, perspectives, and desires, and the humility to maintain this secrecy are considered virtues. This secretive nature has been further nurtured and normalized. Patriarchal structures allow this dissembling and reward people who deny their values and withhold their true thoughts and feelings. Authentic intimate relationships are turned away in the name of respect, humility, and conformity. Patriarchal culture lets people feel burdened by false guilt when offering viewpoint critical of or contrary to public opinion. This "hermit culture," further reinforced by the person's social and societal standing, stems from the teachings of patriarchal father-son relationship.

Kyu-t'ae Yi, a Korean journalist, explains the state of mind for Koreans living in this hermit culture, as *Han* (한, 恨).[28] *Han* is the combination of two words, unmoving (간, 艮) and mind (심, 心). Much like a deep rooted tree that takes all blows from the environment, Koreans in this state of *Han* also take all blows to their emotional well-being, and turn thoughts and feelings inward. Instead of pouring out their hurt feelings to a significant other, Koreans will absorb their hurt feeling inwardly. This is *Han*. Living in this state of *Han*, they will inwardly abhor outsiders hurting them and, further, will mourn quietly for themselves. As the Korean culture frowns upon individuals who lash out at others in expressing their conflicts, worries, and inner feelings, the only way Koreans have to deal with their anger and sadness is to swallow it up inside. I will discuss this concept of *Han* in more detail, especially as it relates to women in their quintessential Korean identity, in chapter 3.

In contrast, Westerners more immediately voice disagreement or complaint, and as a result, they do not carry the weight inside that many

---

28. Kyu-t'ae Yi, *Han'gukin ui Uisik Kujo*, 2:250–52.

Koreans may. However, Koreans, especially women, have no way of venting or letting out frustrations when scolded by in-laws, elder siblings, and teachers because of the prohibitions of rigid hierarchy in Korean society. This is also carried out in the workplace or in other group settings—even when the individual may know that he or she is right, yielding is necessary thanks to the collectivist mindset. The individual, not wanting to deal with backlash from the larger group, is forced to hide real thoughts and emotions. As noted above, *Han*, from this mindset, forces the individual to adopt the mindset of "passive-surrender." As this pattern of passive-surrender is considered virtuous (even beautiful) in Korean society, this ultimately limits the growth of the person, the family, or the group.

The core values of harmony, collectivism, low self-disclosure, and hiding, all prized in Confucianism, have had a negative impact by creating a closed system in Korean family dynamics. Even today, the Korean patriarchal atmosphere still requires the younger generation to fit into the structure of the old. As a result, the younger become passive. Passion and creativity are quickly stifled into submission and routine. Even in the culture of higher education, the students listen passively to lectures given by professors, with no regard for an active learning experience. An American professor remarked to me that Korean students are obviously very smart and good learners, but that they often fail to ask the critical questions, and as a result, many do not complete their PhD courses. Also, Samuel Kim's thesis notes that over 40% of Korean students admitted into Ivy League schools drop out of their courses.[29] With regards to education, he notes that the Korean education, as currently influenced by Confucianism, is not as successful as perceived.

In summary, clearly defined roles and rigid hierarchy are the first results of Confucian philosophy in Korean families. Korean families place a high value on the family unit rather than the individual (this especially holds true for the male members of the family). An individual's personal action reflects not only on himself but also on his immediate and extended family, as well as his ancestors. An individual is expected to function in his or her clearly defined role and position in the family hierarchy, based on age, gender, and social class. Moreover, central Confucian teaching places the child's obedience and unquestioning fidelity to parents as one of

29. According to Kim's thesis, the dropout rate by race is as follows: Jewish, 12.5%; Indian, 21.5%; Chinese, 25%; other races, 34%. See Si-soo Park, "44% of Korean Ivy League Students Quit Course Halfway," *Korea Times*, October 3, 2008, quoting Kim's thesis, http://www.koreatimes.co.kr/www/news/nation/2008/10/117_32124.html.

the most important principles. Though there are precepts of how parents should relate to their child, the most important was the expected fidelity of child to parent. This then sets the patriarchal family relationship as the norm so that bloodlines, familial fidelity, and dutiful obedience bind the society together in an obligational network. To show disobedience or disrespect to the father was akin to showing disloyalty to the king—to quote a well-known and well-adhered-to Korean proverb, "Loyalty to Country, Obedience to Parents."

This family-centered mindset, with absolute obedience to the father, has created the norm in Korean culture that children must unilaterally sacrifice for their parents (even more for the daughters) to the point that it became a virtue. It is natural that the responsibility that was once held by the parents to care for their children will pass down to children to care for their parents. However, to demand this sacrifice unilaterally is improper, and never collaborated by teachings of Confucius. Sacrifice, then, should be the natural outcome of the love and mutual respect that grows naturally between parents and children, fathers and sons. Likewise, filial piety should be the result of love, service, and mutual respect, not of absolute authority and blind obedience.

The Korean Woman's Role and Status in the Family

Confucian exaltation of the authority and domination of fathers and sons over wives and daughters has made the unequal treatment of women natural and normative. The subordination of wives to husbands and daughters to all men in the family, the denial of inheritance rights, inequitable marriage laws, and unequal treatment in genealogical records can be seen as proof of the sexual inequality fostered by Confucianism in a Confucian society.[30] In extreme cases, girls are ignored to such a degree that a father would leave them out of his calculation when asked the number of children in his family. Moreover, only sons can glorify the family through official appointment or perpetuate the family name. Even after death, it is the sons, as sole performers of the ancestral worship, who are responsible for the welfare of their departed parents. So from the day of her marriage, a woman is under pressure to conceive and bring forth a healthy male child, because the clan lineage is acknowledged only through the male line. The

---

30. Kang, "Confucian Familism," 174.

importance of sons is so great that if a wife fails to bear a male child, the husband reserves the right to divorce her and send her back to her family.[31]

Today the importance of sons has diminished significantly, largely due to increasing numbers of people who are educated, experienced in cultural exchanges, and aware of different values. However, Koreans still generally prefer sons over daughters. For example, when a mother gives birth to a son , she feels relief, pride, and joy, because she believes that she has fulfilled one of her fundamental duties to her parents-in-law. When a daughter is born, the mother usually feels disappointed and consoles herself with the thought that her daughter can be helpful to her. Nevertheless, many mothers hope for sons the next time or continue to give birth until they bear sons.[32]

Perhaps no book explains the position of women in Korean society better than *Naehun*. Compiled by the mother of King Seongjong in 1475, *Naehun* (*Instruction for Women*), was the most important and influential textbook used to teach proper Confucian roles to girls and married women.[33] It emphasized the four basics of womanly behavior: *moral conduct*—women need not have great talents, but must be quiet and serene, chaste and disciplined; *proper speech*—women need not have rhetorical talents, but must avoid bad and offensive language and speak with restraint; *proper appearance*—women need not be beautiful, but they must be clean in dress and appearance; and *womanly tasks*—women need not be clever, but must pay attention to such duties as weaving and entertaining guests.[34] The book also elaborated on a married woman's role, including being a self-sacrificing daughter-in-law, an obedient and dutiful wife, and a wise and caring mother. Also, it helped girls prepare for their future functions as moral

---

31. Ibid., 173. There are seven traditional grounds for divorce by husband: disobedience to a husband's parent, failure to bear a son, promiscuity, jealousy, having an incurable disease, talking too much, and stealing.

32. According to research by the Korea Institute for Health and Social Affairs, in 2006 only 10.2% responded that they "must have a son" in their family planning. To the same survey conducted in 2000, the response rate was 16.2%, a decreased of 6% in the 6-year period. In addition, for the first time women who preferred to have a son decreased, from 43.2% in 2000 to 39.3% in 2006. In contrast, women who did not care whether they had a son increased in the same period, from 39.5% to 49.8%. This research shows that Koreans' attitudes on preferring to have a son are changing. See *The 2009 National Survey on Fertility, Family Health and Welfare in Korea*, http://211.252.146.33:8080/bitstream/2 01002/858/1/%EC%97%B0%EA%B5%AC_2009-33.pdf.

33. Deuchler and Mattielli, *Virtues in Conflict*, 5–6.

34. Ibid., 6.

guardians of the domestic sphere and providers for the physical needs of their families.[35]

Korean women were reduced to an inferior role in traditional Confucian society. Traditionally, women were raised and educated to be good girls with the eventual, indeed ultimate, goal of being married by arrangement into a good family and becoming good wives. This reinforced the notion that women were wholly dependent on men in society. Women were socialized to sacrifice their personalities, emotions, achievements, and ambitions for men. Kyoung-il Kim underlines that Confucianism, for Koreans, was an ethic for politics and governance, not for human relationships; for men, not for women; for the old, not for the young; for the privileged not for the ordinary.[36] As a result, the gender roles were further cemented, with women being further subjugated in society. "*Nam Jon Yuh Bi*" (男尊女卑), meaning subjugation of women in male dominated society, was ingrained into the Korean society as high virtue.

In this sense, the most seriously abused victims of Confucianism in Korean society are women. According to a Confucian saying, "When hens crow, the house is ruined." Another proverb concludes that "women and young generation are hard to raise." Korean proverbs such as "loud women will become widows" and "argue with a women in the morning and your day is ruined" (among others), give insight into the status of women in Korean society.[37]

In this regard, Deuchler states that "many Korean proverbs reflect the Confucian ethic embodied in the saying 'respect man and despise women.'"[38] Old sayings and teachings have been ingrained in the Korean culture, shaping the thoughts and mentalities of countless generations. Deuchler also points out well that married women are devalued as women and as wives, and this double curse is accomplished in the proverbs by casting her as a deceitful creature with a potential for causing trouble and bringing bad luck.[39] These twelve particular proverbs made by men for men

---

35. Kim, "Transformation on Family Ideology," 72. Though traditional Korean women's responsibility was restricted to the domestic sphere, the woman as an inside master established her own authority and became a financial manager, symbolized by the right to carry the family keys to the pantry.

36. Kim, *Kongja ka Chugoya Nara ka Sanda*, 7

37. Ibid., 160–161.

38. Deuchler and Mattielli, *Virtues in Conflict*, 49.

39. Ibid.

shows the distinct trait of placing women in the role of submission and muting their voices entirely:[40]

1. 여자는 사흘을 안 때리면 여우가 된다.
   If you do not beat your woman for three days, she becomes a fox.

2. 여자의 웃음은 주머니의 눈물.
   A woman's laughter is a bag of tears. (A woman may be laughing outwardly, but in secret she's crying.)

3. 여자가 셋이며 접시가 깨진다.
   When three women get together, the dishes will break. (Women talk a lot, and it's noisy.)

4. 여자는 제 고을 장날을 몰라야 팔자가 좋다.
   A woman must not know the market day in her own district if she's to have a good life. (Keep a woman at home and ignorant of outside events if you want her to have a good life.)

5. 여자의 말을 잘 들어도 패가하고 안 들어도 망신한다.
   If you listen to a woman's advice, the house comes to ruin; if you don't listen, the house comes to shame.

6. 여자가 울면 삼 년 재수가 없다.
   If a woman cries, no good luck for three years.

7. 계집 둘 가진 놈의 창자는 호랑이도 안 먹는다.
   Even a tiger won't eat the entrails of a man with two wives. (A man with two wives has such a hard life that his insides turn rotten.)

8. 천 길 물 속은 알아도 계집 마음 속은 모른다.
   You do not know what's in water a thousand fathoms deep, and you can't know the mind of a woman.

9. 계집은 상을 들고 문지방을 넘으며 열 두 가지 생각을 한다.
   As she carries the dinner table over the door sill, a woman has a dozen thoughts. (A woman is supposed to be silent, but she has many thoughts. She is always thinking and making things complicated; therefore, a woman is not to be trusted.)

10. 계집 입 싼 것.

---

40. Ibid., 50–66.

A woman's mouth is a cheap thing. (A woman's words are light; she keeps no secrets.)

11. 계집의 곡한 마음 오뉴월에 서리 친다.
A woman's spirit is like frost in the fifth and sixth months.

12. 영에서 뺨 맞고 집에 와서 계집 친다.
Get slapped at the government office; come home and hit your woman. (Like kicking the dog after a hard day at the office.)

All of these, then, lead women to believe that they should obey men, that it is their responsibility to maintain domestic peace, even at personal sacrifice, and that self-sacrifice is part of their lives. When this self-sacrifice is not carried out, a woman is shamed, receives punishment as fate and the heavens have ordained, and is rejected from the society. Even in their own family settings, women could not fulfill their needs and ambitions, had to be constantly wary of what their husbands were thinking, and were invariably driven by fear of ruining their interpersonal relationships. By suppressing their personalities and emotions, they believed that they were committing self-sacrifice for their families. Though some men may have had similar feelings and thoughts, Korean women were driven by fear and anxiety stemming from this. This was the direct result of the patriarchal Korean society.

However, although cultural imperatives—filial piety, ancestor worship, patrilineage, patriarchy, and dominance of men over women, and submission—work together in a complex weave to support practices that require and establish feminine subservience, we should be careful not to be over-enthusiastic in embracing politically correct concepts such as "absolute equality." Rosenlee correctly argues that "this absolute equality would constitute a response that is insensitive to the particular problem that Chinese women face."[41] Rosenlee's proposal for Confucian feminism is characterized by "a qualified inequality among the unequal based on ability and moral authority."[42] In other words, the cultivation of the ethical self should not be grounded in the inner-outer (內外) distinction but rather based on ethical ability.[43] While absolute gender parity is not possible, there must be a change in attitude and perception so that the two genders are

---

41. Rosenlee, *Confucianism and Women*, 152.
42. Ibid., 158.
43. Inner-outer (內外) is commonly associated with masculinity and femininity and recognizes different gender roles.

able to treat one another ethically. Certainly, it must be commended for its attempt to maintain integrity of societal ethics and personal responsibility. What we need is neither a total rejection nor a blind acceptance but an ongoing re-conceptualization of the notion of mutual and equal regard. In order for women to acknowledge themselves as responsible and free agents, not dependent on men, and to reject the patriarchal construction of men (the Subject) and women (the Other), we must pursue a more complete understanding of interdependence. Idealization of the Confucian concept of relatedness between humans without a reflection on the praxis of how women have lived under this Confucian concept of relatedness can result in the perpetuation of women's suffering under extreme androcentric values and institutions in Confucian society.

Acknowledging these cultural backgrounds, which place high value on family-centered lives with each role strictly defined and on membership in a society that stresses harmony among interpersonal relationships, will help immensely when trying to understand the issues surrounding the concept of self-sacrifice for Korean Americans. Understanding this cultural background, pastors and counselors should be better equipped and trained to identify and handle issues of shame, depression, and burnout with Korean Americans, especially women.

Major Transition from Traditional to New Confucian Ethics

Before I finish the chapter, I should acknowledge that these traditional values are often challenged by younger generations who are strongly influenced by Western culture. This challenge could be much more intense for many Korean immigrant families. They struggle in balancing the traditional Korean culture and adapting to the new American culture, putting a difficult strain on marriage and family relationships. I believe that Korean immigrant families have cultural dynamics that differ from Koreans still living in Korea. They have become influenced by Western values, such as reciprocal sacrifice and the importance of mutuality in interpersonal relationship. However, though it is appropriate to be aware that these cultural views may have a great influence on many Korean Americans, one should not assume that all Korean Americans hold traditional cultural beliefs about family relationships.

In the past two decades, Korea has changed rapidly in many aspects, due to the colliding forces of modernization, urbanization, industrialization, the internet, and the growth of IT industry. The socioeconomic revolution and consequent rapid, widespread migration from villages and towns to the city had a major impact on the form, structure, and functions of the family. Korea's industrial transformation had profound effects on the family, substantially reducing the proportion of stem families—patrilineal, three-generation families—as children left their parents in the countryside and started their own conjugal families.[44] This led to the decrease of traditional extended families and the emergence of nuclear families as a predominant form.

Table 1.2 Households by household composition: 2000–2020[45]

	2000	2005	2010	2015	2020
All households	14,609,493 (100.0)	15,827,994 (100.0)	16,962,225 (100.0)	17,730,845 (100.0)	18,379,761 (100.0)
Married couple w/o child(ren)	1,802,054 (12.3)	2,197,596 (13.9)	2,629,902 (15.5)	3,040,288 (17.1)	3,502,709 (19.1)
Married w/ child(ren)	7,034,864 (48.2)	7,436,421 (47.0)	7,669,234 (45.2)	7,691,741 (43.4)	7,541,799 (41.0)
Father w/ child(ren)	224,572 (1.5)	242,383 (1.5)	266,541 (1.6)	279,790 (1.6)	285,157 (1.6)
Mother w/ child(ren)	922,649 (6.3)	1,006,166 (6.4)	1,081,269 (6.4)	1,115,117 (6.3)	1,128,479 (6.1)
Three generation or more	1,223,214 (8.4)	1,153,826 (7.3)	1,075,570 (6.3)	966,560 (5.5)	854,018 (4.6)
One-person	2,269,964 (15.5)	2,695,218 (17.0)	3,158,192 (18.6)	3,576,090 (20.2)	4,016,903 (21.9)
None-relative	162,530 (1.1)	160,078 (1.0)	150,616 (0.9)	143,711 (0.8)	136,810 (0.7)
Other	(6.6)	(5.9)	(5.5)	(5.2)	(5.0)

Note 1: Including unknown (916)
Note 2: Figures in parentheses are the percent distribution of each category of total households.

44. Park and Cho, "Confucianism and the Korean Family," 123.

45. Young-joo Park et al., "Household Projections for the Republic of Korea," National Statistical Office, 20th Population Census Conference, June 19–21, 2002, Ulaanbaatar, Mongolia, http://www.ancsdaap.org/cencon2002/papers/Korea/Korea.pdf.

Comparably, as the number of nuclear families increases, we see dramatic changes in the family structure taking place. The most pronounced pattern in household composition revealed by the household projections is a fast-growing number of one-person households in Korea. One-person households were 2,269,964 (15.5% of the total) in 2000 and are expected to grow to 2,695,218 (17.0%) in 2005, 3,158,192 (18.6%) in 2010, 3,576,090 (20.2%) in 2015, and 4,016,903 (21.9%) in 2020. It should be noted that the households composed of three generations and more and the non-relative households will decrease either absolutely or relatively. In addition, nuclear families will increase in number but their share of total households will remain constant. This suggests that Korea has almost completed the process of family nucleation.

After 1911, the earliest year for which statistics are available, Korea witnessed a steadily increasing divorce rate except for the years from 1946 to 1966, a period that included the Korean War and post-World War II industrialization. Since the 1970s, the crude divorce rate has increased significantly every ten years, almost doubling from 0.67 per 1,000 people in 1970 to 1.16 in 1980 and again to 2.6 in 1999.[46] The divorce rate has been growing for Koreans in their native country, and some research suggests that the reasons for this increase also help to explain the increasing rate of divorce among Asian Americans.[47] First, an increased focus on wealth and career advancement may increase divorce rates, perhaps because family relationships are given lower priority and work stress spills over into marriage. Second, Asian American women have become more educated and economically independent, which has given them greater freedom to leave unhealthy relationships. Traditionally, Korean American women were expected to accept their situation if their husbands had affairs or if their husbands or mothers-in-law abused them, because they had a lack of financial resources and income. However, as more women are completing their education and enter the work force, the divorce rate has increased accordingly. Third, in the past, tight-knit communities within Korean culture kept struggling couples together by providing instruction and pressure to make peace when there was conflict. Extended families are losing the influence that they previously had over couples. This change may be due in part to a growing value of individualism. Traditionally, Korean marriage was

46. "Contemporary Korean Families," *Marriage and Family Encyclopedia*, http://family.jrank.org/pages/1021/Korea-Contemporary-Korean-Families.html.

47. Huang, "Asian Perspective on Relationship and Marriage Education," 161–73.

regarded as the union of two families, not just of two individuals. Family bonds (精, *jung*), reputation, and children all played an important role in keeping married couples together. Divorce was taboo, an unspeakable and unbearable shame. Today, beliefs have moved away somewhat from that view of marriage. Although Koreans tend to value obedience, self-control, and family interests rather than the typical American values of independence, self-expression, and individual interests,[48] Korean American may be less willing to sacrifice personal desires and ambitions for their families than they were in past. This shift in values could possibly make couples less committed to their spouses and less wary of shaming their families by divorcing.

Finally, this transition from old tradition to new is marked by changes in the fertility rate.[49] Korea currently has one of the lowest birth rates in the world, and the lowest among OECD countries. The total fertility rate fell from 6.0 children per woman in 1960 to 1.7% in 1990 and 1.19% in 2003.[50] In 1990, a total of 658,552 children were born versus 493,471 in 2003, a drop of 165,081 births in that decade. More couples are choosing to have only one or no children.

More and more, the increasing divorce rate and the decreasing fertility rate show that Korean society is becoming a self-oriented, individualistic society. In contrast to Korean traditional values, personal rights and self-fulfillment of the individual are now of increasing importance to most Koreans / Korean Americans. The traditional or idealized focus on community and family colliding with this fierce individualism results in a "strange" culture in today's Korea. The Confucian principles of family relationships are perhaps being seen as remote and strange to some of the

---

48. Huisman, "Wife Battering in Asian American Communities," 260–83.

49. According to the Planned Population Federation of Korea, the fertility rate has been steadily decreasing in Korea from 4.53% in 1970 to 2.1% in 1984, 1.47% in 2000, 1.3% in 2001, and 1.17% in 2002, which is below the world average of 1.58% in the same year. According to OECD the 2001 birthrates in other nations were as follows: 2.03% in the United States; 1.24% in Italy; 1.29% in Germany; 1.33% in Japan; 1.9% in France; 1.65% in Great Britain. This thirty-year drop in the fertility rate in Korea is further shocking when compared to the fertility rate drops from 1970 to 2000 in other nations: a decrease of 0.4% in the US; 0.7% in Germany; 0.8% in both Great Britain and Japan; and 1.9% in France. Researchers attribute this large drop in birthrate to increasing levels of education, increasing numbers in the workforce, decreasing rates of marriage and increasing rates of divorce, and delaying birth until later years. Adapted from Planned Population Federation of Korea, http://www.ppfk.or.kr/index.asp.

50. Park and Cho, "Confucianism and the Korean Family," 123.

younger generation of Koreans. As a startling example, studies conducted after 1980 comparing attitudes of survey respondents with those found in earlier studies reveal the extent to which values and practices have changes in both urban and rural Korean families.[51] Table 1.3 shows the differences in opinions of obedience to their parents by now-adult children.

Table 1.3 Opinions about whether children should obey their parents. Korea, 1959 and 1990.[52]

Opinion	1959 (%)	1990 (%)
Children should obey	43.2	18.7
Depends on the situation	50.7	62.4
Parents should do what their children want	5.4	18.9
Other	0.7	0
Numbers	702	402

According to the preceding study, the biggest difference in the opinions of adult children in 1959 and 1990 is that children are no longer obligated to obey their parents. When parental authority is in dispute, one-way obedience is no longer axiomatic in the family relationship. The proportion of respondents who said that children should obey their parents was only 18.7% in 1990 compared with 43.2% in 1959. Likewise, letting children follow their own course of actions contrary to parents' wishes rose to 18.9%, compared with 5.4% in 1959. The values of vertical filial piety characterized by one-way benevolence, authority, and obedience, once thought of as absolute, are now fading away, especially with the younger generation of Koreans. Korean society thus seems more accepting of the egalitarian marriage and equality and mutual love and less prone to traditional attitudes that emphasized one-sided obedience and sacrifice.

However, these changes are not universal; some of the traditional images of fixed patterns of family relationships still strongly persist in Korean society. Despite these changes, Confucian influence on the Korean family is still strong, as evidenced by persistent deference by wives to their husband's status and role, the preference for sons, and strong kinship bonds.[53] Many

51. Ibid., 125–26.
52. Ibid., 125.
53. Ibid., 132.

studies on family values and behavior noted that the changes have not been accompanied by improved social, political, and legal status for women.[54] Despite obvious gains made by women in education and economic participation, the notion of male dominance still persists within the family and the society. Korean families still cherish the ideal image of the traditional extended family. Even though nuclear families are more popular in reality, Koreans try hard to maintain their extended family structure by visiting or calling their parents, struggling to maintain the bonds of the extended family. The ethics and values espoused by the traditional Confucian influence of the past are changing very slowly.

In Korea today, as a result of the rapid transformation of the economy and society in recent decades, there appears to be a conflict between traditional values and the Confucian heritage on the one hand and Western influence through economic and social changes on the other.[55] The conflict is being played out between parents and children, men and women, and superiors and subordinates as they attempt to apply, depending on their viewpoint, traditional Confucian values or modern egalitarian principles—in the family, in the workplace, and in their actions as individuals.[56] This diversity is generating a great deal of tension and threatens social harmony and consensus in Korean society and family relationships.

With these challenges, Byung-sun Oh suggests that the "new Confucian ethics" places great emphasis on education and personal and familial relations.[57] It also stresses personal cultivation, self-improvement, and discipline, both spiritual and psychological. Oh goes on to state that new Confucian ethics also stress harmonious personal relationships among individuals and put great importance on harmony, cooperation, consensus, and social solidarity among members of an organization.[58] This is in sharp contrast to the Western emphasis on competition. Today, the harmonious integration of values stressing cooperation and competition appears increasingly crucial for Korean society's continued development. According to Oh, a new culture of personal cultivation, self-achievement, and cooperation must develop; from a one-way self-sacrifice to mutual sacrifice

54. Ibid.
55. Ibid.
56. Ibid.
57. Oh, "Cultural Values and Human Rights," n.p.
58. Ibid.

in parent-child and marital relationships. There should also be integration between cooperation and competition.

However, a great concern in Korean society and family is that "individualism" will emerge in its most egocentric forms. Koreans have traditionally rejected these expressions of individuality because they have resulted in selfishness in personal choices and narcissism in flight from solidarity of family relationships. Korean culture is in a state of total confusion in wanting and recognizing freedom from collectivism and tradition versus blind and relentless pursuit of individual ambition and greed. Chun-sik Ch'oe calls this "patriarchal collectivism."[59] He defines this as a collective society that places the father-son relationship above all else. Since in Korean culture great emphasis has been placed on one's own parents and family, responsibilities to other people are ignored and sometimes excluded. The ethical system is based on not only the principle of respecting the superior, but also favoring the intimate. Because family members are conceived of as part of a whole body, members of a family residing under the same roof have an obligation to share resources with one another. They should do their best to satisfy the needs of their family members first. Relationships with friends or people outside the family are different from relationship with family members. Koreans increasingly focus on satisfaction of one's own needs and family over all else. Yet, they are still in conflict because of the strict adherence to filial piety, and purportedly placing the community ahead of the individual. This creates inner turmoil and social confusion which ultimately must be resolved in the family.

Conclusion

In this chapter, we have focused on self-sacrifice as practiced in Korean culture and family relationship. For Koreans, self-sacrifice has been considered a natural byproduct of a hierarchical culture influenced by Confucianism, which stressed an interdependent and connected harmony within family, community, and society. This understanding of self-sacrifice often arose out of obligation and duty, not self-giving or voluntary service, which offered true liberation and mutual benefit to each other. To Koreans, if an individual refuses to go along this obligation, then he is branded as an outcast. In all familial relationships (spousal, parental, and sibling) responsibilities to the family come above all else. For Koreans, sacrifice for family

59. Ch'oe, *Han'guk Chonggyo Munhwa ro Ilnunda*, 206.

and others is not only demanded but is considered as an inevitable part of their life. The Korean's future is determined by the needs and reputation of the family and not by individual passions, visions, strengths, and talents.

However, Korean family relationships are undergoing a major transition from the traditional to "the new Confucian relationships." To demand that everyone hold to traditional values and beliefs in a rapidly changing society is naive. While it is important to emphasize the strength of the unity of community and family, we cannot overlook the importance of equality and mutuality in our interpersonal relationships and community. There must be a new set of ethics that balances both the community and the individual and recognize that one has a right to one's own choice to self-fulfillment and self-achievement, yet to serve, sacrifice, and unite with others to preserve and defend community. Sacrificing for unity and personal cultivation are not mutually exclusive. We can be united as individuals without losing our individuality or our love for individual freedom and for others.

Misunderstanding of and improper motives for self-sacrifice can be detrimental to family relationships and Koran society as a whole. In this context, I will be arguing in subsequent chapters that the concept of self-sacrifice in Korean family and culture must change from obligated service to serving each other in reciprocal equality and voluntary self-giving. Now, more than ever, Koreans are seeing that this hierarchical authority for sacrifice no longer holds the power to cement the culture. Koreans look at the concept of self-sacrifice with a different perspective and are incorporating the Western cultural value of individualism. They make sacrifices with different motives and reasons than those characteristic of the traditional Confucian family. Parents can no longer demand that a child do as they see fit because of this hierarchy, nor are they expected to continually sacrifice for their children. Instead of maintaining hierarchical relationship, they should strive to form more flexible, affectionate, and personal relationships in families and friendships where the virtue of self-sacrifice is regarded as graceful self-giving and welcome mutual service, not as socially defined obligation and structural duty.

Self-sacrifice out of duty as a women, a parent, or a first-born son is not true self-sacrifice. This one-way self-sacrifice is harmful to human relationship, especially family relationship. Without reciprocated care and respect, obligatory self-sacrifice will destroy individuals and family relationships. We can also no longer allow self-sacrifice to create scapegoats for the harm that patriarchal hierarchy has inflicted on society. Obligatory self-sacrifice seen in Korean traditional culture should not be praised as a virtue in the name of Confucianism. We must understand self-sacrifice, not as the central virtue, but as one among many virtues, as an act done only in the proper context and out of proper motives.

Jesus says, "I no longer call you servants, because a servant does not know his master's business. Instead, I have called you friends, for everything that I learned from my Father I have made known to you" (John 15:15 NIV). Jesus called us friends, and out of this radical inversion and subversive leveling of the social order, he demonstrated what true self-sacrifice shall be among his disciples. In this, Jesus called each and every one of us to follow that example. When self-sacrifice is motivated by equality and fairness, it becomes something greater than an individual's effort to create harmony and peace by one-sided obeisance in self-sacrifice. Without understanding the dignity, integrity, and equality necessary for authentic interpersonal relationships, self-sacrifice becomes impossible.

In the following chapter, I will provide a case study of a Korean American interracial marriage that will provide the basis for discussion of the patterns of yielding to dominance and the interplay of dominance/submission in Korean American marriage relationships. I will discuss how Korean marriages tend to be imbalanced, and note how intercultural experiences are revealing to Koreans how deeply renewal is needed. In this case study we will discover a clear example of a not atypical interracial couple's marital problems that reveal the injustices and injuries arising from competing and conflicting cultural differences, confusing language barriers, and opposing family backgrounds. We will see self-sacrifice in a living situation.

2
———————————————

Self-Sacrifice and Marital Expectations
Yielding and Dominance/Submission

Introduction

KOREANS ARE ONE OF the fastest growing ethnic groups in the United States. Recent Korean immigrants constitute the vast majority of the Korean American population. As a result, interracial marriages between Korean and Americans have increased, and have become a momentous issue in the Korean community. The most common problem faced by Korean American couples is relating to the multigenerational Korean family, because Korean parents tend not to accept such interracial marriages, and these couples must worry that their interracial marriage will certainly cause distance and may break off relationships with parents and relatives. This is a serious issue for a Korean partner to handle; the unity of family is highly valued in the Korean culture, and the interracial marriage threatens to create disharmony and conflict between family members. In addition to problems related to family, Korean partners face diverse patterns of inequality in their marital life, including social problems such as financial status, language barriers, community activities, etc. These couples, especially Korean women, face a harsh reality and have a difficult time adjusting to the differences in cultural norms and values.

Korean marriage, with dominance granted to the male, submission required from the female according to traditions reaching back to Confucius, is inherently imbalanced, and intercultural experiences such as bicultural marriage are highly revelatory of the effects of this inequality. Renewal is needed.

In this chapter, I will apply the insights on self-sacrifice to Korean American marriage by using a clinical study of an intercultural marriage that offers a CAT scan of the inner dynamics of self-sacrifice when a Korean spouse is confronted with a partner from a non-sacrificial, individualist culture. The case presents the dynamics of a cultural clash, and the vignette will show that the most serious challenges come in regards to assumptions related to yielding or sacrifice as the expected resolution of tensions between wills and goals.

In overview, this chapter will deal first with the interracial marriage of Korean and American spouses. As the chapter unfolds, I will present my own experiences working with Korean American interracial couples in the United States. These examples can be helpful for understanding Korean and American cultures and contexts. The typical Korean American couple struggles with two deeply contrasting backgrounds, such as a Korean woman who has been raised in a collective and sacrificial culture and an American man who is accustomed to an individualistic and self-oriented culture. Second, I will present research on the primary differences in cultures, and family backgrounds faced by Korean American couples in their marriage. Third, I will provide an organized, culturally sensitive theoretical framework that can be helpful for Korean American couples. I believe that such a conceptual framework should take into consideration the couple's cultural differences, language barriers, original family structures, and help-seeking patterns. Among the many theories of family and marital therapy, I will apply the theoretical framework of Bowen family systems theory, which offers the best clinical base for reflection and assessment.

The entire chapter will be unified by frequent references to the story of a Korean American couple who has been married for twenty-five years, which forms the central clinical case for exploration. I believe that this case will provide a good example of a typical interracial couple's marital problems that center in cultural differences, language barriers, and different family backgrounds.

Furthermore, I will evaluate the case of a Korean American couple utilizing Bowen's approach to systems therapy. I want to critique its contribution, as well as some perceived deficiencies in applying this framework to the context of Korean American couples. However, this evaluation will be primarily focused on how to help Korean American women in interracial marriage with American men, because I have a deep interest in and commitment to dealing with the issues of Korean American women in my future ministry. Finally, I will give some theological implications and practical suggestions for pastors and counselors in their ministry.

The Reality of Interracial Marriage

Interracial marriage, like any other marriage, is a continuous process in which two individuals learn to live together. They learn how to adjust to each other to produce a successful marital relationship. When a person marries someone with a different racial and ethnic background, the complexity of adjusting to their partner's expectations increases exponentially. In this section, I will present a story of a Korean American couple who has been married for twenty-five years. Their names have been changed and their permission of disclosure has been obtained. This section discusses traditional characteristics of Korean families and how they contrast with American families, as well as the contrasting ways in which they view the socioeconomic changes that affect contemporary Korean American families. In addition, this section deals with some issues Korean American couples face as a result of their culturally different backgrounds. However, it is important to recognize that the case presented in this chapter is illustrative of the dynamic of self-sacrifice in marriage and not intended to generalize from one case to the larger population of intercultural/interracial marriages.

Case Study: The Story of Vincent and Pokja

Pokja, a Korean woman, and Vincent, an American man, have been married for twenty-five years. They are in their late forties and have two sons. Their sons are married and each has one boy. Vincent is a truck driver and Pokja works for a Korean grocery store.

Pokja and her family first came to America from Korea in search of a better job opportunity for her father. Vincent was introduced to Pokja by his Korean friend. He liked the Korean culture and desired to know more about Korea. In addition, Vincent found her very attractive, not because of her good looks, but rather her good personality and willingness to submit herself to him. Pokja was raised within a very conservative Korean family.

Self-Sacrifice and Marital Expectations

She could speak only Korean at home and her family's activities usually took place exclusively in the Korean community. She was raised to be self-sacrificing, docile, submissive, and eager to please. She tried to listen to and obey Vincent's wishes. He did not see this sacrifice in American girls. After dating her for a while, Vincent asked for Pokja's hand in marriage. However, she worried about introducing him to her family, especially her father and older brother. Her father, a very authoritative and conservative Korean man, would not allow his daughter to marry an American man. This was just the beginning for Pokja and Vincent. On her wedding day, Pokja's family failed to attend the ceremony. Her mother's absence caused Pokja much grief. Pokja said, "It was the greatest shock I have ever experienced. I was very upset. I felt humiliated, and um . . . I wanted to die right away." However, Pokja, intuitively, understood that her interracial marriage would bring shame to her family and the Korean community. From that day, she began to distance herself from, and eventually severed all ties with, her family. However, in spite of this great loss, she was happy with her husband, Vincent. His family welcomed her and helped her adjust to American life.

After their first son, Tom, was born they experienced some conflicts in their marriage. Vincent complained that Pokja spent all day long caring for her son. When he came back from work, he wanted to have some private time with her. However, she refused this request. He could not understand why Pokja would pour out all of her energy and time into taking care of her son. One day, he asked Pokja to leave her son at his mother's house for dinner. This upset Pokja greatly, and she complained of Vincent's lack of love toward his son.

In addition, Vincent was also distressed that his Korean wife, Pokja, would hardly respond to him sexually. Vincent complained to his wife, "You always turn me down when I want to make love to you. I don't understand that you refuse to give a hug and a kiss to me in public." Pokja explained, "I want you to make love to me with words as well as actions. I cannot respond affectionately when I don't feel good toward you and toward our relationship. I do not feel comfortable to express my love in front of others." Pokja considered the Western way of publicly demonstrating affection and expressing their love openly as being overly external, physical, and even unclean. Pokja explained that she was embarrassed when her husband's friends slapped her on the back and tried to squeeze her shoulders from the side. Pokja said, "We just do not do that in Korea, as you know. I get really upset, plus I could not speak good enough English to explain my traditional way to greet each other. I do not want to make my husband angry, but I just cannot do that."

They also have communication problems because of language barriers. Although Pokja has been in the United States for over twenty-five years, she still has difficulty understanding his English. Vincent said that he, sometimes, is not sure if his wife understands his deep feelings for her. She also feels the need to talk about her feelings toward her husband, but is not able to express them easily in English. In an attempt to express her emotions, Pokja tried to talk about her marriage life in detail with her Korean friends and her first son, who can speak Korean. She always feels sorry about the lack of communication between her parents and her husband. This, however, did not seem to be an issue to Vincent.

Another factor contributing to the marital conflicts centered in contrasting attitudes about money. For some time, Vincent had been growing resentful of Pokja's conservative attitudes toward spending money. Pokja, on the other hand, had been feeling uneasy about Vincent's liberal, carefree attitude toward their personal finances. He complained that she did not know how to spend money, but she instead attempted to save for her family's future. Vincent began to distance himself from her and his children. Pokja, on the other hand, was upset about the fact that he was not interested in saving money and making a better future for his children and their marriage. Whenever her husband distances himself from her, she feels lonely and very depressed. She sometimes talks to her mother and sisters, but rarely visits them due to her situation with her father. She sometimes regrets marrying an American man.

Pokja also has a conflict with their first son's wife, Mariah. Pokja complains that Mariah is very lazy and does not want to work for her family. So, Pokja talked about this with her first son, Tom. However, Tom did not listen to her, instead he became very upset about her intervening in his marriage life. When she tried to talk with him on the phone about her feelings, Tom hung up. Pokja was in shock and very upset. She said, "It is unbelievable that Tom just hung up. He used to be a good son. His wife spoiled Tom and provoked him to disobey me. I do not want to talk to him and Mariah." Tom and Mariah did not visit Pokja and they did not talk to each other for a while.

Cultural Differences in Korean American Marriage: General Cultural Backgrounds and Differences

Joel Crohn points out that ethnicity, religion, race, gender, and class do influence every aspect of a person's view of the world and what they consider "normal" or abnormal.[1] Cultural norms affect how anger and affection are expressed, how children are disciplined and rewarded, how strangers and friends are greeted, and what roles men and women play in society. For instance, in cross-cultural relationships, contrasting cultural norms may lead one partner to describe behavior as friendly, while the other sees it as seductive. While one person may regard a little debate to be a friendly disagreement, the other may be just as sure it is a threat. When one says he visits his parents "often," he may mean twice a year; but for another, "seldom" may mean twice a week.

For this reason, the major problem in an interracial marriage is often a result of different cultural values. Each partner is likely to think that his/her own cultural values are "right." Man Keung Ho points out that "once the individual's value system is challenged, especially by a spouse, the individual becomes uncertain and most often reacts defensively."[2]

At first, such contrasts between American and Korean values may form the basis of the attraction, but these different cultural values can lead to conflict in Korean American marriage. Crohn suggests that the values of "hyper-individualistic" white American Protestant culture, which elevate the separate, bounded, and autonomous self, stand in sharp contrast to the collective and communal values of Asian culture in which individual and group identity are tightly intertwined.[3]

In many Asian countries, Lee says, there is a general cultural assumption that the family exists as the basic unit of society.[4] Many Asian American groups, such as Korean, Chinese, and Japanese, value the commitment to the needs of the group over the individual's needs and self-development. These cultures all value obedience, self-control, sacrifice, and family interests rather than the typical American values of independence, self-expression, and individual interests.[5] Although second- and third-generation

---

1. Crohn, "Intercultural Couples," 295.
2. Ho, *Intermarried Couples in Therapy*, 24.
3. Crohn, "Asian Intermarriage," 429.
4. Lee, *Working with Asian Americans*, 9.
5. Esther Ngan-Ling Chow, "Feminist Movement: Where Are All the Asian

Korean immigrants have become more familiarized with the individualistic American culture than their counterparts who are born in Korea, they still maintain a strong attachment to traditional cultural and family values. For instance, most Korean women living in the United States still have a strong sense of faithfulness to their husbands and will readily sacrifice for their families. Due to the influences of a strong Confucian background, a Korean wife values the unity of family and feels the responsibility for caring for the whole family. In Korean culture, the roles of men and women are more clearly, although rigidly, differentiated, and marriage exists in the context of extended family and long-term interfamily relationship.[6] Therefore, the bonds of loyalty and obligation in Korean culture are tremendously strong and extend back through the generations. For Koreans, it is common that a family member can be called upon to make personal sacrifices for the sake of the extended family.

However, in American culture, strong autonomy and independence are emphasized among family members. There is a general assumption that the family exists for the development and protection of individual family members. For example, an American husband may not want to be involved in extended family matters, especially of his wife's side. It is likely that he is more interested in his own business or his children's upbringing. He encourages his own children to pursue their own visions, dreams, goals, wishes, and desires. The primary concern for the typical American head of the household is limited to the immediate nuclear family, to the point that extended family is easily considered as separate, at least to the point that their concerns become secondary or tertiary in value. To make sacrifice out of respect for even the immediate family is not generally regarded to be as important as one's ability to fulfill one's own desires, success, and happiness. These kinds of differences in cultural values may cause marital problems in a Korean American interracial marriage.

In Vincent and Pokja's case, she always forced the children to study hard. It was very important to Pokja that her children attend a good school and get a good job to honor the family. Her children's failures, she assumed, would cause her family to be shamed by the community. Vincent, on the other hand, did not place the same emphasis on the importance of education. Rather, he wanted to raise his children to be self-sufficient and self-reliant, and ultimately to leave their home and lead their own lives. Pokja,

---

American Women?," in *Making Waves*, ed. Asian Women United of California, 362–77.

6. Crohn, "Asian Intermarriage," 429.

with her Korean upbringing, understands the role of an individual to be dependent on societal norms, believing that one's family members are not isolated from society. She placed great importance on the perception of others, especially her elders in the community. For her, one's reputation is very important. "I have to force my children to study. If they do not succeed in studying, other people would think ill of me." This is a strong representation that embodies the prohibitive aspect which guards the norm and standard of Korean society. For Vincent, on the other hand, the importance of his children's education came not from reputation and social standing but fulfilling the needs, goals, and capabilities of his children. This problem stems from the cultural differences, many of which are tacit or unspoken and come to awareness only when one person is in sharp conflict with another.

Korean culture places high value on the motivation to serve, to sacrifice, and to connect with others. This is in sharp contrast to the American culture, which places high value on motivations directed toward achievement of personal goals. One study's finding suggests that Asian Americans are more likely than other Americans to make personal sacrifices that foster harmony and promote the well-being of a relationship.[7] Such behavior may increase the stability of Korean American interracial marriages. Traditionally, Korean marriages were seen as an extension of the parents' family and the joining of two families. Accompanying this type of marriage were the beliefs that husbands and wives should remain devoted to each other and should maintain harmony no matter the circumstances. One researcher notes that, traditionally, Chinese people have viewed divorce as so shameful to a family's honor that they prefer to endure an unhappy marriage than the shame of divorce.[8] This tendency applies to a Korean partner in Korean American interracial marriage.

Another difference is that traditional Korean culture avoids open conflict. A Korean American wife may have communication styles in marriage that differ from the American cultural norm. For many Americans, the ability to talk openly over issues and disagreements is considered one of the most important aspects of marital satisfaction. Open conflict is relatively common and normal and is often part of family communication and

---

7. Huang, "Asian Perspective on Relationship and Marriage Education," 161–73.
8. Lucy Jen Huang, "Chinese American Family," in *Ethnic Families in America*, ed. Mindel and Habenstein, 115–41.

dynamics.[9] In contrast, many Korean Americans do not place high emphasis on verbal communication in their marriage. In Korean families, family conflict is frequently managed by isolation, indirect communication, and polite inattention.[10] The strong hierarchy within the family defines who may voice an opinion and who must suppress it. This tendency often leads the submissive partner to be obligated to unilateral self-sacrifice to maintain harmony or avoid conflict. One study found that many Chinese couples deal with conflicts simply by not bringing the issue up again.[11] This is also seen in Korean Americans. Korean norms discourage the expression of feelings, especially strong negative emotions such as anger and frustration. Koreans were more likely to express love and support nonverbally through doing tasks for each other and sacrificing their own needs.[12] For instance, in Vincent's case, when he brings up some issues to his wife, Pokja tends to withdraw from the conflict and becomes quiet. He complains that she does not try to voice an opinion, but rather suppresses it. He wants to have frank and open conversations with his wife. Vincent does not understand that it is common and normal that a Korean woman does not speak for herself and raise her voice in the family.

Table 2.1 highlights some of these general differences between traditional Asian values and Western values. I cannot describe these differences in detail in this section due to space limitation, but I believe that these differences give us some distinctive characteristics between Eastern and Western cultural values.

---

9. Lee, *Working with Asian Americans*, 11.
10. Ibid., 10.
11. Cheung, "Cross-Cultural Comparison," 51–78.
12. Mortenson, "Sex, Communication Values, and Cultural Values," 59–60.

Table 2.1. Comparisons of Asian and Western cultural values[13]
Asian agricultural system / Western industrial system
Traditional society values / modern society values

1. Family-/group-oriented	1. Individual-oriented
2. Extended family	2. Nuclear/blended family
3. Multiple parenting	3. Couple parenting
4. Primary relationship: parent-child bond	4. Primary relationship: marital bond
5. Emphasis on interpersonal relationships	5. Emphasis on self-fulfillment and self-development.
6. Status and relationships determined by age and role in family	6. Status achieved by individual's efforts
7. Well-defined family members' roles	7. Flexible family members' roles
8. Favoritism toward males	8. Increasing opportunities for females
9. Authoritarian orientation	9. Democratic orientation
10. Suppression of emotions	10. Expression of emotions
11. Fatalism/karma	11. Person control over the environment
12. Harmony with nature	12. Mastery over nature
13. Cooperative orientation	13. Competition orientation
14. Past, present, and future orientation	14. Present, future orientation

Due to these different values, many Korean American interracial couples have a difficult time adjusting to differences in culture, tradition, family background, and language. Many of these couples enter marriage without sufficient preparation to handle the problems that they will soon face. Consequently, a high percentage of interracial marriages end in divorce.

However, it should be noted that although Korean Americans tend to value obedience, sacrifice, and family, today they may be willing to pursue personal desires and ambitions, as well, due to their assimilation into the American culture. This shift in values by comparison makes Korean American partners in interracial marriages less fixated to their spouses and families. They are also less wary of the Korean ethos of potential shame that is associated with the lack of self-sacrifice in a family environment. If an American husband expects that a Korean American wife be obedient and sacrificial to family members, this expectation could become a source of conflict within their marriage.

13. Ibid., 9.

Different Family Backgrounds (Family Issues)

Crohn says that "intermarried couples often discover that they must grapple not only with different culturally shaped behavioral norms, but also with the nature of their blended families' cultural and religious identities."[14] As a result, many couples attempt to deal with their differences by trying to ignore or forget their cultural and family background. Some interracial couples use a kind of voluntary "cultural and religious amnesia" to ease the discomfort of living and loving together in relationships that defy tradition, but even when ties to tradition, culture, and family background have eroded, the need to belong does not disappear.[15] In Pokja's case, she wanted to forget every memory of Korean life and tried to eliminate contact with her family. However, as time progressed, she found that she still missed her family, culture, and tradition and had a strong desire to go back to her family of origin even at the expense of divorce. The failure to clarify and discuss the meaning of cultural identity may lead to conflict in relationships.

The most common problem faced by Korean American interracial couples is family problems, because Korean parents tend not to accept their interracial marriages. Before Korean American couples decide to marry, the individuals, especially the Korean partner, worries that his/her interracial marriage may change his/her relationship with parents and relatives. Studies indicate that extended family ties for ethnic minorities are more cohesive and extensive than kinship relationships among the white population.[16] For Koreans, the support from their family and relatives play a vital role in creating the sense of belonging and security.

For a Korean woman, disobeying her parents who oppose her interracial marriage is a big issue, because parental consent is, according to Korean tradition, required for marriage. The main reason that Korean parents oppose their children's interracial marriages lies in their strong ethnocentrism. Koreans are members of a very homogeneous race. They all speak and write the same language, which has been a crucial factor in their strong national identity. They want to keep this "pure race" by not mixing with any other racial groups. Korean parents believe that the cultural differences in interracial marriages would be in some ways harmful to Korean society.

---

14. Crohn, "Intercultural Couples," 300.
15. Ibid.
16. Ho, *Intermarried Couples*, 9–10.

Many Korean parents also reject their children's interracial marriages, because Korean parents often see their children's choice as an attempt to hurt or reject them.[17] When their children decide to marry Americans, Korean parents feel that they have failed in educating their children and think that they have lost their children. The parents seem to fear that their daughters and sons will turn away from their families and their Korean culture. The parents easily become angry, cold-hearted, and irrational. Sometimes, the parents try to threaten their children to give up their interracial marriage because the parents have a high expectation of their children's happiness in the marriage, of maintaining strong family ties, and of having personal relationship with their in-laws. In addition, in traditional Korean families, the father makes all major decisions for his children. Therefore, without the father's consent, a Korean partner would be forced to choose whether to give up her interracial marriage or leave her parents and Korean community.

For these reasons, before many Koreans make a strong decision to marry Americans, they at times try to keep the relationship with Americans secret in order to maintain their Korean family ties. In *Counseling Multiracial Families*, Bea Wehrly et al. quote Hedgeman, who correctly points out that "isolation and alienation from family, friends, and neighbors have been reported as some of the stressors felt by couples in Black-White marriages."[18] This is also true for Korean American marriages.

Theoretical Framework for Korean American Marriage

Most Western family therapy approaches have been limited in their application to interracial couples focusing primarily on American issues. In this respect, frameworks and family therapy models should take into consideration family history, tradition, and cultural backgrounds when dealing with the problems of Korean and American couples. Also, these models should dialogue with communities of experience, as well as Christian sources and interpretations, with the aim of guiding actions toward social and individual transformation.[19] I believe that among the many theories of family and marital therapy, Don Browning's ecosystem approach and Murray Bowen's

---

17. Root, *Love's Revolution*, 18.
18. Wehrly et al., *Counseling Multiracial Families*, 35.
19. Browning, *Fundamental Practical Theology*, 36.

family systems therapy models will best serve as a theoretical framework for Korean American couples.

I have chosen to utilize Bowen Family Theory as my clinical perspective, selecting it from the wider field of family theories because it offers the most coherent clinical and philosophical base for moving between cultures in both theory and practice. The strength of Bowen's model for cross-cultural work rises from its firm biological base, clear interpersonal stance, and socio-cultural orientation. Bowen's model recognizes that the family system is a subsystem of the community, and the community is a subsystem of the society; the society, of the national culture, and ultimately, of the culture of humanity. These all interrelate; each sets the emotional, rational, relational, and moral tone for all others, because all are interdependent, and any change in one affects the whole.[20] In this context, with Bowen's family systems theory, we can help couples to see their problems within both the extended and immediate families and to differentiate themselves from the unhealthy bonds. In addition, with Browning's model, we are able to grasp the larger context of interracial marriage so that we can converse with cultural and religious experience, personal experience, church history, systematic theology, memory of community, and tradition. The ecosystem approach and Browning's model will serve as a framework within which I will evaluate Bowen's family systems theory as it deals with more specific issues in a Korean American marriage.

The Ecosystem and Browning's Strategic Practical Theology Model

In order to help Korean American couples, it is clear that marital therapy requires an organized, culturally sensitive theoretical framework. I believe that interracial couples' marital relationships should be understood in the ecosystem approach, for such a conceptual framework takes into consideration the couple's cultural differences, language barriers, original family structures, and help-seeking patterns.

An ecological model originally developed by Urie Bronfenbrenner (1977) utilizes four factors affecting human development and interaction: individual, family, culture, and environment.[21] If pastors or Christian counselors miss one of these aspects, the counseling or therapy will not be useful in helping the interracial couples, especially Korean Americans.

20. Augsburger, *Pastoral Counseling across Cultures*, 179–80.
21. Ho, *Intermarried Couples*, 36.

An ecosystem model is presented below.

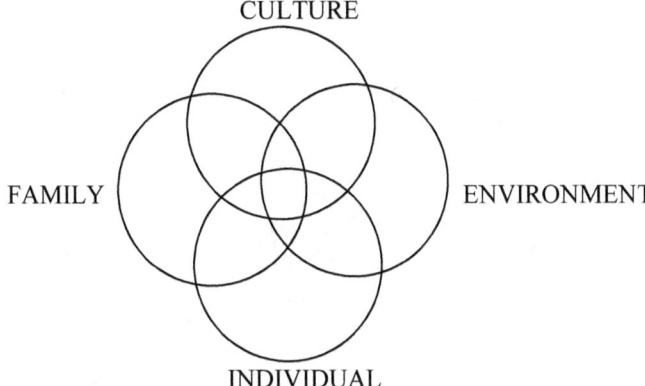

Ho points out that although an interpersonal relationship is the primary concern of marital therapy, problem-solving and enhancement of the marital relationship cannot occur without a clear analysis of the four ecological factors.[22]

According to the ecosystem approach, in order to understand interracial couples' problems better, we should focus on the individual level (personal strengths, communication and language skill, emotional temperature, and habit formation), the family level (family life style, culture, tradition, ritual, and relationships), the cultural level (value systems and social norms), and the environmental level (economic and social structure).[23] An ecological perspective helps pastors or Christian counselors understand how these four factors function, even when they interact in complex ways, within an interracial marriage situation and accept interracial couples' unique cultural backgrounds and life styles.

In addition, Ray Anderson employed Don Browning's model, which offers a compelling and critical model that is developed from what he is calls "practical reason."[24] "The concept of practical reason, for Browning, places the theological task at the center of the social context, where the theologian stands with and alongside the church mediating the gospel of Christ from the center."[25] Browning claims that "practical reason has an

22. Ibid.
23. Ibid., 36–37.
24. Anderson, *Shape of Practical Theology*, 26.
25. Ibid.

overall dynamic, an outer envelope, and an inner core."[26] The components of practical reason are presented below.[27]

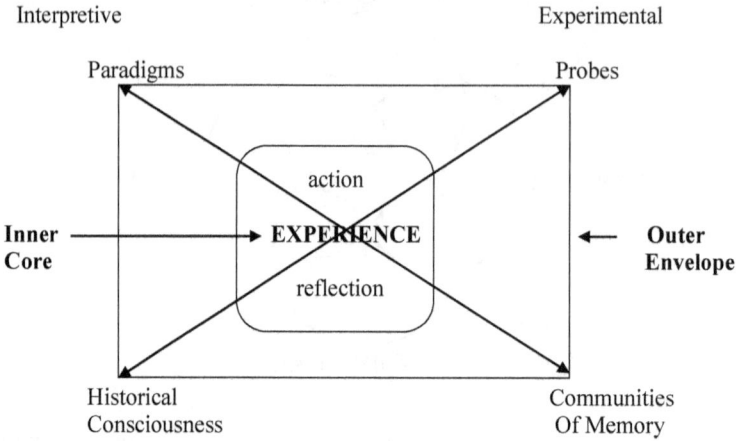

For Browning, "The outer envelope of practical reason is its fund of inherited narratives and practices that tradition has delivered to us and that always surrounds our practical thinking."[28] He continues to explain that "the inner core functions within a narrative about God's creation, governance, and redemption of the world. It also functions within a narrative that tells how the life and death of Jesus Christ furthers God's plans for the world. This narrative is the outer envelope of practical reason. It constitutes the vision that animates, informs, and provides the ontological context for practical reason."[29] By focusing on practical reason, we practical theologians need to ask, "What should we do?" and "How should we live?"

This approach of strategic practical theology helps not only to interpret the issue of interracial marriage with practical and theological perspectives, which goes from practice to theology and back to practice, but also to respond to difficult questions that the couple is facing in their interracial marriage within the larger context of historical background, church tradition, communities of memory, and individual's concern.

---

26. Browning, *Fundamental Practical Theology*, 10.
27. Anderson, *Shape of Practical Theology*, 27.
28. Browning, *Fundamental Practical Theology*, 11.
29. Ibid.

Bowen's Family Systems Theory with Interracial Marriages

One prime factor influencing an interracial couple's response to stress and problems is the organizational structure of each partner's own family prior to the conflict.[30] Interracial couples bring two different family systems and communication patterns which they have previously used to deal with the problems in their family life. The different family systems can be understood only through their original cultural and familial contexts.

In this sense, Bowen's family systems therapy will help interracial couples, especially Korean American partners, better understand conflicts within their original cultural contexts and family backgrounds. Bowen's theory will assist in understanding self-sacrifice in the context of Korean American marriage, because in many cases, the female Korean American partner interacts with a fear of being abandoned. She tries to maintain close contact with her partner, but with a coping mechanism of either *merging with* or *distancing from* her spouse. She believes that husbands and wives should maintain harmony at all costs. I believe that Bowen's theory helps to identify the situation on an objective scale between union and separation, reducing the chance of conflict-avoidance, which can turn unhealthy in the long run.

Bowen's family systems perspective also can provide a new view of family problems and can cross cultural boundaries and contribute to a fuller understanding of broader macro-sociological forces within and between cultures. To understand self-sacrifice within the traditional Korean culture, Bowen's theory lends the view that this self-sacrifice must be understood within the context of the traditional Korean family, the principle of filial piety and societal patriarchy, and the vertical virtue system of the traditional culture. Because many Korean American interracial marriages still function with the belief that vertical benevolence is of the highest virtue (despite the influence from the more individualistic American culture), Korean American marriages can be highly revelatory of the inequalities stemming from this belief. By utilizing Bowen's systems theory, one can see the differences in vertical benevolence vs. mutually reciprocal relationship, in relationship building pattern, in family background, and in cultures within the Korean American marriage.

In addition, Bowen's theory tends to focus on issues related to a partner's family of origin and how these issues may affect his/her marital

---

30. Anderson, *Shape of Practical Theology*, 26.

relationship. Dealing with issues from the family in which a partner grew up can be valuable, but ongoing relationships with parents and in-laws may be particularly important for Korean American women in interracial marital relationship. In this sense, Bowen's theory is a powerful tool to help Korean American couples to understand their differences in family background, culture, the way to relate others, vertical vs. mutual reciprocal relationship.

Bowen's family systems theory consists of eight basic interlocking conceptions. No single concept can be fully understood without the other seven concepts, and each has evolved in complex and distinct ways. In the following discussion, I will not discuss the meaning and difficulties involved in utilizing all of Bowen's eight concepts, but I will describe selected elements of concepts to pinpoint their applicability, usefulness, and limitations within the context of Korean American marriage.

Murray Bowen proposes that "the most central theoretical premise of family systems theory concerns the degree to which we all have poorly 'differentiated selves,' or the degree to which we are 'undifferentiated,' or the degree of our unresolved emotional attachments to families of origin."[31] When a self is less differentiated, behavior is largely emotionally responsive or reactive and controlled by emotions and the anxiety of the moment.[32] When a self is more differentiated, behavior is goal directed, with a clear awareness of distinctions between thinking and feeling activities.[33] Thus, the most important goal of family systems therapy is to help family members toward a better level of "differentiation of self" within interpersonal relationships. Edwin H. Friedman states that Bowen defines differentiation as "the capacity of a family member to define his or her own life's goals and values apart from surrounding togetherness pressures, to say 'I' when others are demanding 'you' and 'we.'"[34] However, the concept should not be confused with autonomy, independence, or narcissism. Instead, this concept needs to recognize the capacity for the individual to remain as an individual while remaining connected to the family. A critical point in Bowen's theory is that differentiation is not achieved through cut-offs but by balance between separation and connections. Cut-offs rather, implies reactivity and fusion, which is the opposition of differentiation.

31. Bowen, *Family Therapy in Clinical Practice*, 529.
32. Hall, *Bowen Family Theory*, 17.
33. Ibid., 23.
34. Friedman, *Generation to Generation*, 27.

Self-Sacrifice and Marital Expectations

In Pokja's case, by Bowen's differentiation of self-scale, she is still living in the degree of the "stuck-together" domain and has a hard time separating herself from the painful experiences of the past. She is intensely related to her family and its cultural issues. Therefore, she tried to leave her family by making an emotional "cut-off" from her family. However, she may still stick to deeply rooted anger, grief, and unresolved personal conflicts that may lead to marital troubles. These unresolved issues have caused Pokja to avoid openly sharing her problems with her husband. The way Pokja seeks to distance herself from her family of origin is by having no communication with her family. Pokja felt that she was rejected by her family of origin, especially by her father. At times, she also felt isolated from her husband and American society because of cultural differences.

Bowen has dealt with this concept within the marital relationship, but also within the larger context of the extended family. According to Bowen, anxiety increases in one or both partners when they allow emotional forces to dominate intellectual functioning.[35] If each spouse depends on the relationship patterns developed in their families of origin and they continue to stick to the patterns in their marriage, this leads them to marital conflict. One spouse who was relatively undifferentiated in his or her original family will continue to be undifferentiated when they form a new family. In other words, if the partners are still intensely and emotionally influenced by their families of origin, they may bring unresolved conflicts from their family into interactions with each other. The lack of differentiation in the family of origin may lead to an emotional cut-off from parents, which in turn leads one to distance him/herself from the partner. In fact, many interracial couples deal with their unresolved emotional problems from original families by merging into or totally separating from their family. It is obvious that if the pattern remains, problems between the interracial couples are likely to persist.

For example, Pokja, with her background in patriarchal Korean family, handled her anxiety by distancing herself through withdrawal or unilateral sacrificing because she was afraid of confronting her husband. Displacing the focus, making it less personal and less threatening, was an excellent way for her to decrease her anxiety. Sacrificing her own needs was the pattern that she has learned from her family of origin, to avoid conflict and maintain harmony. In order not to repeat this in her new family relationship, it is important for Pokja to understand this inescapable link to her family of

---

35. Bowen, *Family Therapy in Clinical Practice*, 305.

origin. Also, unless Vincent makes proactive attempts to understand her family of origin, he will continue to face this unresolved issue with his wife, as well.

Another important concept offered by Bowen's theory that gives insight to interracial marriages is the transmission of the problem to offspring. Bowen calls this the "family projection process."[36] This is the process by which parents transmit their immaturity and lack of differentiation to their children. It is important to note that projection is different from caring concern, but it is an anxious and enmeshed concern. The child who is the object of the projection process becomes the one most attached to the parents (positively or negatively) and the one with the least differentiated self. In this sense, a family project can be considered a scapegoating process in which one person is singled out as a family "problem."[37] The family projection process is so common that Bowen says "it exists to some degree in all families."[38]

Family "triangles" are also important factors that we should take into consideration for understanding the interracial couples' conflicts originating from their different family origins. Celia Jaes Falicov points out that most symptoms of family distress have been regularly linked to the presence of family triangles.[39] The concept of "triangles" describes the ways that any persistent tension, conflict, or anxiety between two people can be diffused by involving a third party. Bowen has defined the smallest relationship unit in the family as a triangle, or a three-person system.[40] This triangle relationship unit can be found in any family in any culture and society. Especially in a marital situation, the conflict is often manifested as disagreements over a third party, such as a child or an older parent.[41] Falicov calls this alliance between two members of different generations (usually a parent and child against the other parent) the "cross-generational coalition."[42] Many therapists not only believe that unresolved marital conflicts cause the intrusion

36. Ibid., 308.
37. Hall, *Bowen Family Theory*, 24.
38. Bowen, *Family Therapy in Clinical Practice*, 308.
39. Celia Jaes Falicov, "The Cultural Meaning of Family Triangles," in *Re-visioning Family Therapy*, ed. McGoldrick, 37.
40. Hall, *Bowen Family Theory*, 23.
41. Falicov, "Cultural Meaning of Family Triangles," in *Re-visioning Family Therapy*, ed. McGoldrick, 37.
42. Ibid.

Self-Sacrifice and Marital Expectations

or the recruitment of a third party, but also believe that a triangle has the effect of weakening necessary boundaries around the couple, and thus further precludes the resolution of the underlying marital discord.

Features of Bowen's Family Systems Theory in Clinical Application

The relevance of Bowen's family systems theory with interracial couples is that the theory helps us to see the effect and impact of unresolved emotional conflicts from the family of origin. In other words, the family system theory's theoretical concepts describe the range of ways family members are emotionally "stuck to" each other, and the ways this "stuck togetherness" continues to operate in the family background, no matter how much people deny it or how much they pretend to be separated from the family origin.[43]

In this sense, Bowen's concept of differentiation will help to strengthen Korean American marriages. The partners who are clearly differentiated selves are freer to relate to one another in mature patterns and are not bound by dependency needs and insecurities which both limit relationships and the persons within those relationships.[44] Therefore, differentiation of self contributes to the healthy functioning of individuals and thus enhances the functioning of the marriage. To interpret this differentiation with an ecological perspective, one needs to differentiate "within" as an individual, and differentiate "between" his family, environment, and society. As a differentiated individual, he does not seek to control others or merge his identity into others and he is not afraid of being rejected; rather, he freely and mutually interacts with others and is able to separate himself from his culture and environment, despite the togetherness pressure exerted, and connect with others freely.

Through Bowen's theory, one can see clearly how the act of self-sacrifice occurs in Korean American family relationship dynamics. People with good differentiation are capable of clear thought and rich feeling, without tendencies to overpower or control the other. They interact freely without fear of being either absorbed or abandoned. They maintain close contact with all the significant people in their family relationships but without being flooded by others' anxieties or fleeing to manage stressful times. David Augsburger emphasizes that "the crucial insight for understanding

---

43. Bowen, *Family Therapy in Clinical Practice*, 529.
44. Waanders, "Ethical Reflections," 100.

differentiation is that it is always balanced between union and separation. Differentiation is not radical independence but centered responsive interdependence."[45] Augsburger continues to offer useful insight to help us see this phenomenon with different cultural lens. He observes there is a "theoretical centering between the two poles," but notes that "cultures vary on the degree of dependence or independence appropriated to the particular context."[46] The Western nuclear family, when congruent with its social context, is centered toward independence. In contrast, the Asian family is centered toward unity and dependence on one another. Understanding this family dynamics will provide an invaluable tool in realizing the pattern of self-sacrifice in Korean American women. It helps us to understand that the optimum balance between union and separation in the forming of a self is relative to the cultural understanding of personhood.[47]

In addition, through the lens of Bowen's theory, Korean American couples can be helped to see complicated "triangles" in their relationships—with each other, children, and extended family members—that can aggravate their marital conflicts. As Hall states, Bowen's theory emphasizes the importance of an individual's ability to objectively observe the primary emotional system and the part the individual plays in it.[48] Once this ability is sufficiently developed, each member of the family can interact with one another without emotional intensity and fusion. However, triangular patterns cannot be isolated from their cultural context, nor can they be judged as universally troubled or dysfunctional.[49] In Western cultures, triangles are viewed with mistrust or a sign of disruptive relationships (high anxiety). Healthy, functional relationships are person-to-person, featuring dialogue; conflicts are managed and resolved between the two; clear, open communication of thoughts and feelings allows rational discussion, as well as emotional investment.[50] However, within Korean culture, conflicts are immediately referred to a third party—family members, especially parents, friends, or a trusted person from the religious community. This triangle relationship can be seen as serving to save face for both parties and to reduce

---

45. Augsburger, *Pastoral Counseling across Cultures*, 181.
46. Ibid.
47. Ibid., 182.
48. Hall, *Bowen Family Theory*, 67–69.
49. Augsburger, *Pastoral Counseling across Cultures*, 183.
50. Ibid., 181.

Self-Sacrifice and Marital Expectations

shaming in the system.[51] However, it would be an unhealthy process to draw in persons who are emotionally involved and likely to be impaired by the process.[52] Therefore, in order to help married Koreans and Americans interact with one another without leaving each other overloaded and over-engaged in their relationships, the crucial issue is not the presence or absence of triangles but whether they are healthy or unhealthy; the question to ask of third-party involvement is whether or not it is conducive to resolving the conflict.[53] It is interesting to note that the act of self-sacrifice can be explained as an instrument of conflict resolution. As tension increases beyond the ability of either partner in a Korean American marriage, self-sacrifice, as a fictive entity assuming third party, is imposed into the stability of a triangular relationship to reduce anxiety and to avoid conflict. Many Korean American women try to maintain harmony or to avoid conflict by making one-way self-sacrifice. On the other hand, Korean American men throw themselves into work, sport, and hobby in order to avoid conflict.

In Pokja's case, she desperately devoted her emotional energy to the children, especially her first son, Tom. It is possible that Pokja wanted to regain her cultural identity through Tom. By understanding the fact that her family is away from her both emotionally and physically and that Vincent is usually out of town because of his job as a truck driver, we can see that Tom was the only available one with whom she could identify herself as a Korean. However, her intense focus on her children has caused Vincent to further distance himself from her. Because his wife was not available to him all the time, Vincent often went with his friends when he was off duty. On the other hand, when Vincent left home, Pokja focused more on her children. Consequently, she made a fixed and rigid triangle relationship between herself, Vincent, and her children. This emotional fusion between Pokja and Tom may have taken the form of warm, dependent, and close bonds, but the emotional fusion often created another conflict. As Friedman notes, one side of emotional triangle tends to be more dysfunctional than healthy.[54] In relationship systems that are not as healthy, the conflict tends to be located on one particular side of a triangle. Pokja said, "I often felt envy, anger, and jealousy when Tom did not listen to me, and took his

---

51. Ibid., 183.
52. Ibid.
53. Ibid.
54. Friedman, *Generation to Generation*, 38.

father's side." Pokja, through her son (identified patient), made her triangle relationship and attempted to restore the balance in the family.

According to Bowen's theory, the emotional fusion may distract her from her own anxieties but does not resolve her own problem. She may transmit her anxieties and her marital problems to Tom because she cannot deal with her problems. It is possible that she does not want to face the painful and traumatic experiences of her past. To deal with her own issues, she expresses her anger toward Tom and tells him almost everything about his father. This emotional fusion with her family of origin and Tom may interrupt the process of differentiation of self for both Pokja and Tom.

If we take Bowen's family systems therapy to help Pokja's family, the main task is to reduce the emotional fusion between a mother, her children, and her family. In other words, the therapist may encourage Pokja to differentiate herself into a clearer relationship with her family of origin and her children. This would require exploration of ways of bridging the cut-off and restoring a new level of connection with her family. It is obvious that the concept of Bowen's differentiation of self can help Pokja recognize her emotional cut-off from her family of origin and emotional fusion with her children in order to differentiate herself from the frozen situation of being "emotional stuck," thus allowing her to step back to see her marital problems with a different angle. It is no doubt that pastoral counseling or therapy should help Pokja to deal with her problems by reversing the triangles and beginning to deal directly with Vincent rather than projecting these on Tom. Pokja and Vincent should see the ways in which their triangulated relationships lead them to conflicts. They must reframe their family communication structures and break the "triangles" between Pokja, Vincent, and the children. The differentiation will strengthen their marital relationship and maintain a more stable and healthy family. If they are differentiated from fixed and frozen triangles, they will be able to relate to one another more freely and maturely.

At this point, the question should be raised whether any and all triad relationships have a harmful effect on human relationships. In other words, is it possible that a third parties or issues in relationship can work positively within human relationships? Suppose a wife and a husband have a common interest or hobby. They can enjoy this together and build up their marital relationship with common interests in a constructive way, thus helping them manage potential tension in their marriage. In other words, by bringing a common third party into the relationship, they can share their resources, find love and friendship in their relationships, and mitigate the possible strain or pressure in their marriage, rather than distorting and subverting real issues and placing all blame on others. Bowen's concern is with imbalance in triads, when one side of the triangle is close and the other is pushed far away. He is concerned about fixed and frozen triangles that do not allow clear, healthy, dyadic or person-to-person dialogue and conversation. In Pokja's case, it would be helpful for her to make some meaningful relationships with her women friends. Within these relationships, she could release stresses caused by emotional separation from her family of origin and her husband. She could get gratification and emotional support rather than distorting and subverting the issues in her marriage. I hope some further study about his positive effect of triangle relationships within Korean American marriage will be done in the future.

In this sense, we as pastoral counselors should not ignore the presence of different cultural values. The concept of the differentiation of self has different meanings and methods in American and Asian cultures. In Western culture, people believe that optimal development requires a stance of differentiation from one's family of origin.[55] Within a Western perspective, we may easily pathologize the lifelong connectedness and interdependence that is characteristic of many Asian cultures, including Korean, whose life conditions often make of the parent-child dyad a more enduring or stable relationship than the marital bond.[56] For example, in Korean American marriage, Korean wives are blamed for fusing their identities to their children's. However, Korean spouses should not be blamed for social arrangement that is culturally sanctioned. Korean women grew up in hierarchical and patriarchy system in which a man and woman have different roles that are rigid and unequal. It is possible that Korean women may be encouraged to be in fusion with other family members. In their marriages, there is still inequality in power based on gender or culture. Korean women are searching for their identity through their fusion with other members of the family. Consequently, their search and values from this fusion must be acknowledged by the family. For this reason, it is always a mistake to evaluate people from one's own cultural perspective. Instead, the culturally capable counselor must be equipped with a multicultural perspective to help interracial couples. In Pokja's case, she may discover her true self in

---

55. Falicov, "Cultural Meaning of Family Triangles," in *Re-visioning Family Therapy*, ed. McGoldrick, 39.

56. Ibid., 38–39.

her connectedness and emotional involvement to her children rather than attachment to her husband. It may be natural or possible that Pokja wants to devote her time and energy to her children and sacrifice herself for her family because she was raised in a collective culture where the parent-child relationship was more emphasized than Western culture.

In this respect, Bowen's family systems theory may have some weaknesses in applying the concept of the differentiation of self and triangles to Korean and other Asian cultures. However, for Bowen, differentiation is not *from* but *with*, and his concern is to maintain a balance of separateness and connectedness. He would point out that differentiation of self for Pokja is made difficult by her cut-off and would seek to find alternatives to staying distant from her family; he would see differentiation as choosing how close to be to her son and not using him as a substitute relationship for what she is missing in her marriage; he would look for parallels in Korean marriages that allow an effective marital intimacy as well as a vital mothering commitment. He would not support confusion of relationships where Tom becomes the stand-in for Vincent and isolation from her family is accepted as necessary to obey cultural hierarchy. Bowen's theory recognizes that an affective closeness between the mother and children may be culturally expected to be a more intense alliance in one culture versus another. With Bowen's theory, pastors or counselors should discourage Pokja from completely devoting herself to her children and family and encourage her to focus on her job. If they are encouraged to separate from family with ignorance or without balancing differentiation and connectedness, the Bowen's strategy may make Pokja more puzzled and depressed because this can be perceived as selfish or disrespectful to Pokja who may not have a cultural code about the autonomy and separation of the children.

In addition, in the hierarchical and patriarchal Korean society, it is acceptable for the father to distance himself from his wife and from his children for a social life related to his job and for the mother to have an affective closeness with her children. With the different cultural perspective, in which the mother-child bond is emphasized and father can be a "less involving" outsider, a "light" triangle relationship is not always harmful to a Korean woman because she does not have to confront her husband, an authoritative figure, and she can ease her anxiety and fear through others with whom she can build a more comfortable relationship. They can receive some emotional support and gratification of releasing their stress. These triadic relationships may make Korean partners feel more security

Self-Sacrifice and Marital Expectations

and enhance the stability of the marriage. At this point, Falicov gives us an insightful example of a first-generation Filipino American family making use of triangles to grow together. I think that this example can well apply to Korean culture. He says:

> The process of triangulation, so often seen as dysfunctional by Western-culture clinicians, can be successfully employed by first-generation Filipino American families, and their second-generation offspring, especially in dealing with their parents. That is, concerns or complaints about a person can be relayed to that person without straining relationships or exacerbating conflict.[57]

Like Filipino Americans, Korean women also wish that the third person act as a go between and delivers their message to their husbands in an attempt to induce a change in their spouse. Therefore, when pastors or counselors can detect triangle relationships in interracial families, they should not automatically consider these relationships as destructive or harmful to this family, but ask what is the function of the third-party process. They should take into consideration the cultural backgrounds and communication styles.

In Vincent and Pokja's case, their problem lies in a dysfunctional communication between his wife's family and his family, his wife and himself, his wife and his children, and so on. It is especially sad to see that there is no communication between his father-in-law and himself at all. If they experience any conflicts, their communication style is to become quiet and angry at each other indirectly, rather than to have an open talk and solve problems directly. This dysfunctional communication style should be understood in different cultural situations. For example, Vincent immediately voices disagreements or complaints and does not continue to carry this burden inside. In contrast, Pokja has few ways of venting or letting out her frustrations when confronted by her husband and in-laws because of the prohibitions of rigid hierarchy in Korean society. Even when she knows that she is right, yielding is necessary due to the influence from the patriarchal hierarchy. She does not want to deal with the criticism or disrespect from her husband and his family and may be forced to hide real thoughts and emotions.

Also, Koreans wish to preserve family connectedness and avoid interpersonal conflict. They like to take an indirect, implicit, and covert

---

57. Falicov, "Cultural Meaning of Family Triangles," in *Re-visioning Family Therapy*, ed. McGoldrick, 41.

communication style. They agree with others in order to make them comfortable. Falicov argues that "this superficial harmony may be accompanied by talking behind a person's back to a third party for two reasons: first, simply to decompress and reduce tension about some difficult aspect of the relationship; or, second, actually to engage the listener as a helper in changing the other person, with whom the speaker does not wish or dare to negotiate directly."[58] If pastoral counselors understand the Korean communication style in the patriarchal and hierarchal society, they will be in better position to help Pokja to solve her conflict with Vincent.

As for Vincent, he also may feel that Pokja is not listening, understanding, or caring about his problems and his issues. He may believe that they are on different level, "talking to the wind," and "passing right by each other." There is no doubt that the cultures in which they were raised in can be detrimental to their marriage. However, the truth is that different communication styles apply to different people, and true communication between Vincent and Pokja requires that they learn to understand, accept, and accommodate each other's style. However, it is important that they also learn to accept the fact that they probably will never completely understand the each others' true states of mind. They must also accept that their problems will not automatically go away despite the realization of each other's different communication styles.[59] Realization will help to alleviate some of the perplexity, scapegoating, and negative judgment from their different cultural perspectives.

Furthermore, many therapists believe that the actual process of change is begun by learning about one's larger family history—which made up of the family, where they lived, what they did, and what they were like.[60] Augsburger states that "no symptom is ever just one generation deep. A minimum of three generations is involved in any personal problem—self, the parents one is reacting or responding to, and the grandparents who are the repetition or reverse of the parents' emotional style."[61] To see the lager family history and dynamics, Bowen uses a genogram as a multigenerational family map. Genograms are schematic diagrams of families, listing family members and their relationships to one another. In a Korean American interracial marriage, the genogram will serve to describe the

58. Ibid., 40.
59. Romano, *Intercultural Marriage*, 139–40.
60. Ibid.
61. Augsburger, *Pastoral Counseling across Cultures*, 185.

Self-Sacrifice and Marital Expectations

dynamics of relationship within each partners' family. The recognition of both strengths and weaknesses (whether biological, psychological, or in interpersonal relationships) from generation to generation is instrumental in helping Korean American couples to understand the differences in behavioral responses of members of different culture or family backgrounds.

In Pokja's case, it will be helpful to see how much she is differentiated emotionally from her family when we look at her family genogram. Pastors or pastoral counselors are able to get much of Pokja's information about both past and present relationships with other family members. In Pokja's genogram, she had "conflicted" relationships with her father and brother. Conversely, she had a very close relationship with her mother and sisters. She was completely "cut off" from her father. Whenever she felt the need for family support, she was forced to turn solely to her mother and sisters. This triangular pattern continued until she married Vincent. Interestingly, she has a similar relationship pattern with Vincent's family. She also has a conflicted relationship with her father-in-law, but a good relationship with her mother-in-law. She may see her own father's image in her husband's father. As she used to do, she goes to Vincent's mother or her children to gain their emotional support.

If pastoral counselors detect severe intergenerational conflicts in Pokja's family, they may want to interview all family members involved. However, all of Pokja's family members do not reside in the United States. It is very difficult to bring them together into a therapy session. Although chances are, even if they did reside near her, they would still be reluctant to cooperate. Due to this dual-fold limitation imposed by circumstances in space and culture, it will be helpful for pastoral counselors to use the genogram of both Pokja and Vincent to get all information of how closely they are related, what they do, how old they are, and so on. This genogram can be used as an alternative to finding out about intergenerational conflicts that have long been hidden. In addition, this genogram will help Korean American couples to understand that family is a system and that individuals have a direct impact on the family's behavioral patterns, functions, and relationships; the potential for change in the individual members and the entire family; and to find and understand unresolved issues within the family.

Also, the method of family systems theory is directed at the entire family unit, but Bowen's theory is also focused on the nuclear family unit. Bowen believes that meaningful changes are followed by observable changes in the levels of functioning of significant members in the family.[62] Change is initiated by individuals or couples who are capable of affecting the rest of the family. Differentiation of self, which begins as a personal and individual process, is the vehicle for transforming relationships and the entire family system. This seems appropriate in helping interracial couples see their conflicts within not only a family's cultural context, but also the nuclear family they had formed in the United States. However, there still is a level of inequality in power based on gender and culture within Korean American marriages. So although one person is changed, if he or she is in the weaker position, it will be very difficult to influence changes of the whole family. For Korean women, even within a Korean American marriage, taking the initiative is difficult, as they are still living in a sexist society. Therefore, when we examine interracial families, we must look deeply into an individual's ecological background: individual, family, culture, and environment.

Theological Implications and Practical Suggestions for Pastoral Ministry

Today, interracial marriage has become a major issue in pastoral ministry. How can pastors, pastoral counselors, or practical theologians help interracial couples, especially Korean Americans, adjust to their partners' different culture, family backgrounds, and traditions and to see their problems within a theological perspective?

First, when counseling Korean American couples, pastors and pastoral counselors must acknowledge and pay careful attention to the fact that racism, sexism, and prejudices exist in our societies and families. If the theology of the pastors and pastoral counselors is informed through a culturally hegemonic hermeneutic, which tells them that the Bible really condemns interracial marriage as sin—effectively pronouncing one race as "superior" or "inferior" to another—they may be paralyzed by a socio-neurotic distortion or a false consciousness which will render them ineffective as counselors to the intermarried.[63]

Even today, the prejudices of racism are worldwide. There are a significant number of Christians, particularly in Korea, who would claim that such "interracial" marriages directly violate God's principles in the Bible

---

62. Hall, *Bowen Family Theory*, 196.
63. Harris, "Interracial Counseling," 114.

Self-Sacrifice and Marital Expectations

and should not be allowed. But does the word of God really condemn such marriages? In other words, is interracial marriage sin? How can we see this social pattern, as it relates to interracial marriage, within a biblical and theological perspective? How can we practical theologians interpret a biblical text from the theological discourses? How can we offer a sound theological foundation to better see the prejudices of racism in our social contexts?

Before we answer these questions, we practical theologians must first look at what the Bible says about "race." The Bible does not even use the word race in reference to people, but does describe all human beings as being of "one blood" (Acts 17:26 KJV). This, of course, emphasizes that we are all related, as all humans are descendants of the "first man," Adam (1 Cor 15:45 NIV). Jesus Christ also was a descendant of Adam, being called the "last Adam" (1 Cor 15:45 NIV), this is why the gospel can be preached to all tribes and nations. Any descendant of Adam can be saved, because our mutual relative by blood (Jesus Christ) died and rose again.

However, some people think that there must be different races of people because there appear to be major differences between various groups, such as skin color and eye shape. The truth is that these so-called "racial characteristics" are only minor variations among people groups. For example, if a white person is looking for a tissue match for an organ transplant, the best match may come from a black person, or vice versa. What is important is that there are differences among us, but they stem from culture, not race.

The only reason many people think that these differences are major is because they've been brought up in a culture that has taught them to see the differences this way. Today, many scientists support the biblical view that all people are rather closely related—there is only one race biologically. For this reason, there seems to be in essence no such thing as "interracial marriage."

Then, we need to go to this question, "Is there anything in the Bible that speaks clearly against men and women from different people groups marrying?" Throughout the Bible, there are no explicit grounds to prohibit interracial marriage. Some argue that marriage with foreigners (implying people both of different cultures and races) was prohibited throughout the Old Testament. However, it should be noted that the prohibitions were not strictly against Jewish-Gentile marriage as racial mixture, but against believer-unbeliever marriage (Deut 7:3–6). The marriages of Rahab to

Salmon (Josh 2:1; Matt 1:5) and Ruth to Boaz (Ruth 4), both Gentile women of faith, can be good examples of interracial marriage in the Old Testament. It is worthy to note that they were both accepted into the community of believers, and they are even in the genealogical line of Jesus (Matt 1:5). In accordance with the Old Testament teaching, Paul appears to prohibit believers from intimate fellowship with unbelievers. However, the context speaks nothing of skin color, race, and culture.

When pastors and theologians legalistically impose non-biblical ideas such as "no interracial marriage" onto their cultures, they are helping to perpetuate prejudices that have often arisen from evolutionary influences. If we are really honest, in countries like America and Korea, the main reason for Christians being against "interracial" marriage is really because of skin color. Pastors and pastoral counselors should inform interracial couples that two people from very different cultures can have a number of communication and other problems, but such problems have nothing to do with race.

Second, cultural mixing is another issue centered in interracial marriage. Most Jewish people do not allow interracial marriage to come into their own community. They worry that interracial marriage would dilute their own culture and faith tradition. They do not like the practice of cultural mixing. However, today our culture and context is changing. As Litonjua says, our context is no longer local, but global.[64] It is common to see cultural diversity all around the world. The nations share their goods and resources and learn many things from each other.

In addition, we need to understand the issue of cultural mixing within theological perspectives. There are passages in the Bible that also encourage us to include differences, rather than exclude them. For example, on the day of Pentecost, when God poured out the Holy Spirit on the disciples, they began to speak with other tongues, declaring of the mighty deeds of God (Acts 2). This event revealed God's plan to allow Gentiles to hear the gospel in their own language and to be accepted into the body of Christ. The Apostle John also saw a heavenly vision in which before the throne of God a great multitude was standing, and they were from every nation, tribe, people, and language (Rev 7:9ff).

In all of this, God is working to redeem for himself a people who are one in Christ. The Bible makes clear in Galatians 3:28, Colossians 3:11, and Romans 10:12–13 that in regard to salvation, there is no distinction

---

64. Litonjua, "Global Capitalism," 210.

Self-Sacrifice and Marital Expectations

between male or female or Jew or Greek. In Christ, any separation between people is broken down. As Christians, we are one in Christ and thus have a common purpose—to live for him who made us. This oneness in Christ is vitally important to understanding marriage, even interracial marriage.

However, Paul states in 2 Corinthians 6:14 (NIV), "Do not be yoked together with unbelievers. For what do righteousness and wickedness have in common? Or what fellowship can light have with darkness?" Nevertheless, this statement has nothing to do with race, but emphasizes the priority in marriage that a Christian should marry only a Christian. However, sadly, there are some Christian homes where the parents are more concerned about their children not marrying someone from another "race" than whether or not they are marrying a Christian. When Christians marry non-Christians, it negates the spiritual (not the physical) oneness in marriage, resulting in negative consequences for the couple and their children. Therefore, within a theological perspective, these two issues do not present big problems in dealing with the interracial marriage.

However, if they see the basic unity of the human race (Gen 3:20), holding equality in Christ (Gal 3:28) and real love as the true signs of faith (John 8:42), they can be very helpful in what one counselor called one of the most demanding of counseling situations.[65] The church could greatly relieve the tensions over racism, particularly in Korea, if only the leaders of the church would teach that all people are descended from one man and woman; all people are equal before God; all are sinners in need of salvation; all need to build their thinking on God's word and judge all their cultural aspects accordingly; all need to be one in Christ and put an end to their rebellion against their Creator.

Theologically, interracial or cross-cultural marriage can become a means of reconciliation between people of different cultures. The full acceptance of interracial marriage in our society today has come a long way. However, further effort is required to improve our attitude, understanding, and acceptance of other cultures by means of cross-cultural communication. God has lifted the wall of culture which has separated men from each other for thousands of years through the person of Jesus Christ. In Jesus Christ, all mankind has become one again. Through faith in Jesus Christ, culture becomes transparent.

Second, we as practical theologians also need to think realistically about self-sacrifice, the domination, injustice, and hardship that a woman

---

65. Ibid., 114.

often faces in an interracial marriage. In reality, even some Korean women living with American husbands still experience some degree of patriarchal and hierarchical inequality because American men bring to their marriage their stereotyped expectation that Korean women are docile, obedient, and submissive. For example, a Korean interracially married woman says, "My American husband is like a Korean man. His attitude, thought, and behavior are like my father's. I don't like this stuff." On the other hand, if the Korean wife brings with her the stereotypical expectation of the American husband, which is one that fosters mutual, reciprocal acceptance, equal regard, not hierarchy, she is often hurt by the betrayal of her expectations. In some cases, the American husband still wields dominant power and at times ignores or diminishes the importance of his partner's cultural background. He might even take away his wife's right to enjoy and live with her own cultural things. From my personal experience working with Korean American interracial couples, I have seen some American husbands who do not allow their children to learn Korean heritage, including language, and demean their wives' Korean culture, family background, and heritage in front of their children. Consequently, their children develop negative impressions of their own mother's cultural background. The restrictions go so far as to not allow his wife to spend time with her family. Instead expectations are enforced that she will spend all her time sacrificing for their family and yielding to his wishes and his demands. This domination and hierarchical power make the relationship twice as difficult for Korean women in cases of interracial marriage with such expectations. These women have a hard time not only adjusting to cultural differences, but also to being dominated by American society and by their husbands. They are living in both Korean and American cultures. Falicov labels this family as being in "cultural transition"—that is, in a state and process of coexistence of different cultural ideologies and codes.[66]

In this respect, pastors or pastoral counselors should be aware of all signs of the husband's domination over the wife and children and the ways the power struggle hurts the Korean partner and often results in divorce. Within this theological perspective, pastors and counselors should lead the interracial couples into justice, equality, reconciliation, and love in their marriage. The pastors and counselors should help the couples find and

---

66. Falicov, "Cultural Meaning of Family Triangles," in *Re-visioning Family Therapy*, ed. McGoldrick, 45.

experience God's unconditional love, grace, forgiveness, active reconciliation, and renewed community in their marriage.

Third, pastors and pastoral counselors have to understand that there is no such thing as cultural "neutrality." In other words, pastors and pastoral counselors must be aware of their own values about culture, family, and community and appreciate the validity of a wide range of cultural perspectives.[67] Pastoral counselors should be aware of and allow for cultural differences in healthy relationships and family boundaries. For example, what may appear as an intrusive family relationship to some American partners, such as in-laws' involvement in the couple's decision-making, may be acceptable to their Korean American partner. Furthermore, pastoral counselors should be aware of the level of traditional beliefs of the Korean American partners and the degree to which they have accepted or rejected Western culture. It is important for pastoral counselors to demonstrate their understanding of each partner's differences relating to cultural values, traditions, and family backgrounds so that they feel more comfortable and secure and can more openly express their feelings to the pastors. Bea Wehrly, Kelly R. Kenney, and Mark E. Kenney give useful suggestions that pastors and pastoral counselors should know before jumping into counseling:

> The counselor must be aware of the biases and assumptions that he or she may have with respect to interracial couples and interracial union. The counselor must also be willing to gain knowledge and understanding of each partner and the cultural values and worldview that each partner brings to the relationship. The counselor must be willing to learn and use strategies and skills that are culturally appropriate for each partner, keeping in mind the need to help the couple understand that his/her partner's different cultural frameworks may dictate the use of different approaches when the counselor is working with each of them. Ultimately, the counselor must be open to working with the couple around the issues and needs the partners present, not around what the counselor assumes the problem to be.[68]

In addition, one of the more obvious problems that may occur in interracial marriage is conflict created by different individual expectations that are brought into the marriage. These expectations are rooted in the cultural values, the past experiences, and relationships between family

---

67. Ibid., 43–45.
68. Wehrly, *Counseling Multiracial Families*, 50.

members. If these differences are not fully explored, the possibility for conflicts is increased. In this sense, the pastoral counselors must help partners understand their different expectations for each other.

Fourth, pastoral counselors must have emotional contact with the couple while avoiding emotional entanglement. When interracial couples feel confident, secure, understood, and affective, they will be more involved in helping the counselors and solving their conflicts on their own. It is particularly important for pastors and pastoral counselors, in working with immigrant Korean women, to recognize that they have been victimized by years of sexism, loss of power due to language barriers, role reversal, and racism in the new country.[69] Pastors and pastoral counselors must help Korean women realize the reality of where they become oppressed and powerless, and empower them to interact successfully with external systems and change the relationship as much as possible.

It would be helpful for couples if pastors or pastor counselors were able to speak Korean and English. They need to understand the couples' different languages in order to have a better understanding of interracial couples' problems. With the help of an interpreter, pastors or Christian counselors easily fail to comprehend each partner's emotional and psychological issues. Ho accurately points out the disadvantages of a mono-lingual therapist.

> If they can speak only English, the partner whose native language is not English will be placed in a severe disadvantaged position. A coalition, based upon similarity of spoken language between the therapist and the English-speaking partner, can create an unsatisfactory triad. Furthermore, a spouse's use of nonstandard English can lead to a misdiagnosis and a distorted conceptualization of the martial conflict by the therapist. Hence, when presented with a client whose native language is different, the therapist may better refer to another therapist who is bilingual.[70]

Fifth, as Joseph Harris proposes, "Pastoral counseling with interracial couples must be theologically based in its approach in order to avoid ineffective or misleading counseling."[71] The pastors or pastoral counselors should be prepared to address the biblical meaning of marriage and family relationships. The Bible says that marriage is honorable for all (Heb 13:4).

69. Lee, 31.
70. Ho, *Intermarried Couples in Theraphy*, 9.
71. Harris, "Interracial Counseling," 113.

Jesus says that it is to be a permanent bond (Matt 19:6) because it was instituted by God (Gen 2:18–24). The significance of the marriage relationships in the Bible helps interracial couples understand their presupposition that there is something unhealthy about their marriage because of its interracial nature. However, nowhere in the Bible are distinctions made about interracial marriages being less honored by God. It is helpful for interracial couples if they see that their problems or conflicts stem not solely from their interracial marriages, but from basic problems that all married couple are handling.

As a practical matter, the triangle relationship can be understood positively and theologically. James David suggests an unwitting congruence between Bowen's triangle theory and marital stability for Christian couples.[72] David insists that "the more central an authentic relationship with Christ is to the marital dyad, the greater the likelihood of enduring, dyadic commitment."[73] It is necessary to say that the third person in the central triangle could be anyone or anything. For example, Pokja chose the third person as her first son, Tom, and her friends. However, for Vincent, it was his work or hanging out with his friends. Their marriage may be stabilized by these triangle relationships. However, David argues that these relationships are inadequate for the Christian couple who realizes that they are called to be a sign and symbol of Christ's intimate love relationship to church (Eph 5:25–26).[74] They can invite Christ to be the third person of the inevitable triangle. This concept is very helpful for Pokja to make her marriage more stable and stronger. In the light of Pokja's family background and cultural value, in which direct confrontation and voicing her opinion in public are discouraged, Pokja has a difficult time carrying all of the burdens from disapproval of family, a disconnected husband, and her own work stress. She needs to release her feelings and emotions, which have been suppressed or oppressed. She may create some meaningful relationship with the third person. She can develop her relationship with God to help to love her husband and God. This relationship with God can help her see who she is and hold a balanced stance between fusion and individuality. This triangular way of viewing the traditional marital proposition of two people being united in Christ will stabilize many interracial marriages.

---

72. David, "Theology of Murray Bowen," 259.
73. Ibid.
74. Ibid., 261.

Despite these apparent benefits, if it means adopting a "take it all to Jesus," pietistic stance as a means to avoid relational tension and anxiety, then it is not helpful for either Pokja or Vincent in dealing with their marital issues and their spiritual development. It becomes a utilitarian quest, to make Jesus a destination of religious escapism. I suspect that there may already be much of this endemic in the Korean church and community.

Korean American partners in interracial marriages, and Korean people in general, are hesitant to seek counseling because of aversion to shame and the stigma of making public the private problems of the family. Because they place a high value on learning, they rather rely on education. Pastoral counselors should frame marital programs as learning opportunities, rather than to present them as counseling opportunities that offer a clinical solution to nagging problems. For example, pastoral counselors or family educators may conduct a seminar that highlights these issues. First, allow partners to focus on issues related to the Korean American partner's family of origin and how these issues come to affect his/own own marriage relationship. Second, encourage partners to achieve healthy and balanced marital roles by presenting the value of equal partnership in marriage as important in all marriages. Third, bring to the awareness of both partners their own individualistic communication styles (based on their culture) and facilitate the development of effective means of communication within the marriage. Fourth, educate partners in parenting, especially by focusing on issues that may be exclusive to raising biracial children. Finally, inform partners how to be sensitive to individual cultural differences.

In the following chapter, I will explore more how Korean cultural background and the church's teaching affect Korean women's self-sacrifice. I will present a relational model based on equality, mutual love, and respect, which can help Korean women understand self-sacrifice in a broader context and maintain their self-respect and self-esteem within their family and faith communities.

3

Self-Sacrifice and Gender Inequality

Yielding as Women's Destiny

Introduction

Christian tradition has frequently placed special emphasis on pride or self-regard (self-interest) as a particularly destructive sin and promoted denunciation of self as a virtue. For centuries, the notion of what a good Christian ought to be was shaped by this single virtue, self-denial, and in its most potent form, self-sacrifice. Indeed, self-sacrifice was considered the highest value of the Christian life, a virtue to be sought in familial solidarity, loyal friendships, and consistent covenantal and social relationships. Within this Christian teaching, women were given the supreme privilege of exemplifying this virtue in its fullest expression as the gender most called upon to give of self without hesitation or limitation.

Quoting selected texts from the Epistles, women were consistently exhorted to submit to their husbands or to the appropriate authority, to care for others' needs, and to sacrifice themselves willingly for others. Drawing on the oppressed role of women in the Korean community, women's traditional duty of self-sacrifice and self-denial was reinforced by Korean Christian theologians, pastors, and, quite happily, husbands, as Biblical behavior, as virtuous action, admirable and highly praised obedience to the will of God. As a result, women raised in a Korean Christian home learned to see themselves as substitutional surrogates, carrying the whole family's weight on their shoulders in obedient sacrifice as divine duty and godly obligation. They came to know themselves as roles, not persons, as functions, not as those with an identity. Absorbed by spouses, exploited by children, used by the church, they often did not know how to love and find themselves.

For example, many Korean Christian women often believe that their self-sacrifice or suffering is the means by which they can carry the cross of Jesus in their lives and prove their love and commitment toward God on the earth. They believe that it is through tolerance or patience, obedience, and self-denial that they can receive forgiveness and a reward from God. They also believe that this self-sacrifice and self-denial is the way for them to come closer to God. To make this worse, many Korean pastors and Christian leaders encourage women to be passive and accept their own victimization and internally suffer, just as Christ suffered on the cross. If they teach that self-sacrifice and self-denial are God's will, why do they not put emphasis on men's self-sacrifice and self-denial? Obviously, self-sacrifice and self-denial can make someone feel fulfilled. But if women are passively accepting suffering, and positions in which they feel the need to care for others by sacrificing themselves, this kind of sacrifice and denial cannot make them feel fulfilled. It is obvious that if women are forced to sacrifice themselves without emphasizing their own needs and values, this can contribute to the perpetuation of patterns of domination and subordination between men and women.

If women's self-sacrifice and self-denial are fueled by Christian teaching, pastors and Christian counselors should acknowledge that they have failed to help women maintain their own value and identity. Furthermore, pastors or Christian counselors should transform these Christian teachings to a practical theology which can help women find their true selves and new possibilities within the community of faith and lead them into the fullness of humanity in God's grace.

Many Korean scholars tend to put too much emphasis on Korean women's self-sacrifice in the family and society, based on their heritage of Confucian patriarchal perspectives. However, Korean men in the family are also pressured to achieve and take responsibility for their own families, as well as their extended families. They face demands for a different kind of self-sacrifice within the Korean family system. Knowing this, Koreans can expand the concept of self-sacrifice for the Korean family and church.

We need to pay careful attention to the structuring of gender roles and the profound impact of women's subordinated and devalued status in their families of origin and in their marriages. The ways in which women have suffered from the traditional structure of Korean family life need to be explored.

It is important that those who are involved in helping others be concerned with their own development, have come in contact with their own emotions, and should be allowed to strive for their own happiness. For this reason, Kurt Remele quotes Eugen Drewermann, who vigorously attacks a traditional Christian spirituality of permanent self-sacrifice, self-hatred, self-emptying, and self-abasement. He holds such Christianity of masochistic self-denial mainly responsible for the neurotic personality structure that is characteristic of large numbers of Catholic clergy.[1] He continues to report from his clients that strict obedience to the authoritarian structures of their communities has alienated many members of religious orders from their true feelings, has undermined their self-regard, and stifled their personal growth.[2] This kind of self-denial and self-sacrifice can sap their strength, keep them from taking responsibility for their lives, and suffocate their attempts to grow in freedom and authenticity. There is no life for others as long as one has not learned to live oneself.

Carol Lakey Hess argues that Christian theology that promotes self-sacrifice and self-denial can inhibit the growth of the individual, especially women.[3] The Christian tradition frequently has put a special emphasis upon pride as human sinfulness and denunciation of self as a human virtue. Within this Christian teaching, women consistently are exhorted to submit to their husbands or the appropriate authority, to care for other's needs, and to sacrifice themselves for others. Especially, in the community of faith, women's self-sacrifice and self-denial are reinforced as admirable and considered rewarding. As a result, women raised in a Christian home or church often do not know how to love themselves and do not know how to find themselves. They do not have a true identity, they do not know who they really are.

If women do not know and love themselves, how can they be forced to love others? If women do not know who they are and what they need, how can they see other's needs? It is very ironic that women are forced to please other's needs without knowing their own. In this sense, it is possible that

---

1. Remele, "Self-Denial or Self-Actualization?," 19.
2. Ibid., 20.
3. Hess, *Caretakers of Our Common House*, 55.

Christian teaching conveys a dangerous and potentially destructive message for women's self-development in many ways.

The church's emphasis on the virtue of self-denial and self-sacrifice can be a harmful obstacle to spiritual growth for women. It can become spiritually abusive. Many Christian women understand suffering, self-sacrifice, and self-denial in the context of a "Christ-like" way of redemption.

How has Christian teaching affected women's self-sacrifice and self-denial? What are the negative effects of self-sacrifice on women? These questions can help pastors and Christian counselors to have a better understanding of how theological teachings in a community of faith pose a dangerous and potentially destructive effect on women's self-development.

This chapter focuses on the shadow side of self-sacrifice, the negative effects of self-denial in Christians,' and particularly in Christian women's, self-development. In addition, I will deal with a unique cultural background of Korean women that can magnify the negative effect on their service in the home and in the faith community. Since, as I argued in the first chapter, Korean society has been established by patriarchal Confucian thought, Korean women have been dehumanized and trained to serve others and to live lives of complete self-sacrifice, neglecting their own needs, wishes, and desires for the sake of family and others, especially men. In looking at cultural background, I will look further at the characteristics of Confucian society and the theology of *Han*. I will also deal with how Confucian and patriarchal culture contribute to Korean women's self-denial and self-sacrifice in the context of their "*Han*-laden" life. In addition, I will suggest how Korean pastors and Christian counselors can help Korean women release their *Han* and redirect *Han* into more positive outlets in their lives. In exploring this issue, I understand that the behavior of self-sacrifice and self-denial occur at all socioeconomic levels and within all psychological and cultural levels. However, I want to limit my focus on women's self-sacrifice and self-denial to theological and cultural perspectives, looking at how a theological and cultural tradition can contribute to a woman's self-sacrifice and self-denial.

In the conclusion of this chapter, I will propose some theological and practical suggestions of how pastors and Christian counselors can help women to maintain their self-esteem and self-care at home and in their community.

How Do Christian Teachings Affect Women's Self-Sacrifice and Self-Denial?

First, Christian theology often teaches women that submission to their husbands' authority, the practice of self-sacrifice, and the duty of self-denial are ideal goals of Christianity. This teaching tends to stress only one side of Christ's servanthood—Christ's suffering—encouraging women to take not only their own suffering, but also that of others, upon themselves by "giving themselves away" without concern for their own values and needs.

In addition, as Gill-Austern argues, their identities as women and Christians are shaped by a theological tradition that views self-denial and self-sacrifice as the defining attributes of Christian love.[4] In the equating of love with self-sacrifice, self-denial, and self-abnegation, Christian theology can be dangerous to women's psychological, spiritual, and physical health, and we must add, it is contrary to the real aim of Christian love.[5] Many Christian women understand suffering, self-sacrifice, and self-denial in the context of a "Christ-like" way of redemption. For example, many Korean Christian women believe that their self-sacrifice or suffering is the means by which they can carry the cross of Jesus in their lives and prove their love and commitment toward God on the earth. As we observed in chapter 1, Korean women have been the most prominent victims of patriarchal Korean society. When Christianity was accepted by Korean women, they believed that it is through tolerance, obedience, and self-denial that they could receive forgiveness and a reward from God. They also believed that this self-sacrifice and self-denial was the way for them to come closer to God. To make things worse, many Korean pastors and Christian leaders have encouraged women to be passive and accept their own victimization and internally suffer, just as Christ suffered on the cross. If self-sacrifice and self-denial are the center of God's will, why do they not stress the same for men?

Obviously, self-sacrifice and self-denial can bring happiness, satisfaction, and fulfillment to some women, but for many, only passively accepting their suffering and their need to care for others by sacrificing themselves cannot make them feel fulfilled.

---

4. Brita L. Gill-Austern, "Love Understood as Self-Sacrifice and Self-Denial," in *Through the Eyes of Women*, ed. Moessner, 308.

5. Ibid., 304.

In addition, the belief that self-sacrifice and self-denial are the ideals of Christian love often creates great stress and strain for women. In other words, Christian teachings of self-sacrifice and self-denial that require the denunciation of women's own needs, interests, opinions, and desires and force women to live only to please others can contribute to depression caused by suppressed or unresolved anger and can hinder women's self development.

It is interesting to note that Valerie Saiving describes self-denial and self-sacrifice as "the sins of women." Saiving argues that

> the specifically feminine forms of sin—"feminine" not because they are confined to women or because women are incapable of sinning in other ways but because they are outgrowths of the basic feminine character structure—have a quality which can never be encompassed by such terms as "pride" and "will-to-power."[6]

The sins of women are rarely about excessive pride or overt abuses of power but are more likely to be sins against the self and others born out of a self-destructive tolerance and self-sacrifice. Hess also speaks of the "sin" of giving herself away. She correctly points out that "giving up oneself—sometimes even in service to another—can be an act of sin if it is passive, splits community into those who care and those who assert, and fails to hold other people accountable for their actions."[7] The reason woman is guilty of the sin of "giving up oneself" is that she tries to abandon herself and throw herself into others.

According to Kierkegaard, woman was by very nature devoted to others, and thus tended to lose herself in the others.[8] Women tend to accept self-sacrifice and self-denial as their own destiny and do not question Christian teachings and the social or cultural systems forcing them to give up themselves for others. The self must be grounded in God alone; this means that the self must not be lost in conformity or convention or give up its spirit to that which is a "matter-of-course," which results in the spirit being "secured against becoming aware."[9] In that sense, women's self-sacrifice is not faithful to God's purpose and can lead to sin.

---

6. Valerie Saiving, "Human Situation," in *Womanspirit Rising*, ed. Christ and Plaskow, 37.

7. Hess, *Caretakers of Our Common House*, 38.

8. Ibid., 40.

9. Ibid., 41.

Self-Sacrifice and Gender Inequality

When Christian theology defines ideal love as self-sacrifice and self-denial, it can unwittingly contribute to exploitation and domination of relationships by the more powerful party. In this sense, Gill-Austern quotes the great American reformer Elizabeth Cady Stanton, who argued that "men think that self-sacrifice is the most charming of all the cardinal virtues of women . . . and in order to keep it in healthy working order they make opportunities for its illustration as often as possible."[10] It is obvious that if women are forced to sacrifice themselves without emphasizing their own needs and values, this can contribute to the perpetuation of patterns of domination and subordination between men and women.

If women's self-sacrifice and self-denial are fueled by Christian teaching, pastors and Christian counselors should acknowledge that they have failed to help women to maintain their own value and identity.

Second, Christian teachings also direct the way in which women dare react and respond to the demands for self-sacrifice and self-denial. Pastors or Christian counselors often place a special emphasis on biblical passages that emphasize a wife's submission to her husband, the obligation for women to sacrifice themselves for others and to forgive those who hurt them, thus forcing the women to give themselves away without caring for self and receiving care from others. This theology of rigidly defined sex-roles, focusing on submission, forgiveness, sacrifice, denial, and tolerance on the part of the women, often causes the suppressed women to become depressed, ashamed, and even victimized. For instance, Ephesians 5:21 and following can often be used for claiming that the wife should submit to her husband. However, there is no way that it can be shown that the intent of this passage can include the physical and emotional abuse of a woman by her husband, though some have erroneously used it as a justification. The Bible should be interpreted within a larger context, looking at all possible levels and backgrounds. The expression in verse 22, "Wives, be subject to your husbands, as to the Lord," is clear enough in itself: "Subject . . . as to the Lord," that is, as one is subject to Christ, who "loved us and gave himself up for us" (Eph 5:2). And, in verse 21, establishing mutuality in spouses as the norm for Christian marriage: "Be subject to one another out of reverence for Christ." Then follows, "Wives, be subject to your husbands," and later (v. 28), "Husbands should love their wives as their own bodies." Both the larger

---

10. Gill-Austern, "Love Understood as Self-Sacrifice and Self-Denial," in *Through the Eyes of Women*, ed. Moessner, 315.

context and the specific words, all based on what the love of God in Christ asks of us, cannot be translated as tolerating physical and emotional abuse.

In addition, the concept of forgiveness is also misunderstood as a Christian woman's responsibility to overlook others' mistakes without justification. However, forgiveness should not be considered to be just forgetting nor simply restoring unless those who have power show evidence of true changes over a significant period of time. It is abusive for pastors to encourage women suffering violence or psychological oppression to pray harder, to have more faith, and to be tolerant for their children's future. In his book *The Shape of Practical Theology*, Ray Anderson lists popular false assumptions about forgiveness: forgiveness is good for you; forgiveness is demanded of you; forgiveness is a shortcut to reconciliation.[11] Many Christians believe that forgiveness is a quick fix for ruptured and broken relationships. However, fast forgiveness is not good for restoring broken relationships; it is dangerous, because people tend to forgive quickly in order to avoid their pain. They forgive quickly in order to get an advantage over the people they forgive. This sort of instant forgiving only makes things worse. Forgiveness that fails to lead to personal and social renewal at the human level also fails to reach God at the spiritual level.[12] Bonhoeffer gives a good definition of forgiveness:

> Why is it that it is often easier for us to confess our sins to God than to others? If we do, we must ask ourselves whether we have not often been deceiving ourselves with our confession of sin to God, whether we have not rather been confessing our sins to ourselves and also granting ourselves absolution. A man who confesses his sins in the presence of a brother knows that he is no longer alone with himself. He experiences the presence of God in the reality of the other person. . . . Mutual brotherly confession is given to us by God in order that we may be sure of divine forgiveness.[13]

There is no shortcut to forgiveness. Forgiveness is a journey that we must take. True forgiveness takes place when we are finally able to push through the self-deception that blinds us, and we can experience personal healing and reconciliation with others.

Third, Korean Christian teaching and theology still show a strong tendency toward bias on sex-roles that offers a secure ideological basis for

---

11. Anderson, *Shape of Practical Theology*, 292–94.
12. Ibid., 295.
13. Ibid.

Self-Sacrifice and Gender Inequality

the permanent patriarchal or hierarchical control of women. A theology is oppressive when it teaches that the patriarchal system of family is the order of creation, that male authority is based on God's direction and on God's very nature, that insists that female inferiority was simply the result of God's appointment in the ordering of higher and lower place.[14] Within family relationships, such theologies teach that the husband is the wife's head in the family, so the duty of a wife is to be submissive to, directed by, and advised by her husband. Within this perspective, the relationship between a husband and a wife is clearly a male dominant, unjust, and unequal, controlling climate.

Even though injustice, inequality, and dominance are common in our society, they often go unrecognized or overlooked, forcing women to suffer in isolation, feeling a lack of support from outside the home. At worst, even in church, the powerful, controlling members take advantage of women's self-sacrifice by imposing traditional cultural norms and buttressing these claims with selected proof texts from Scripture. Such teachings have served not only to keep women silent, but also to make them vulnerable to injustice and inequality. Cynthia Ezell points out that for many Christian women, the greatest dilemma comes from having to repress their anger toward their husband, because they have been taught they must not challenge the husband's authority.[15] Hess also criticizes St. Benedict's teaching on humility and obedience. For St. Benedict, humility is understood to be the antidote to the vices of anger, ambition, and pride. "Rather than express anger at another, the spiritual person is to see the wrong in oneself; rather than control one's life, the spiritual person is to patiently endure suffering; rather than assert autonomy in relation to one's spiritual leaders, the spiritual person is to obey and submit."[16]

How Has Korean Cultural Background Impacted Self-Sacrifice and Self-Denial in the Context of the "Han-laden" Life of Women?

It is sad to observe how deeply these understandings of sacrificial virtues are embodied in Korean women's lives. Korean women have historically

14. Barton, *Family in Theological Perspective*, 110.
15. Cynthia Ezell, "Power, Patriarchy, and Abusive Marriages," in *Healing the Hurting*, ed. Kroeger and Beck, 26.
16. Hess, *Caretakers of Our Common House*, 43.

experienced oppression and domination with deep roots in a both patriarchal culture and religion. Korean society and dominant religions (Buddhism and Confucianism) have taught Korean women to be subordinate to the husband and to authority. They must serve and obey in both the home and public. For Korean women, responsibility and obligation to husband and family always come first. Korean women always take all suffering of the family upon themselves. This results in suppressed anger and resentment that often causes Korean women to be depressed, feel helpless, and become isolated from society, so that they suffer in silence and cannot seek help from relatives, church, or the community. In addition to these traditional values, if the Korean church emphasizes rejection of one's own will and desire, submission to others, enduring one's suffering, concern for self as sinful, and caring for others as utmost in spiritual maturity, this limits the possibilities for women's self development.

For this reason, it is necessary to examine a typical and prevailing feeling of the Korean people, especially women, called *Han*, and to look at the nature of *Han* for Koreans and how Korean women have developed *Han* in their lives.

First, three major religions, Shamanism, Buddhism, and Confucianism, have had a profound influence on Korean social and cultural development, and have also had an impact in shaping the lives of Korean women. These religions have actually influenced social and political attitudes toward women. Under Shamanism and Buddhism, women were relatively free, but when Confucianism was adopted as the official religious during Yi dynasty, women became the objects of severe restraint. As mentioned in chapter 1, Confucianism imposed a moral code for women that was very strict and oppressive.[17]

Because Confucianism discouraged progress but preserved the established order and assured power and position for the literate and educated, especially men, it stressed a rigid vertical order of relationships based on age, gender, and inherited social status. Confucianism thought strongly supported men, thus, Confucianism's infiltration into Korea had negative consequences for women.[18] A daughter is considered as "robber women," who carries household wealth away when she married. Men are honored, but women are abased. This is called "Nam jon yo bi sasang."

---

17. Kim, "Oppression and Han," 55.
18. Ibid., 60.

Self-Sacrifice and Gender Inequality

The rituals and ceremonies of ancestor worship exclude women, which reinforces their marginality. Women can only function as assistants to the men. They manage any necessary preparations, such as cooking or setting the ritual table. This ceremony offers a clear picture of the sexual dichotomy between men and women. In Confucian society, women were born to obedience. A woman was to obey her father while at home, her husband when married, and her son if widowed. From Confucian cosmology came the notion that the female "um" force, essential for harmony, ought to be passive and docile, following the lead of the more important male "yang" force.[19]

In addition, for a woman, marriage meant becoming the housewife of another family, performing ancestral sacrifice, giving birth to a son, and serving her husband's parents. The obligation of providing a male heir became a woman's sacred duty, which assured the continuation of the ancestral cult.[20] So, in the case where the first wife is childless or only had daughters, the husband was given an excuse to take a second or a third wife. The practice of taking concubines eventually reduced women to sex objects for men to manipulate and enjoy. Thus, the more Korean society became Confucian, the more subordinate and oppressed women became.[21]

In Confucian society, a woman dare not commit one or more of the seven evils, called *Chil-Guh-Ji-Ak*, which were the accepted reasons for a man to arbitrarily divorce her. The seven evils were disobedience to the parents-in-law, failure to bear a son, adultery, jealousy, hereditary disease, garrulousness, and larceny.[22] Even though divorce was simple for a husband, a woman had no grounds for divorce. She was expected to endure any hardship, injustice, and unhappiness for the sake of the family, children, and even herself. When a woman was divorced, she had no economic resources. This inequality enforced the ideal, so women had no choice but to be passive, quiet, and chaste, an obedient daughter-in-law, a devoted wife, and a dedicated mother.

Another example of the inequality that existed between men and women during the Confucian era is that women were also identified by their positions relative to men and, thus, lost their sense of identity as

---

19. Ibid., 61.
20. Ibid., 63.
21. Ibid.
22. Kim, "Healing of Han in Korean Pentecostalism," 126.

individual persons.²³ A woman was called someone's daughter or someone's mother. When a woman was married, the name of her original family was entered into the husband's family registry. Even in her family registry, her husband's name was recorded, but women's names were never entered. Married women belonged to their husbands' families, permanently unable to separate their own identity from those of their husband and children. Their social selves became subjective selves. Their existence was immersed in their men, and their self identity was negated.

With the influence of Confucianism in Korean society, one can clearly see a severe measure of oppression against women. Korean women suffered unjustly at the hands of cruel men and an oppressive system that continuously denied or, at best, downplayed women's rights. Koreans have articulated a mode of responding to the sinful situation of the oppressed called *Han*.²⁴ *Han* is a psychological term that denotes the suffering of a person who has been repressed by her actions or through the oppression of others. *Han* also can be a psycho-social term that inevitably appears in the stories of Korean women. Through their suffering and oppression, Korean women inevitably experience and accumulate much *Han* throughout their lives. *Han* is an underlying culture-wide characteristic feeling of Korean people. It is essentially untranslatable; even as a Korean, its meaning is difficult to articulate. Andrew S. Park's definition of *Han* as "wounded heart" is worthy of notice.²⁵ A wound is an injury caused by the separation of living tissues of the body due to external violence. *Han* is "the division of the tissues of the heart caused by abuse, exploitation and violence. It is wound to feelings and self-dignity."²⁶ Park compares physical pain with emotional suffering well:

> When the heart is hurt so much, it ruptures symbolically; it aches. When the aching heart is wounded again by external violence, the victim suffers a yet deeper pain. The wound produced by such repeated abuse and injustice is *Han* in the heart.²⁷

Han as wounded heart is closer to the experiences of ordinary people in Korea, especially of women, than any other definition of *Han*. As discussed

---

23. Kim, "Oppression and Han," 65.
24. Ibid., 66.
25. Park, *Wounded Heart of God*, 20.
26. Ibid.
27. Ibid.

above, Korean women have experienced oppression and discrimination under Confucian and patriarchal society. Few social systems existed to protect a Korean woman's rights in a patriarchal society. However, strangely enough, woman's anger was typically targeted at herself, not at her husband nor the husband's family who exploited her. The woman's sentiments of anger, resentment, and sadness, caused by an unjust social structure, turn "inward," become hardened and inflicted this deep wound to the heart.[28]

For this reason, *Han* is a distinctive feature of Korea even though *Han* is a Chinese character widely used in Asian countries.[29] In Chinese, *hen* is "to hate or to feel resentment"; in Japanese *kon* (or *uramu*) is "to bear a grudge."[30] In both languages, *Han* is a type of desire for revenge and a counter-attack. Whereas *hen* or *kon* is a feeling related to hatred of others, *Han* is a feeling of inward frustration. The distinctive feature of Korean *Han* is that it has no concrete target of anger while *hen* or *kon* has. *Han* is similar to a yielding spirit; it is a feeling of defeat, resignation, and nothingness. It is obvious that the feeling of *Han* comes from the sinful interconnections of racism, sexism, classism, colonialism, and Confucian ideology that Korean people have experienced for a long period of time.

Today in Korean society, patriarchy structured by racism, sexism, classism, and colonialism still prevails. It limits the options of women in defining themselves and their roles in equal regard. As Hess accurately points out, if women, whose voices are already suppressed, with self-esteem already lowered to negative degrees, are forced to follow the prescribed spiritual exercises—humility or spirituality understood as seeking the wrong in oneself, enduring suffering, obeying the common rule—these Christian exercises can lead to damaging intensification of suppression and oppression.[31]

When Christian teaching supports and even prescribes those patriarchal beliefs, the one possessing power uses theological resources to validate presumed superiority and to claim a superior position over women. Therefore, women have a lack of options and suffer from the poor support of their faith community. In that sense, Anson Shupe et al. argue that men used religion as a rationale to dominate women and to excuse occasional

---

28. Ibid., 15.
29. Kim, "Healing of Han," 126.
30. Ibid.
31. Hess, *Caretakers of Our Common House*, 43.

violence as necessary discipline.³² In that sense, Christian theology can prevent women from knowing the truth that shall set them free.³³

A culture and society based on a patriarchal system causes women to be prone to unquestioning acceptance of not just a role but an identity shaped by self-sacrifice and self-denial. Brita L. Gill-Austern, in "Love Understood as Self-Sacrifice and Self-Denial," identifies six psychological, cultural, and theological issues that motivate self-sacrifice and reinforce this behavior in ways that are often detrimental to self and others.³⁴ These six issues give important clues to understanding the motives behind self-sacrifice committed by Korean women.

First, self-sacrifice is deeply rooted in women's experience of identity as essentially defined in connectivity and relation; and in a culture that substantially informs this sense of self by raising women to consider the needs of others, to take care of men, and to care for children. Second, women are motivated toward self-sacrifice because they have grown up in a culture that gives them the message that in order to remain connected and maintain relation they must sacrifice themselves and their needs. They are taught that love becomes associated with selflessness, relationship without lack of conflict. Third, self-sacrifice is motivated by women's economic and social dependence. Fourth, women are motivated toward self-sacrifice by the unholy trinity of self-abnegation, self-doubt, and false guilt which is always knocking on the door of women's lives. Women often behave in self-sacrificial ways because they believe they are less important, less valuable, and less essential than men. Fifth, women are motivated toward self-sacrifice not primarily because of distortions of caring and love, which are individual neuroses, but by the structural inequalities in which they are embedded. Self-sacrifice can be a means of controlling as much as of loving. Sixth, women are motivated toward self-sacrifice because their identities as women and Christians have been shaped by a theological tradition that views self-denial and self-sacrifice as the defining attributes of Christian love.

Generally speaking, feminist theology has tended to attack Christian theology as furthering the exploitation of women rather than facilitating women's sense of self and empowerment. Feminists believe that existing

---

32. Shupe et al., *Violent Men, Violent Couples*, 97–98.

33. Hess, *Caretakers of Our Common House*, 94.

34. Gill-Austern, "Love Understood as Self-Sacrifice and Self-Denial," in *Through the Eyes of Women*, ed. Moessner, 304–9.

theologies, even when they are explicitly biblically based, have been interpreted in ways that exploit women. Frequently it criticizes aspects of "patriarchal religion" such as the "maleness" of God in imagery, language, and function, the origin of sin, the history of human origins, hierarchical structures. So they criticize the evangelical and fundamentalist Christian traditions for creating and complicating the problem of identity in women in a society structured by a patriarchal worldview. They also seek to pay particular attention to how this biased patriarchal theology affects women's identities and roles in the church.

There is a great need for the church to be in conversation with feminist theology that concerns women's needs and concerns and helps them to ground gender relationships within a proper understanding of biblical texts and contexts. When feminist theology promotes women's quest for identity, equality, personal improvement, and empowerment to call for change in patriarchal society, it can be a powerful and useful tool to liberate women to personal creativity and self-confidence by enabling them to remember that they, too, are created fully and equally in the image of God.

However, it is sad to note that my Korean conservative tradition has intentionally ignored this feminist theology without any effort to pay careful attention to these legitimate concerns. They have disregarded these feminists by reason of their less "fundamental" approach toward gender and sexuality issues and interpretation of the Scriptures. So, Korean conservative groups have no opportunity to discover the necessary and good aspects of feminist theology that can be helpful for women in finding their true identity and equality in Korean society. Even worse, Korean churches have interpreted many aspects of the Bible in misogynistic ways that maintain idolatrous traditional values and elevate the power of the male to exploit women. However, now it is the time to listen, to learn, to be taught by our sisters, and to explore the good aspects of feminist theology that call us to make a careful reinterpretation of many aspects of the Bible in ways that provide a genuine avenue for women to know their needs and their true self-image. Only with a proper biblical interpretation can women freely and fully serve human needs.

In any change to deeply held cultural values, great care is advisable, and this is particularly true in applying feminist insights to conservative Korean churches. Feminist theologies are quickly seen as attacking traditional biblical understandings of headship and sex-roles, replacing male images with female ones and thereby changing the balance of power. This leads to increasing closing of the ears and minds of traditional groups. What is needed is the hard work of constructing a biblically sound theology of gender and sexuality with roots in Korean thought and practice. Korean conservative churches strongly reject many aspects of feminist theologies that have a tendency to disrespect dominant male narratives and hold to an exclusive understanding of God's image as male, even though the new teaching is explicitly biblically based. Change will come slowly, and from within, as we rethink and recommit to the task of seeing the Bible through less culturally colored lenses.

In fact, both women and men should be seen as created in God's image within a biblical context that requires that both submit to God's will. Rather than rejecting Scripture as "patriarchal and hierarchical," as some feminists argue, we need to hear the deeper insights of a feminist biblical theology that leads to a deeper understanding of the complexities of God's word as it applies to our situation where male and female may be treated differently but fairly. Thus, Korean churches will need to enter a difficult period of discernment that allows them to learn from a biblical feminist theology on women, to have a more sensitive interpretation of women within more biblically based traditions that give us a balanced understanding for women, and not be defensive, avoidant, or closed on the one hand, or too quickly and easily accepting of all that is new and challenging on the other hand.

How Can Pastors and Christian Counselors Help Women to Maintain Self-Esteem and Self-Care?

The Proper Understanding of Self-Sacrifice and Self-Denial from a Biblical Perspective

In an earlier section, I briefly addressed a passage of Scripture—Ephesians 5—to develop a revised theology of submission. Here, I want to explore a more a proper understanding of self-sacrifice and self-denial within a biblical perspective.

Jesus is our ultimate model for a right understanding of self-sacrifice. He lived life as it was created to be by the author of life, giving an example for all humans to follow.[35] Jesus did not glorify himself, instead he described

---

35. Benner and Hill, *Baker Encyclopedia of Psychology & Counseling*, 1079.

Self-Sacrifice and Gender Inequality

himself as a suffering servant (Mark 9:35).[36] He lived out his life with an unparalleled ability to give, to love, and finally to die for all humankind. His life has often been summarized as self-sacrifice and self-denial. He also lived with unparalleled assertiveness, self-disclosure, courage, steadfast obedience, and witness to the truth. He calls us to follow his example of self-sacrifice to fulfill our mission in our lives just as he did.

The phrase "deny himself" occurs in only one event, although that is recorded in three Gospels (Matt 16:24–25; Mark 8:34–37; Luke 9:23–24).[37] Self-denial is described in other passages (Matt 10:37–39; Luke 14:25–27; 17:33; John 12:25–26) in terms of our putting service to God first and giving up self-needs as our highest priority.[38] The most profound picture of self-denial is found in Philippians 2:5–11, which describes the example that Jesus set for us in emptying himself in order to be a fully human person and to die for us on the cross.

However, Jesus takes up the cross as a voluntary act, not by being obliged by God. If we follow his example, "self-denial" or "self-sacrifice" will not be seen as something imposed upon us by God against our will, the imposition of power overwhelming the will of the week. Following the model of Jesus' self-sacrifice does not mean that we become people of no value and need; instead it means that we become the very best that we can be. Of course, through service to God and to others we may have personal satisfaction and fulfillment. However, when people learn to value themselves and know themselves and their needs, they more freely give themselves in loving service to others. This is a proper understanding of self-giving and self-denial. If a person believes that he or she is of no value and yet feels obliged to serve God and others, that person has not discovered the center and soul of truly serving God and others. The biblical way to build self-esteem is to do the best we can and be rightly proud of what we have accomplished (Gal 6:4).[39] In biblical self-denial, we seek to be good steward of our talents by cultivating God-given skills so that we will have even more to contribute to God's work (Matt 25:14).[40]

However, the problem lies in the situation of systemic cultural oppression. When the value of sacrifice is used manipulatively to motivate

36. Ibid.
37. Ibid.
38. Ibid.
39. Ibid., 1080.
40. Ibid.

sacrificial behavior and to justify the power of the dominant group, the poor and weak can be victims of prejudice and exploitation.[41] Within oppressed society, those who are less powerful, such as women, racial minorities, and the poor, are doubly targets of this kind of manipulation, for both members of the socially dominant group and persons of their own group may demand self-sacrificing behavior of them.[42] In this sense, true self-sacrifice should come from a position of strength and not weakness; it is a matter of choice, not of self- or other-imposed necessity; it is in the service of truth and not of delusion; and it is an expression of free self-giving rather than compensation or compulsion.[43]

In exploring the proper understanding of self-sacrifice, the Korean cultural background, which emphasizes the importance of the collective and communal value, has a great potential to contribute profoundly to a reconstructed model of self-sacrifice and denial. The Korean emphasis on collective solidarity as a ground for balanced identity in community is biblically rooted. In the story of creation in Genesis, there is no such thing as an individual, we are created as inter-dividuals. There is no such thing as a pure collective, we are created as distinct persons. Rather, God creates man as an inter-dividual, who from the beginning stands in need of woman in the community of the family. The Genesis statement "male and female created he them" reflects God's intention for humanity. We also experience this intention in our own creation. We are not born pure individuals, but only with potentiality of individuality. Our individual selfhood depends on community and society. We learn to talk by hearing others talk, to walk by watching others walk. Individual human consciousness emerges out of the communal activities of family and society. From the beginning, man is not an individual but individual-in-community.

In Korean culture, due to the influences of a strong Confucianism background, the value of the unity of family and community life are highly prized, with a strong sense of responsibility for caring for the whole family and community. For Koreans, it is common that a family member is called upon to make personal sacrifices for the sake of the extended family and community. However, in Korean families, family conflict is frequently managed by isolation, indirect communication, and polite inattention.[44]

41. Hunter, *Dictionary of Pastoral Care and Counseling*, 1102.
42. Ibid.
43. Ibid.
44. Lee, *Working with Asian Americans*, 5.

The strong hierarchy within family defines who may voice an opinion and who must suppress all impulses to speak.

So, Koreans need to learn to share opinions and feelings in a trusting, open, and accountable community. When such an open and caring community emerges, we can enjoy others' interests above our own and thereby reduce our tendencies toward individualism and isolation. Within a trusting and caring community, we may freely give ourselves to others and experience in ourselves more delight in serving others' needs. We are able to be subject one to another (Eph 5:21) rather than practice power and dominance over the less powerful, such as has been the practice of men over women.

The Role of Pastors and Counselors for Growth in Women's Self-Giving and Care

Then, in a more practical sense, there must be concerted study on new means for pastors and Christian counselors to help foster growth in women's self care and self-esteem in the faith community.

What is the proper role of pastors in providing answers to these problems of women's self-development? How can pastors help women promote an understanding of the sacredness of human life and of the importance of justice and human dignity?

First, many Christians, even women, often take for granted that women should serve others and give themselves away as much as they can. Even though many feminist scholars raise crucial and challenging issues regarding women's rights, equality, and justice as the desirable Christian virtues and point to self-sacrifice as living too weakly, as the "sin of unbelief and failure to claim God's promise and intentions," these issues are still largely ignored in the Korean community of faith. For this reason, pastors and Christian educators should break the silence and teach what is the true meaning of self-sacrifice and self-denial to their congregations. A good place to start teaching the negative effects of self-sacrifice and to begin advocating self-care and the sacredness of a human being is from the pulpit of our churches. The sins of distorted self-sacrifice and self-denial need to be addressed as actively as any other sins that plague the body of Christ. Pastors and Christian counselors should address the fact that abandoning themselves and losing their "true self" given by God in the name of self-giving is wrong and even sinful. Through sermons, prayer, and Bible study groups, both women and men will have an opportunity to bring the issues of self-sacrifice and self-denial as "sin" into light of confession and to learn the importance of self-care and of relationships for self-identity in women.

In addition, pastors and Christian counselors also need to give renewed attention to reexamining all patriarchal teachings adapted from the selective use of the Scripture and installed in the established male-entitled church structures. As I mentioned above, the destructive power of patriarchy has negative effects on women's self-sacrifice and self-denial in the homes and the faith community. If churches and pastors continue to foster "beauty of self-sacrifice and self-denial" as the ideal for women and teach imbalanced sex-roles, submission, and self-sacrifice or self-denial as the basis of the patriarchal system, Christian theology and teaching will keep women in the box of self-sacrifice and self-denial without an opportunity for self-recognition and true fulfillment. For this reason, pastors must first understand their own belief on the issue of self-sacrifice and self-denial under which they are able to give advice and counsel to women. This self-examination or self-reflection helps pastors articulate the moral, psychological, and theological dimensions of self-sacrifice and self-denial.

Next, pastors and Christian counselors should challenge women to break from their traditional beliefs of submission and self-sacrifice as the ideals of Christian love and their beliefs in their obligation to maintain the patriarchal structure by sacrificing themselves. The pastor can ask, "Where did you learn that women must be submissive to their husbands?" or "What do you believe are the responsibilities of wives in a marriage relationship?" or "What does the Bible teach about equality, justice, respect, self-care, and mutuality in marriage?" These questions give the pastors valuable information about what the woman believes and how she should be helped and challenged with the teachings of the Bible.

Christian leaders should take a "prophetic" stance for women who are suffering from a patriarchal system. If they overemphasize self-sacrifice and self-denial as the utmost virtue, this may blunt their prophetic voice. It is through a prophetic voice that Christian educators or pastors can empower women by condemning negative forms of self-sacrifice as sin against justice, against trust, and the true love in God. They can help to rediscover sympathetic stories of women from Scripture in which women make a positive contribution to the community, and they can invite women to find their true selves and to know how to love and care for themselves.

Self-Sacrifice and Gender Inequality

In that sense, Hess suggests that church ought not to be "the community of pretense," rather it should be a place where all are free to tell the truth.[45] The church should be viewed as a safe place where women bring their concerns, where women will be heard, where women will be cared for, and where God's love and grace will be demonstrated. When the church is a supportive community for women, they can come to the church not only for emotional and spiritual support, but also for sharing their pain and suffering with other members and even with God.

For example, among Korean women, there are two modes of dealing with *Han*. One is to accept (*Jung Han*), and other is to refuse (*Won Han*). With the teaching of Confucian philosophy, Korean women have been taught to be at peace with their situation and live a dutiful life for the reward of a better fate in the next life. Even some missionaries perpetuate *Han* in Korean Christian women's lives by encouraging them to be passive and accept their own victimization. By use of a substitutional atonement story from Christian theology, they were encouraged to internally suffer, just as Christ suffered on the cross, because it was God's will. However, this acceptance mode (*Jung Han*) does not change anything, as it is submission or resignation to fate.

The second way to deal with *Han* is to refuse it, which is called *Won Han*. Women need to attend to the pain of their *Han* and dare to refuse or act to overcome the oppressive situation where they find themselves. Women need to be taught that it is okay to be angry about their situation and seek transformation and revolutionary change. Of these two modes of dealing with *Han*, I believe *Won Han* is the more needed path for Korean women to take if they are to change their situation rather than just accept their suffering and inequality. Many Korean scholars describe *Han* as a very negative force for Korean women. However, I strongly believe that we can use *Han* as a positive force to refuse the oppression and fight back to change injustice in society. They need no longer remain in the passive mode and accept things as they are, but must take positive action to resist old structures and change their situation.

It is interesting to note here that there is a way for Korean people to release their *Han* in the shaman rituals, called *Gut*. In the *Gut*, Korean women have been helped to release the *Han* that came from oppression, self-sacrifice, and the denial of their own identity and worthiness. When the reality of pain was recognized and the community was brought to

---

45. Hess, *Caretakers of Our Common House*, 46.

awareness and repentance there is the possibility of finding healing for women. All kinds of *Gut* are closely related to the real lives of people: healing *Gut*, initiation *Gut*, *Gut* for rain, *Gut* for the dead, *Gut* for the disease, *Gut* for the exorcism, etc.[46] For example, at the *Gut* for a drowning victim in Korean shamanism, a possessed shaman replays the process of the drowning step by step and shows the bereaved and friends the way the victim was drowned.[47] The shaman speaks and acts as if she were the victim, reliving the traumatic accident. This ritual helps the bereaved and friends recognize the *Han*-filled reality of accidents and the uselessness of fostering *Han*, and seek positive ways to divert their energy from *Han* into the prevention of future drowning. In the midst of watching the reenactment, the bereaved and friends experience the releasing of *Han*. It is important to recognize that the reality of the painful *Han* and to determine the diversion of *Han*-energy is the avenue by which one's *Han* is released. The shamanistic ritual gave the voiceless the opportunity to tell their stories of *Han*, then the community can collectively resolve the sufferer's *Han* by eliminating the source of oppression and comforting the victim. *Gut* has been an opportunity for collective repentance, group therapy, and collective healing for the ghosts and their human communities in Korean society.[48]

Constructing community rituals that fulfill these same needs within the community, but utilizing the riches of the good news of Christianity, can enable Korean women to resolve their *Han*. I believe that there are resources of confession, public witness, shared grieving, and preparation for and the institution of the Lord's Supper that can be used as venues for proclaiming that justice has come, repentance is real, change is being created, and a new covenant of respect and mutuality is being celebrated that are already present in our Christian tradition. These can be employed in creating rituals that are truly helpful to Korean woman to actualize and solemnize their freedom from their *Han-laden* life. When pastors and Christian counselors listen to physical, emotional, and psychological questions, yet at the same time listen for the word of God as grace and forgiveness, all these rituals of faith can be endowed with new meaning. Pastoral care can be a type of proclamation, speaking the word as it has spoken to us. I believe that pastors or Christian counselors are mediators through whom the word and will of God are delivered to those in need and crisis, offering an

---

46. Kim, "Healing of Han," 127.
47. Ibid., 128.
48. Kim, "Oppression and Han," 69.

authentically Christian means, just as *Gut* served as the traditional channel, though which women were given the opportunity to see a new reality and to be freed from their pain. As mediators, pastors should not only hear the word, but also try to bring people into appropriate response to the word.

Howard W. Stone says, "If we neglect to speak to them of God, offering only uncritical warmth and affirmation, we give the people a stone rather than the Bread of Life; instead of providing eternal nourishment, we simply nurture good feelings for the short terms."[49] For Stone, the essence of pastoral care, as of all ministries sharing in the legacy of the Reformation, is the proclamation or communication of the Word—that Word which became flesh, lived among us, and died reconciling us with God.[50] Truly, pastoral care means proclaiming this message, which is not something on the fringes of ministry, but at its very center. However, it is also important for pastors and Christian counselors to be aware that God communicates to and establishes relationship with people not only in a "spoken" word, but also in a "visual" word. A hug, at times, a touching, an attending glance, or an attentive listening ear will be enough to show the love of God to others. Though we do not speak or proclaim the word of God to people verbally, the people can experience an undeserved true love and grace for building supportive relationships, which would help people openly share their suffering and problems.

As a personal witness, during my experience of CPE, I had many opportunities to prepare for and lead worship services in a hospital setting. Participating in a worship service, I have witnessed that true pastoral care happened when we gathered together as a faith community where the word of God was preached and shown by my/our presence and preaching. In a sense, a worship service can be a more effective way to care for people than one-to-one counseling and daily patient visitation. During our worship, people have opportunities to see their painful reality and meet God's presence and to see God's love and grace in the midst of suffering. They also find new possibilities and hope through the word of God.

How, then, can we as pastors communicate God's word and grace to a person who is not ready to receive his word and care because his/her suffering is so painful? How can we assure people that they are forgiven or that God is at work for them even in the midst of their crisis? What is the proper role of prayer in pastoral care? If pastoral care takes place when the

49. Stone, *Theological Context for Pastoral Caregiving*, 51.
50. Ibid., 40.

word of God is proclaimed at a worship service, is that enough? When is the right time for us to bring the word of God to people in suffering? When is the best time to challenge the people with a prophetic voice?

My conservative Korean Presbyterian faith allows me to believe that the task of pastoral care is to address and to dress an individual's injury, relieve the pain, and resolve the problem by proclaiming God's word. Without this, pastoral care and counseling is the same as secular counseling. However, I do not advocate that pastoral care is nothing more than preaching to people and prescribing the only answer for their suffering lies in the Scripture or in finding the will of God. I am assured that we as pastors are not able to give the right answer to all people's problems with our limited knowledge of the word. We have a limited access to know God's word. Our job is not to cure people's problems, but to care for these people in need and suffering. We cannot solve all problems and alleviate all pains people carry on in their lives, but we are able to care for people in the midst of their suffering. We can help them in their crisis by delivering God's word to them, listening to their pain, and by giving genuine presence to them. Pastoral care takes place where God's story and human stories meet.

In this sense, we need to reexamine our Christian tradition and discover the liberating elements that can help release *Han* and affirm the value of the woman as a person and teach a mutual relationship as an ideal for love as taught in Christian theology. We are able to deliver the freeing Word to women with a deep and comprehensive understanding of their painful situation and contexts. For this reason, human context should be viewed from a biblical and theological context. On the other hand, theological and biblical context should be considered with an awareness of personal experience. The two perspectives should be seen in parallel in considering the healing process of pastoral care and counseling. Our church tradition and theology should bring Korean women's suffering caused by hierarchal and patriarchal cultural background to full awareness of the reality of the suffering it evokes, and give them opportunities to look at their painful stories and discover new possibilities and find hope in God's love and grace. Also, the church and pastors should teach them that God is always concerned with our problems and meets us in every experience of life, especially crisis experience. God is suffering with them in their own contexts and prepares the way for women to experience the continuing incarnation of God in the midst of their suffering.

Healing Images of Self-Giving

Healing images of self-giving in the New Testament can give women ways of conceiving of self-giving love as life-enhancing, for both giver and receiver.[51] A new reading of the story of the Good Samaritan can be a helpful example for both caregiver and care-receiver (Luke 10). Gill-Austern points out that in the story of the Good Samaritan, we have a model of love that is based on interdependence.[52] In this story, the good Samaritan did not sacrifice his journey and plans for himself. Rather, he took care of the wounded he met on the road, and then he asked the innkeeper to care for him. He then continued on his travel. Understanding self-sacrificing love as self-giving, women and men are called to care, but care does not mean a relinquishment of all their own needs or agendas for the sake of the other, nor does it mean that we are required to care alone.[53]

A second example for self-giving as life-generating love and care is seen in the story of Mary and Martha. In this story, caring requires active doing, and it also requires time to sit, to be nurtured, and to receive love. Love in the story is not related simply to serving, but also to receiving and knowing what is required, as well as waiting for the appropriate time. As Nel Noddings points out, if caring and love are to be maintained, then the one caring must be maintained.[54]

With a new understanding of the familiar and much-loved biblical stories, Christian counselors or pastors can teach both women and men that Christian love is not characterized only by sacrifice or endurance of suffering but by mutual love and care.

One important concept that can help women maintain their self-esteem and move in this direction of life-giving love is friendship with others. In the context of friendship, we have a good opportunity to clarify our beliefs, values, and life goals and to learn the places of our own deepest gladness and passion so that we may give out of our own sense of fullness.[55] Thus, in the community of faith, pastors make an effort to create an environment that encourages women to participate in "friendship or

---

51. Gill-Austern, "Love Understood as Self-Sacrifice and Self-Denial," in *Through the Eyes of Women*, ed. Moessner, 316.

52. Ibid.

53. Ibid., 317.

54. Noddings, *Caring*, 100.

55. Gill-Austern, "Love Understood as Self-Sacrifice and Self-Denial," in *Through the Eyes of Women*, ed. Moessner, 318.

support groups" in which they are given the courage to express their own needs and beliefs and to practice mutual loving and caring relationships with others.

Care is typically understood as not hurting others, having compassion for others, or tending to the needs of others; however, care is not simply tending to others, but rather also includes a nurturing relationship with others.[56] The tragedy of self-sacrifice is the loss of relationships with others. True relationships cannot be found in the context of simply "giving away" and sacrificing for others to please them and maintain their relationships. As Carol Gilligan correctly notes, "Making connections with others by excluding oneself is a strategy destined to fail," for "relationship implies the presence of both self and other."[57] As Christian counselors and pastors, we should celebrate and rediscover a true meaning of relationship in our faith community. When women are cared for and nurtured and are strong and capable of joy in mutual relationships, they can continue to give voluntarily and powerfully, not by simply giving or sacrificing themselves. A true relationship does not mean "giving ourselves away"—in fact, it may mean "taking ourselves back."[58] The relationship should involve give-and-take, speaking and listening, and caring and being cared for. In that sense, pastors need to help women transform their relationships from self-sacrificial, or "giving away," to more mature and respectful relationships.

Image of God as Father

Finally, we need to renew and clarify our image of God to include the forgotten side of God as nurturer and nurse. The image of "Father" has been one of the most dominant images of God throughout Christian history.[59] By emphasizing the images of God as king, ruler, judge, or the Almighty, religious leaders could exclude the marginalized and the weak, such as Gentiles, women, the unclean, and tax collectors. As Erick H. F. Law points out, the inclusion of the mother image of God can allow women to include themselves as part of what God has given them.[60] This other side of God's

---

56. Hess, *Caretakers of Our Common House*, 91.
57. Gilligan, "Teaching Shakespeare's Sister," in *Making Connections*, 9.
58. Hess, *Caretakers of Our Common House*, 92.
59. Law, *Inclusion*, 69.
60. Ibid., 72.

image can invite women to see part of themselves in God's image and to participate more actively in the ministry.

Christian counselors and pastors can empower women by using inclusive language which makes women noticed and visible in the faith community. According to Hess, exclusive language can contribute to a feeling of invisibility, reduce women's participation, and mark women as deviant.[61] Rather, inclusive language can help women feel more invited and attentive, so they can actively participate in the community and share their resources. Hess also suggests that the women can be empowered by recognizing or developing women's expertise, setting up collaborative situations, and encouraging the sharing of personal stories.[62] If pastors are aware of women's strengths, potential, and capacities, they can promote women's self-worth and self-respect, so that they can take part in something to which they can contribute.

However, on the other hand, women need to resist the increasingly widespread tendency to condemn all forms of self-giving. Self-sacrifice is not always harmful to human relationships. Self-sacrifice can be an essential element of authentic and faithful love—the self-fulfilling and self-transcendence to which Jesus calls us.[63] Within a mutual loving relationship, self-sacrifice can be understood as the means to recognizing our own needs, values, and beliefs so that we may freely give ourselves to others in our own sense of fullness. This kind of self-sacrifice should be contrasted with imposed suffering or passive submission to an oppressive status quo.[64] When women voluntarily give themselves to others and assertively suffer from a lack of power in the sense of their strengths, not in the sense of their weaknesses, this self-sacrifice can be beneficial to women themselves and the whole community.

Conclusion

As we have seen above, Christian teaching and Korean cultural background often convey a dangerous message to women that emphasize women's suffering and self-sacrifice as an ideal of Christian love. They often consider

61. Hess, *Caretakers of Our Common House*, 109.

62. Ibid.

63. Gill-Austern, "Love Understood as Self-Sacrifice and Self-Denial," in *Through the Eyes of Women*, ed. Moessner, 315.

64. Hess, *Caretakers of Our Common House*, 49.

pride as human sinfulness but self-sacrifice and self-denial as mature spirituality or utmost virtue in women. In addition, those who hold the power in the church often take advantage of women with this truncated theological teaching. Alberta D. Wood and Maureen C. McHugh argue that

> the ideas of dominant/submissive sex roles were reinforced and maintained, and these patterns of power and authority sanctioned by the church created an atmosphere for abuse. . . . The abuse of power occurs in the context of power inequality, i.e., a more powerful person takes advantage of a less powerful one; since traditional roles imply an inequality between the sexes, the conditions are ripe for abuse. The church, therefore, by confining women to an inferior position, unwittingly set the stage for abuse.[65]

Subsequently, women become invisible and voiceless in the community of faith. They simply take it for granted that they should obey the will of others. Theological teaching, rather than being a positive invitation to experience grace, has offered a graceless negative effect on women's self-development.

It is time for the church and pastors to acknowledge their failure to help women maintain their self-esteem and self-care in the body of Christ. In the face of the destructive effects of self-sacrifice and self-denial on women, Christian educators and pastors should break the silence and take responsibility to reconstruct our theology and practice of self-sacrifice and self-denial. They need to affirm the value of the woman as a person and teach women a mutual relationship as an ideal love of Christianity.

"Self-giving" is not all about denial of self, but rather offering up one's very fullness and caring for each other within mutual relationships. As Gill-Austern proposes, women's hope for loving and just relationships lies not in self-sacrifice, but in seeing clearly that mutual self-giving and receiving are at the heart of divine love and in women's courage and strength in insisting upon and working for mutual loving relationship.[66]

However, it is not an easy process for women to maintain a mutual loving relationship in their lives, even in the faith community. Sometimes, such a loving relationship requires hard work, determination, courage, forgiveness, an abundance of good will, and even God's grace. For this reason, pastors and Christian counselors need to take actions to help women by

---

65. Wood and McHugh, "Women Battering," 188.

66. Gill-Austern, "Love Understood as Self-Sacrifice and Self-Denial," in *Through the Eyes of Women*, ed. Moessner, 320.

providing supportive groups and by creating an environment where they can serve others voluntarily and be served in return, care for others freely and be cared for as they deserve, nurture and be nurtured, find who they are, and grow in mutual love. They also need to model good relationships with a Christocentric model based on equality, mutual love, and respect, which can help women maintain their self-care and self-esteem in the faith community.

Furthermore, patriarchal social systems and religious teachings can have a strong influence on wife beating. In *Violence Against Wives*, R. Emerson Dobash and Russell Dobash state that

> the seeds of wife beating lie in the subordination of females and in their subjection to male authority and control. This relationship between women and men has been institutionalized in the structure of the patriarchal family and is supported by the economic and political institutions and by a belief system, including a religious one, that make such relationships seem natural, morally just, and sacred. . . . Christianity, as well as most other religions, has provided the ideological and moral supports for patriarchal marriage, rationalized it, and actively taught men and women to fit into this form of marriage.[67]

Theological beliefs become an integral part of one's being. These beliefs are very powerful for the Christian woman in a battering relationship. The way one interprets the Bible, particularly in relation to women's status and position in society, is critical for a battered woman who already believes a patriarchal and sexist ideology. Using theology and the Bible to support the subordination of women just reinforces her belief that this doctrine is the infallible truth from God. For example, views of God as only male, of suffering as virtuous, of forgiveness without justice, and of divorce as sin keep a battered woman in her abusive situation.

Let's explore the most relevant theological problem as a way to gain insight into better directions for pastoral care for victims of intimate violence.

---

67. Dobash and Dobash, *Violence against Wives*, 33–34, 44.

4

Self-Sacrifice and Marital Violence
Yielding and Chronic Abuse

Introduction

Domestic violence occurs at all socioeconomic levels; it is inflicted by members of higher as well as lower classes. Its roots are psychological, social, cultural, theological, personality, family of origin, etc., but these aspects lie outside the scope of this chapter. Rather, this chapter will focus on domestic violence against the spouse—wives in particular—from social, cultural, and theological perspectives, and will offer some practical suggestion for pastors and counselors.

Particularly, I am exploring how the concept and practice of self-sacrifice is taught, modeled, rewarded, and coerced upon women in Korean culture and its relation to domestic violence. In addition, I will present some deficiencies in Christian teaching and theology that inhibit addressing the issues of domestic violence and self-sacrifice out of true concern. Finally, I will propose several theological resources that can deeply and positively inform our pastoral directions with the victims of domestic violence. With this understanding, we will have a broader perspective of the behavior of self-sacrifice of Koreans.

The Scope of the Problem of Domestic Violence

We live in a culture created by violence, sustained by the threat of violence, entertained by the myths of violence—we are immersed in violence. Whether we listen to the world news on the radio, watch it on television, or read of it in print, we are exposed to sensationalized stories about violence, statistical reports on violence, and the constant watch on countries at war, terrorist attacks, or ethnic resistance to oppression or discrimination. At the local level, we are troubled by the unpredictability of street crime, the possibility of armed robberies, the recurrent events of school shootings, or gang warfare. We all worry about being victims of violence.

Yet for many, especially women, their worry is not of violence on the streets—it is for violence in their home. It is both tragic and appalling to note that women are more likely to be assaulted in their own homes by someone with whom they have or have had a trusting, caring relationship than they are to be attacked on the streets in even the most violent American cities.[1] US Department of Justice (1998) statistics indicate that people are twice as likely to be victimized by an acquaintance, friend, relatives, or intimate partner.[2]

Women are the most likely victims of physical violence. Unfortunately, the majority of the perpetrators against these women are the victim's spouse or partner.[3] There are occasions in which men are reported to be victims of abuse; however, it should be noted that perpetrators in these rare situations are often acting in self-defense or in vengeance. The National Criminal Victimization Survey (NCVS) reports that between 1987 and 1991, females annually experienced over ten times as many violent incidents by an intimate than males experienced.[4] In over 90% of the violence by intimates recorded, the victim was female. On average, each year women were the victims of over 572,000 violent victimizations committed by an intimate, compared to approximately 49,000 incidents committed against men. These figures highlight the disparity of victimization between the two sexes.

---

1. Barnett et al., *Family Violence across the Lifespan*, 4.
2. Schewe, *Preventing Violence in Relationships*, 3–4.
3. Martin, *Counseling for Family Violence and Abuse*, 32.
4. Buzawa and Buzawa, *Domestic Violence*, 8.

Another statistics show that annually, 2.1 million American women were battered by their husband or partner during the mid-1990s.[5] Among these, 75% of married women report having received threats of violence from their partners, and 50% are estimated actually to have fallen victim to spousal abuse of one form or another; and 13% suffer partner abuse that is chronic and severe. Another source reports that 15 to 25% of murdered women are killed by their spouse, among those murdered in the United States.[6] The National Family Violence Research survey found that 39% of all incidents of violence toward wives were serious, involving punching with a fist, kicking, biting, beatings, and attacks with knives and guns.[7]

Data on homicides are more complete and indicate a serious domestic violence problem. Unpublished data from the Supplementary Homicide Report, collected as part of the Uniform Crime Reporting Program of the FBI, show that from 1980 to 1991, of women age 18 or older, over 50% of fatalities were killed by a husband, ex-husband, common-law husband, or boyfriend.[8] Furthermore, according to one FBI report, a woman is abused by their domestic partner every thirty seconds. Annually, the number of women who are victimized by domestic violence reaches 1,051,200 (about 2,880 women are victimized daily).

Domestic Violence among the Korean Population

Domestic violence is not exclusively a problem for Americans, it is worldwide, and it is particularly high in incidence in Korean populations. According to KIC (1992), out of 1,200 married Korean women, 64.2% of them had been battered by their husbands more than once during the course of their marriage, 28.5% were battered more than ten times, and 5.9% more than 50 times.[9] Out of 544 women, 10.1% were seriously beaten by their husbands. The Korean Institute of Criminology (KIC) found that 50.5% of husbands battered their wives more than once during the course of their marriage. According to this report, of the total reported 9 million families in Korea, at least 2 million families reported experiencing at least

5. Anderson et al., *Family Handbook*, 164.
6. Martin, *Counseling for Family Violence and Abuse*, 15.
7. Buzawa and Buzawa, *Domestic Violence*, 9.
8. Ibid.
9. Yosong Han'guk Sahoe Yon'guso, ed., *Kajok kwa Han'guk Sahoe: Pyonhwa hanun Han'guk Kajok ui sam ilk'I* (Seoul: Kyongmunsa, 2005), 306.

one episode of domestic violence annually. Over 34.1% of families report experiencing at least one episode of domestic violence annually, which is twice the reported rate of the United States overall, 1.5 times the reported rate for all Koreans living in the United States, and 3 times the reported rate from Hong Kong. Of these, 15.6% were husbands battering wives, 3.5% were wives battering husbands, and 12.3% were cases of mutual battery. Finally, nearly 7.9% of cases of husbands battering wives were considered serious cases of domestic violence, where weapons such as belts, rods, and golf clubs, as well as use of excessive physical force were involved. In conclusion, the report by KIC showed that in all cases of domestic violence, women were the victims in 4.6% of the cases, and men were the victims in 1.6% of all cases.

In addition, according to counseling statistics by Seoul Women's Hotlines in the year 2000, 30.1% of all the counseled cases (13,656) were the direct result of violence against women.[10] According to the Korea Legal Aid Center for Family Relations (2009), 69.8% were victims of domestic violence by their husbands. 12.1% were fatally threatened. Nearly 33.3% were reported to have been battered by their husbands due to distrust; 23.1% were related to drinking problems; 21.3% were financially related; 13.9% were due to challenging the husband's authority.[11]

Based on above statistics, we can infer that the deep motivations for this violence are rooted in patriarchal hierarchy. The harsh realities of the battered wives are much more serious than expected.

However, what is most troubling is that the victims of domestic violence have no place to go with their pain. Abuse often goes unrecognized or is overlooked for extended periods of time. Not surprisingly, in view of the power of patriarchy, there are few women's shelters in Korea. The first women's shelter, which started from "Korean Women's Hotline," opened in 1987. Six shelters belong to private organization with poor financial resources. According to Korean social welfare institutions, the numbers of shelters available in the entire country to women (59) were vastly outnumbered by the shelters available for the children (269), the elderly (250), and the disabled (196).[12] Battered women receive little economic or emotional service from Korean family and society, therefore, victims are forced to suf-

---

10. Ibid., 307.

11. Korea Legal Aid Center for Family Relations, http://www.lawhome.or.kr/law1/sub012/detail.asp?code=news&no=161.

12. Ministry for Health and Welfare, *Yearbook of Health and Welfare 2010*.

fer in isolation, feeling a lack of support from any agency, group, or person outside the home. Sadly, Korean battered women who fail to get emotional, social, or legal protection from the family and community tend to stay in their violent home without alternatives; those who utilize the shelter facilities are more likely to return home to resume the dangers of an explosive spouse, more than is the case of American battered women. Furthermore, these statistics are alarming, especially in light of the fact that they are very likely underreported, due to the stigma against "hanging out dirty laundry" in a culture that places a high value on harmony, saving face, and positive public self-presentation.

Likewise, domestic violence is endemic in Korean families living in the United States. Domestic violence is pervasive among all Asian immigrant groups, with Korean Americans ranking at the top. Spousal abuse, especially wife battering, has become the most pervasive type of domestic violence in the Korean American community. In April 2006 alone, three homicide/suicide incidents called attention to domestic abuse, since all of them appeared to have stemmed from domestic violence. One center for family counseling, the Hanmi Family Counseling Center, is not atypical; the director, Susan Lee, reports that 97 cases of spousal abuse were referred to her organization in 2007.

What reason could motivate Korean women to tolerate and even accept physical and emotional violence against themselves? Many empirical and theoretical studies conclude that possible reasons for the higher rate of spousal violence in Korea are family-oriented structure, excessive attachment to blood relations, patriarchal headship and dominance of men over women, public prejudice toward divorce, public ignorance and tolerance of spousal violence, and finally, lack of legal support and community networks.

As a result, battered women in Korea face a great dilemma. With family-centered ideology, for example, the notion that "staying at home, even one's own violent home, is much better than staying at public facilities" or "living with a violent husband is better than being without" or they conclude fatalistically, "I die, you die, we die." Until their lives are at stake, these women place false hope in naive expectations that things will eventually improve. So they remain in the abusive situation although alienated and continually victimized in the home without social, marital, or psychological help.

The Social and Cultural (Korean) Context of Domestic Violence

It is of paramount importance that we explore the social and cultural context of domestic violence in order to understand the high incidence of domestic violence within traditional Korean cultural patterns. It should be a great concern that the church, pastors, and pastoral counselors have long exempted themselves from responsibility to accept the crucial role they should be playing, if they are true to their central values and callings, in responding to the needs of abused victims, to signal forms of injustice in families, and to bring a halt to familial and marital violence. When counseling battered Korean women, many pastors and pastoral counselors are not aware of the obvious and distinct relationship between domestic violence and the oppressive roles of the women in Korean culture where they are obligated to be both obedient and self sacrificial. Furthermore, they offer selective attention to the gender situation, closing their eyes to how patriarchal and hierarchical values and attitudes laid down by Korean culture and by the teachings of the church affects the victim of domestic violence, especially women and children.

Korean cultural beliefs and Christian teachings have major deficiencies, and serious violations of human justice, in their failure to address the issue of domestic violence and perpetuating the abuse by putting high emphasis on the necessity of self-sacrifice and promoting stated doctrines and popular understandings of theology that work against women's safety, equality, and justice.

Violence in families is a part of a larger cultural pattern; family violence would not be as common if the culture did not condone such violence. When relationships between family members are not horizontal, but vertical, filial piety excuses domination, and all relating is characterized by the interplay of unilateral authority and required obedience. When in the Korean culture women's primary role is to be subservient to men, any resistance leads to an intensification of strategies of dominance, any refusal is met with contempt and coercive conflict patterns.

Patriarchal Family Structure

First, as noted in chapter 1, relationship in Confucianism, based on hierarchical ethic, stresses the duties of the female to the male, the child to the parent, the younger to the elder. While faults and mistakes of the elder are easily dismissed, the faults of the younger are often magnified. Unfortunately, this is evident in all aspects of Korean society. No matter how reasonable the younger's decision may be, the truth is, if the elder disagrees with the decision, it will be easily overturned. As a result, the younger must cater to the elder's wishes and decisions. One's actions are likewise justified so long as they are in obedience to, imitation of, or approved by the elder. This becomes a structural form of latent violence that Korean society has normalized as appropriate filial behavior. For example, as a young man enters a new school or goes into military service, the elder will demand and receive immediate respect. In any case where such respect is not immediately granted, physical violence results to restore the natural order. Because of age and position, this ritualistic violence is normalized and through this, the elder maintains his rank position.

For women, this ritualistic violence (both physical and mental) is much more severe. When Confucian ethics are seen through a woman's perspective, there are many inequalities and unjust practices levied that have no recourse or redress. In a patriarchal society like Korea, women were not only ignored and actively oppressed, but their social status as persons was denied. A woman would achieve status (however small) when she married and when she had given birth to a son to maintain the clan. If she failed to bear a son to her family, she was treated like an animal. Mangja, one of the students of Confucius and regarded as a great Confucian scholar, said that the "not giving birth to a son is the biggest disappointment to the parents and family." In Confucian patriarchal society, men's faults are readily forgiven and overlooked, but women's faults or failures cannot be overlooked or resolved. They must be dealt with punitively and coercively, much like the relationship between younger and elder males. One knows one's place, must never question or step out of place. For example, the rank of women in Korean society has been demonstrated historically in the axioms of the book, "Tangryul (당률)," written in the times of Tang Dynasty in China[13]:

> "남자가 여자를 때리면 법으로 묻지 않는다. 여자가 남자를 때리면 징역 2년이다."
> When a Man hits a Woman, he will not be prosecuted. When a Woman hits a Man, she will be imprisoned for 2 years.

---

13. My translation, from Kim, *Kongja ka Chugoya Nara ka Sanda*, 161.

"남자가 여자를 죽이면 징역 3년이다."
When a Man kills a Woman, he will be imprisoned for 3 years.

"여자가 남자를 죽이면 즉시 목을 벤다."
When a Woman kills a Man, she will be immediately executed.

"남자가 부모를 때리면 곤장 100대를 친다."
When a Man hits his parents, he will be flogged 100 times.

"여자가 부모를 때리면 목을 졸라 죽인다."
When a Woman hits her parents, she will be hanged.

Unfortunately, this is still the case in Korean society. For example, when a woman crosses the path of a man, it was considered bad luck. Likewise, it was considered unlucky for a woman to be the first customer. It was the new wife who was blamed when trouble visited the family. In the male-centered and dominated Confucian society, women were ignored and blamed for all the misfortunes of a family. With this knowledge, one can easily see the potential for domestic violence against women being blamed, justified by the hierarchical culture and society.

In addition, in this patriarchal culture, wives were naturally expected to sacrifice for her family and to be subservient to her husband. Raised and educated in the teachings of Confucianism, a girl was expected to be respectful and subservient to her parents. When married, she was expected to obey her husband absolutely, and as a mother, to be respectful to her son. The rule of "threefold obedience"—of daughter to their fathers, of wives to their husbands, and mothers to their sons in later years—was observed.[14] It was laid down by this society who the woman was to live for.

Traditionally, Korean women had no social standing or privilege. They were wholly dependent on men's status in society. Women were socialized to sacrifice their goals, careers, and ambitions for men. As we have seen in chapter 1, *Naehun* (Instructions for Women) elaborates on married women's roles an obedient and dutiful wife, and a wise and caring mother.[15] The book emphasized the role of daughters only as future wives, mothers, and daughters-in-law, because they were considered *ch'ulgaoiin* (outsider of the family after marriage)[16]. Considered an outsider, the only thing that was expected of her was to obey and sacrifice for her husband's family, because she belonged to her husband and his family.

14. Park and Cho, "Confucianism and the Korean Family," 119.
15. Deuchler and Mattielli, *Virtues in Conflict*, 5–6.
16. Kim, "Transformation on Family Ideology," 71.

The Motives of Self-Sacrifice in Korean American Culture, Family, & Marriage

Even today, despite obvious gains made by women in education and economic participation, they are often wholly and totally dependent upon their husbands for their financial and social needs. Because they lack the skills to become financially independent, they will not leave the relationship no matter how abusive it becomes. As they have lived with this dependent lifestyle, they are further consumed by helplessness as the abuse worsens. In this helplessly dependent situation, a wife easily becomes the target of emotional abuse by her husband, unable to escape. This emotional abuse includes unrequited love, denying physical relationship, belittling or ridiculing, and needlessly criticizing the wife's personal and family life.[17] All of these serve to destroy wife's self esteem and confidence and can be considerably more harmful than actual physical violence. For the victim, love and respect for the family are replaced with fear and uncertainty.

The husband, on the other hand, was raised with the expectation that his will should manifest on his family. If there was even the remotest possibility that his wife would shirk her responsibility, it was up to the husband the correct her by any means, including the use of physical force. As an old saying goes in Korea: "A woman must be hit once every three days in order to preserve peace and harmony in the family."

Marital relationships were not based on mutual and interpersonal affection but on strict hierarchy and unequal power, and maintained by threats of physical and emotional violence. One Korean American woman complained that her husband thinks men are kings and women their servants, saying, "It's not important what I like, what I'm thinking." A hierarchical culture considers wives and children to be personal property or servants of men, so violence against wives and children can be condoned and tolerated, violence as an appropriate tool to maintain discipline and solve problems in the family is expected and recommended. Martin Grant has named this "utilizing the marriage license as a hitting license."[18]

When this obligated and even coerced self-sacrifice is challenged, he can force her to sacrifice through coercion, power, cultural shame, and even violence.

This is shown quite demonstratively when we break down the Seoul Women's Hotline's cases of domestic violence against women.[19] When

---

17. Martin, *Counseling for Family Violence and Abuse*, 45.

18. Ibid., 38. Jan Stets and Murray Straus also suggested that the marriage license might well be renamed a hitting license. Stets and Straus, "Marriage License."

19. Seoul Women's Hotline, 2007 (서울 여성의 전화, 2007), http://womanrights.org.

asked about the situations when they were battered, the victims reported the following:

- Husband's current emotional state: 20.3%
- Talking back against their husband: 19.3%
- Refusing husband's sexual advances: 24%
- Challenging husband's authority: over 60%

When husbands were asked why they battered their wives, they answered:

- Ignored by their wives: 25.8%
- Talking back against them: 21.1%
- Annoyed or pestered by their wives: 10.5%
- To maintain their authority: 57.4%

Finally, when victims were asked why they thought they were the targets of abuse, 22.1% of the respondents answered "as a result of their husband's violent personality" and 19.9% answered "as authoritative actions against them." As one can see from these results, even the victims realize that patriarchal hierarchy and domestic violence are deeply intertwined.

In this sense, Michael Johnson discusses in his recent article that couple violence in families is divided into two major categories: patriarchal terrorism and common couple violence.[20] Patriarchal terrorism, a product of patriarchal traditions of men's right to control "their" women, is defined as "a form of terroristic control of wives by their husbands that involves the systematic use of not only violence, but also economic subordination, threats, isolation, and other control tactics."[21] Of these two forms, common couple violence may occur more often in Korean families. Patriarchal terrorism, however, is almost exclusively initiated by the husband, and most wives never attempt to fight back. Thus patriarchal terrorism becomes more severe over time. There then must be a connection with such cases of domestic violence in Korea and the culture that adamantly demands self-sacrifice, especially for women. As Johnson stated earlier, if women living in this patriarchal society are living in a constant state of terror and unequal power, the family is no longer a safe place for them.

For this reason, wife battering is not only a personal and family problem, but must be regarded as a social systemic problem because historical

---

20. Johnson, "Patriarchal Terrorism," 283–93.
21. Ibid., 284.

traditions of the patriarchal and hierarchical family system in Korean society make escape difficult for women who are systematically oppressed. The markedly unequal position of women and men in Korean society, cultivated by deep Confucian philosophical patterns and values, supports the promotion of violence as a solution on every level of the society; all contribute to the negative spiral of a hostile environment on which domestic violence thrives.[22]

Children Growing Up with Violence (Socialization of Violence)

According to numerous research and studies, when one grows up in a family where domestic violence is the norm, there is a high chance that he or she will perpetuate that cycle of violence in adulthood. Of course, not all children who grow up in this environment will continue to perpetuate this cycle of violence. And likewise, one who did not grow up with this background may become a perpetrator in the future. However, studies support that in a majority of cases of domestic violence, the perpetrators themselves were either the direct witnesses or victims of violence or otherwise grew up in a household where domestic violence was the norm.[23] This is supported by social learning theory, which presumes that humans learn social behavior by observing others' behavior and the consequences of that behavior, forming ideas about what behaviors are appropriate, trying those behaviors, and continuing them if the results are positive.[24] This theory views violent behavior as a social behavior that is learned and shaped by its consequences, continuing if it is reinforced. From this perspective, male violence against women endures in human society because it is modeled both in individuals and families and in the society more generally and has positive results.[25]

In addition, Clements and Mitchell cite Richard Hyman and Amy Smith Slep who found that the risk of both domestic violence and child abuse in families was increased incrementally by the exposure to different types of violence in the family of origin.[26] Specifically, women who both

22. Lee, *Working with Asian Americans*, 440.
23. J. A. Fagan et al., "Situational Correlates of Domestic and Extra-domestic Violence," in *Dark Side of Families*, ed. Finkelhor et al., 49–67.
24. Crowell and Burgess, *Understanding Violence against Women*, 60.
25. Ibid.
26. Mari L. Clements and Alexandra E. Mitchell, "Noncoercion, Nonviolence, and

were abused as children and observed inter-parental violence were more likely to abuse their own children, to perpetrate domestic violence, and to be abused by their partners.[27] Men in this study who were both abused and witnesses to interpersonal violence were twice as likely to be victims of domestic violence.[28] Exposure to either type of family violence placed men at increased risk for both abusing their children and abusing their partners. Other studies suggest that children of violent marriages are at increased risk for being abused as children, for developing a variety of emotional and behavioral difficulties, for perpetrating abuse on their own partners and children, and for being victims of domestic violence as adults.[29]

For instance, in a different 1997 study, the KIC investigated the backgrounds of 482 Seoul-area high school students and 284 parents and compared this with the backgrounds of 174 juvenile delinquents and 175 parents.[30] One of the results from that study indicated that the parents of the juvenile delinquents were more likely to be involved in serious cases of domestic violence. For example, the fathers of delinquents were involved in 12% of the cases of serious battery against their wives vs. 4% for non-delinquents. The background of violence in the family has had definite negative impact on these children's development.

Families are where all socialization begins, including socialization for all types of violent behavior. Studies also support that men raised in patriarchal family structures in which traditional gender roles are encouraged are more likely to become violent adults, to rape women acquaintances, and to batter their intimate partners than men raised in more egalitarian homes.[31] In a very real sense, violence in families appears to feed upon itself, spilling over from one generation into another.

Unfortunately, family is where one not only experiences violence for the first time in life, but also learns that violence is part of the common life of the family. Though the parents do not intentionally teach violence

---

Sacrifice," in *Why Psychology Needs Theology*, ed. Dueck and Lee, 91.

27. Ibid.
28. Ibid.
29. Ibid., 92.
30. Yosong Han'guk Sahoe Yon'guso ed., *Kajok kwa Han'guk Sahoe: Pyonhwa hanun Han'guk Kajok ui sam ilk'I* (Seoul: Kyongmunsa, 2005), 316.
31. Ibid., 62.

to their children, children by example learn that violence is a normal and appropriate behavior in human and family relationships.[32]

So, what do the children learn about violence in family? First, they learn that violence is intertwined with love. That is, because there is love, there must naturally follow violence. Second, they learn that violence is a result of training or discipline for the children. They then learn that violence becomes an appropriate tool to train and ultimately benefit others' lives in as much as it has benefitted them. Finally, violence against children accompanies anger, disappointment, irritation, and frustration, and children learn to deal with their own negative emotions with violence.

Uichol Kim and Soo-Hyang Choi cite Rohner and Pettengill's interesting contrast when they compare parent-child relationships in the United States and in Korea.[33] In the United States, strict parental control is perceived by adolescents as a manifestation of parental hostility, aggression, distrust, and overall rejection. This view is consistent with the fact that American parents, by and large, encourage independence and self-reliance. Rohner and Pettengill noted that for the American sample, parental strictness infringes upon the youths' sense of their right to be autonomous and self-directing.[34] However, Korean adolescents view parental strictness, control, or even punishment as an indication of parental warmth and low neglect. This result is consistent with the fact that in a relational mode, parental involvement is an essential ingredient. Parental involvement is necessary to ensure the success of children. Parental strictness is not viewed as control but as an essential component of academic, economic, and social success.[35]

Another interesting observation is that from birth, a Korean boy experiences corporal violence as a means of punishment and control. When a boy is disobedient at home, he is spanked by his parents as punishment. At school, teachers maintain classroom discipline through corporal punishment, as well. When he enters the mandatory military service, he is routinely and severely punished by his superiors. His life experience and corporal punishment are nearly inseparable. In all critical stages of his life, when he enters a new developmental stage, when he adapts himself to a new environment, he witnesses and experiences violence against him. Peter

---

32. Ibid., 316–71.

33. Kim and Choi, "Individualism, Collectivism, and Child Development," in *Cross-Cultural Roots*, ed. Greenfield and Cocking, 247.

34. Ibid.

35. Ibid.

Self-Sacrifice and Marital Violence

Chang, an executive director of the Korean American Family Service Center, says that "when you look at a man's life history, their life is related to physical punishment. . . . Then they marry, they have a problem, they use the same behavior."[36] The fact that he witnessed interpersonal violence affects his decision-making when he has difficulties in relationships. He uses violence to solve his marital issues.

In Korean society, where violence in family and the general society is somewhat permitted, where physical means of disciplining children are permitted, he learns that violence is appropriate in certain situations, especially when it involves his own wife and children. If violence is continued to be taught as a beneficial tool in others' lives, then it naturally follows that those in position of power will continue to perpetuate this cycle of violence.

Societal Tolerance for Domestic Violence in Korean Society: The Culture of Non-Interference

Korean society, because of its Confucian influences, believes that interfering in the matters of other families is wrong. In Korean culture, the issue of domestic violence is seen as an individual family issue rather than a greater social issue. Therefore, for Koreans, there is the tendency to not interfere with other families' issues and problems, and despite the high occurrence of domestic violence, the perpetrators, most likely males, go unpunished and without shame from society. Rather, battered women are shamed for getting themselves into an abusive situation and remain silent, not wanting their personal lives exposed to the community. This fear causes abused women to conceal the abuse or deny it outright, so it is difficult to estimate the actual number of victims of domestic violence. Because domestic abuse commonly is underreported or the batterers, the victim and the community minimize the severity of violence. Silence and denial are not solutions, instead, numerous studies indicate that the abuse increases in both severity and frequency over time.

When a problem erupts in a family, Koreans assume that it is the responsibility of that family to solve the problem without outside assistance. Even in cases of extreme physical punishment, from the parents, from the mother-in-law to the daughter-in-law, or likewise, there are no repercussions or reproach from society. "This is our family matter, you do not belong here!" has been a sufficient response to end any attempted intervention.

36. Mona Gable, "The Fathers," *West Magazine*, October 29, 2006, 19.

While it is common for Westerners to intervene when neighbors are alerted to instances of domestic violence, the opposite is true for Koreans. Because of this extreme focus on one's own family, the society reveres familial and societal harmony, putting a high premium on privacy and exclusivism. As noted in chapter 1, Chun-sik Ch'oe, a sociologist of religion, calls this "patriarchal collectivism."[37] Korean culture, focused exclusively on the father-son relationship, based on hierarchy, makes rank and assigned power central to all relationships. Even though Korean culture emphasizes relatedness and oneness, Koreans also have a strong exclusionist mindset which makes it easy to define boundaries with people designated inside or outside the collective, be it family, current community, community of birth place, school, family, etc. S. W. Lee notes that "according to Confucianism, social relations are nothing more than an expansion of this family relationship."[38] While Koreans are genial toward one another within the collective, outsiders are shunned to the point where they may be considered enemies. This exclusionary mindset condones the denial and concealment of domestic violence.

Family Crisis and Stress as Precipitator of Domestic Violence

Straus et al. have found that stresses caused by low income, unemployment, part-time employment, and four or five children in the home are related to incidents of violence toward children and between spouses.[39] Each of these conditions can precipitate stress and consequent misbehavior. Domestic violence cuts across all categories of families, regardless of social or financial standing; however, cases of domestic violence increase as the income level of the family decreases. Parents' career choices affect the level of domestic violence, especially where the father has either recently lost his employment or did not have a stable career. Straus et al. also assert that if having a lower status and lower-paying job is more likely to increase the rates of family violence, then we could predict that not having a full-time job or not having a job at all would dramatically raise the likelihood of violence in the home.[40]

37. Ch'oe, *Han'guk Chonggyo Munhwa ro Ilnunda*, 206.
38. Kim and Choi, "Individualism, Collectivism, and Child Development," in *Cross-Cultural Roots*, ed. Greenfield and Cocking, 238.
39. Straus et al., *Behind Closed Doors*, 181.
40. Ibid., 149–51.

Self-Sacrifice and Marital Violence

This is especially true for immigrant Korean families. Kye-young Park, associate professor of anthropology at UCLA, terms this an active gender war among Korean immigrants.[41] When a Korean family immigrates to the United States, the wife often adapts more easily than the husband. She can find a decent-paying job more easily and learn the language more willingly and voluntarily. As a result she becomes more independent. Though many Korean husbands come to United States with college degrees and professional backgrounds, these qualifications may not be recognized in the new context. Moreover, poor proficiency in English limits their ability to find a stable career. Due to these limitations and lack of resources, many husbands turn to labor-intensive small businesses for their livelihood, such as grocery stores, dry cleaners, fast-food restaurants, and garment manufacturing.[42] These small businesses require members of a family, especially wives, to become full-time participants in the business. As a consequence, the two have difficulty providing enough support for their family. The husband, as the typical breadwinner back in Korea, has an extraordinarily difficult time dealing with this new reality. When the wife brings in a larger salary than the husband, this can become the focus of the competition in the family. If the husband fails in his business, puts his family in financial difficulty, or finds that he cannot handle both his financial and family problems, he becomes engulfed in helplessness and becomes discouraged, even suicidal. He then might act irrationally, exploding with the built-up stress. However, he has no normal culturally approved outlet for dealing with this stress. Moreover, when his self-sacrifice goes unacknowledged or is ignored by his family, he may respond violently. His problems are seen as his family's problems, his failure their failure, and the only apparent solution is to dissolve the family in a tragic and violent manner.

For a tragic example, a Korean-born man allegedly killed his spouse, children, and then himself. His daughter, the only one who survived, said of her father, "Besides being proud, he was a perfectionist. He tried to hide his weaknesses. But he struggled with English and worried about money. He was ashamed because he could not provide the life style he had envisioned for his family. He wanted a big house. Instead, they lived in an apartment in Echo Park. However, he had leased a Mercedes-Benz."[43]

---

41. Erika Hayasaki, "The Daughter," *West Magazine*, October 29, 2006, 50.

42. Kim and Choi, "Individualism, Collectivism, and Child Development," in *Cross-Cultural Roots*, ed. Greenfield and Cocking, 249.

43. *West Magazine*, October 29, 2006, 16.

Three significant factors are demonstrated by this case of domestic violence. First, when resources are in short supply, frustrations and conflicts arise with escalating anxiety. When the father is involved in difficult situations, his frustrations are transferred to his family members and increase the likelihood of violence against them. This is especially the case when he feels that he is ignored and takes action to reassert authority over the family. Second, when the family is isolated from the extended family and the surrounding community, domestic violence increases. The network of extended family and the greater local community serves to absorb the stress experienced by the immediate family by providing additional resources and support when necessary. In situations of domestic violence, the community acts as watchman to the threatened members of the family.[44] However, when the family is isolated and does not have the social support of the community, the family is more likely to be subjected to domestic violence, as there are fewer external controls to prevent aggression from occurring. Third, the prestige car indicates that social approval and appearance are more important than internal health, safety, and justice.

Until now, I have explored characteristics of Korean culture, specifically structural characteristics, and how the concept of self-sacrifice relates to cultural and societal background regarding domestic violence. I have explored how domestic violence results from the control of husbands over wives in Korean families, the inequalities in patriarchal hierarchy, the helplessness of wives due to their financial dependence on their husbands, the tolerance of violence by the Korean Society, the modeling of violence to children that grew up with violence as an accepted and appropriate tool, and the stress placed on immigrant families with limited resources. These are key cultural factors influencing domestic violence in Korean families.

It is essential to understand these cultural differences when addressing the suffering of domestic violence. Basic to working with victims of domestic violence is an acceptance of their perception of self as relevant and coherent in their own terms and an understanding of the individual worldview and the dynamics of the family of origin. For example, when a Korean woman perceives that physical abuse is occurring, she might be concerned about the social perceptions of her family and children, not her own. Though she has a strong desire to end her pain, she is conscious of not wanting to cause harm to her family and community. She may be afraid that

---

44. Cazenave and Straus, "Race, Class, Network Embeddedness and Family Violence," 566–74.

revealing her abuse will cause trouble and shame for other members of her family and community. Without understanding the overwhelming power of these cultural differences, the culturally encapsulated counselor or pastor may believe that the abused wife must throw out all such restraints and consider only her own welfare. However, if individually oriented counseling is pursued, it will likely terminate prematurely, ending counseling before the situation is resolved. After this negative experience, it is highly likely that the victim will continue in this abusive relationship. Furthermore she will be even more reluctant to seek counseling in the future.

However, we must note the limitations of relying exclusively on cultural explanations in regard to the issues of domestic violence. Responsibility for domestic violence should not be attributed exclusively to the culture, even to hierarchical Korean culture. The causation is invariably due to multiple factors.

Domestic Violence in Christian Families: The Church's Silence

Are Christian Families Safe from Domestic Violence?

Most Christians see the family as a sacred institution, ordained by God, with lifelong partners who share life's journey together, in good times and amid trials. Through toil and celebration, husbands and wives have been instructed to love and nurture their children and to pass on the story of faith and obedience. Taught from pulpits and internalized within the hearts of Christians, the message that the family is sacred is unquestioned. Given this premise, it is clear that domestic violence and child abuse has no place in Christian marriages and families.

In reality, that is not the case. Personally, I know the tragic impact of violence, since I have witnessed how my mother has been a long-term victim of my father's verbal and physical abuse. Both of my parents are committed Christians; my mother has served as an assistant pastor in the church for fifteen years. Yet no one in the church was able to recognize that my mother was a victim of long-standing domestic violence. I have heard my mother crying to her closest friend on the phone, saying, "I would never in my wildest nightmares have dreamed that my husband would ever abuse me, but he did. My husband is a Christian, but his rage at things is unreal. I took my children and fled after the fourth time he struck me, but I received counsel from my pastor that it was my duty to stay in the relationship for myself, my children and suffer for Jesus' sake."

Annemie Dillen presents the relationships between sacred family, sacrifice, and domestic violence.[45] According to her argument, even when the family is designated as "sacred," the danger of family violence is as real as in secular families. When the family is promoted as an untouchable value, "sacred" by the Christian world, by family members and by the church, the risk exists that family members will want to keep all injustice and violence that occurs inside the family a secret. A woman and child often receive the message to sacrifice her or himself for the sake of family—to behave in a proper way and tolerate the violence in order to sustain the family. Most will really want to keep the family intact, because it is, in spite of the violence, invaluable for them. So, the high risk exists that religion is used as a means to legitimate power imbalance and inequality in the family that can become very oppressive.[46]

The concept of the sacred family emphasizes the traditional family with a pattern of traditional roles. In this traditional family, women are more likely to become victims of domestic violence than men. One reason, among others, is inequality; a family based on inequality is not safe and runs a greater risk of family violence. When people stay together in unequal relationships, founded on relations of dependency and power, rather than on voluntary choice or mutually committed cohesion. If the operational theology of the family supports inequality and ignores the consequent violence and injustice, the family will not be safe place for women and child.[47] A theology of family should mark the signal forms of injustice, offer alternatives to the victims, guarantee safety, and welcome interventions in to stop violence.

Many women and children in our congregations experience the family not providing a safe haven from the pressures and strains of contemporary life; instead, for millions of women and children going home is something to fear.

Lenore Walker, in *The Battered Woman Syndrome*, compares the religious affiliation of four hundred women who were battered by their husbands. The table below shows a summary of the data.[48]

---

45. Dillen, "Holy Families?," 260–71.
46. Ibid., 267.
47. Ibid.
48. Walker, *Battered Woman Syndrome*, 156–58.

Self-Sacrifice and Marital Violence

Table 4.1. Socio-demographic data for batterers and non-batterers at time of relationship, as reported by women

Reported Religion	Batterer		Non-batterer	
	Number	%	Number	%
None	114	29	71	37
Agnostic/atheist	16	4	6	3
Protestant	147	37	64	32
Catholic	110	28	42	21
Jewish	4	1	3	2
Other	9	2	10	5

It is interesting to note that 37% of the women from homes where the husband was alleged to be Protestant are victims of domestic violence, while 37% of the non-batterers were non-religious. Further, 65% of batterers were Protestant and Catholic. Clearly, a religious home is no guarantee of freedom from violence. Data and clinical experience also reveal that the incidence of physical abuse, common within the church, goes untreated. Christian women who come to church every Sunday suffer from physical battery from their husbands. Christian women cry for pastoral support, understanding, and help, but in reality, they do not receive the needed help or support from their pastors and church.

With the knowledge that Christian families are not excluded from domestic violence, churches or pastors should admit that they have failed to recognize the issue of domestic violence, especially wife abuse, in order to address domestic violence from the pulpit, to confront it in open conversation in a public forum, and to respond compassionately to the pain of victims.

The failure is clearly related to Christian teaching or theology that tends to advocate the male dominance that leads to domestic violence, encourage women to take suffering upon themselves, prescribe quick and easy forgiveness, and emphasize the model of traditional family in which there is a pattern of unequal roles.

The concern for gender justice has been ignored in the Korean church where strong attention is paid to traditional and orthodox beliefs, but little concern is expressed for victims of domestic violence. This belief has must be challenged and confronted with proper biblical interpretation and broader gender perspectives. Without challenging traditional doctrines that support a patriarchal power system, the church cannot be a safe and healing place for victims of domestic violence.

How Should Pastoral Counselors Respond to Domestic Violence?

In fact, when women who are committed to their religious traditions turn to pastors for help, it takes a great deal of courage to disclose the abuse that has been happening at home. However, it is disappointing that pastors have not been useful as a voice for justice for women and children who have experienced abuse in their families. Most studies find that pastors are rated as both the least used resource and the least helpful resource compared to family, friends, psychotherapists, family doctors, and social service agencies. Only 54% of the religious victims sought out religious leaders for guidance, while 38% of the non-religious victims also saw clergy about their abuse.[49] Interestingly enough, recent statistics indicate that women who turn to their clergy for marital guidance stay longer with their abusers and the abuse does not subside.[50] Unfortunately, of the religious victims who consulted religious leaders, one-third regarded these leaders as the "least helpful" care providers, whereas only 13% of the non-religious victims rated them in that category.[51]

What kind of help is given to abused women by pastors? What advice is offered? Many battered women received some of the following "pastoral" advice:

Stay and work things out. God expects that.
Christians do not get divorced unless adultery is involved.
Pray. Hope for the best. God will change him.
He is hopeless and cruel but you are married to him.
Try harder not to provoke him.
Be a better and more thoughtful, more understanding wife.

For example, a Korean American woman reports that when pastors and Christian counselors suggested if women were simply more understanding of their husbands' difficulties, their husbands might stop beating them, she felt infuriated, discouraging, and helplessness. She said, "That was a turning point, when I felt I needed to leave the church."

---

49. Horton and Williamson, *Abuse and Religion*, 241.
50. Steinmetz, *Cycle of Violence*, 168.
51. Horton and Williamson, *Abuse and Religion*, 242.

Self-Sacrifice and Marital Violence

In addition, many battered women testify that their pastors often focus on their behaviors and attitudes rather than on their husbands, and advice that they are the ones to change. In many cases, pastors still counsel battered women to return home and, in the spirit of prayer, become more accommodating to her husband's needs so he will not have reason or cause to attack her again. Pastors' counseling attention is simply on the wife who is the victim in the case of domestic violence. The assumption is that if the woman is sufficiently compliant to her husband's demands, marital harmony will be automatically restored and that the abuse will stop.

Second, pastors usually direct the woman to examine her personality to see what is wrong with her that any man would find her hard to live with and be driven to acts of violence because of the defects in her character.[52] Certainly, the assumption goes, if she were less hostile or less passive or less seductive or less whatever the pastor dislikes, there would be no reason for her husband to beat her up. This has been called "blaming the victim."[53] This kind of advice causes the abused women to suffer in silence and tolerate the abuse longer.

Third, the reason why pastors are rated as "least effective" in helping the victims of domestic violence may be explained from pastors' endorsement of traditional teachings concerning the sacredness of marriage and traditional sex roles.[54] It was supposed that the pastors lacked interest in this problem or denied that it even existed in their congregations due to their lack of counseling training and their limited knowledge of treatment programs, legal options, and programs for abusers.[55]

However, it is more important to note that pastors are often torn by conflicting theological perspectives that pit concern for the sanctity of marriage against concern for the sanctity of the personhood of battered women. Pastors' effectiveness is undermined by their truncated theological beliefs and male-entitled church dogma. These can be very serious issues if indeed pastors are feeling that they are not able to be very helpful to victims of domestic violence, especially wife battering, because they are trapped by a theological doctrine that mandates patriarchal power.[56]

---

52. Rassieur, *Pastor, Our Marriage Is in Trouble*, 110.
53. Ibid.
54. Wood and McHugh, "Women Battering," 191.
55. Ibid., 192.
56. Neuger, *Counseling Women*, 96.

However, when battered women were asked to identify the most important source of help used to convince their husbands to stop abuse, it came from a new understandings and vision, such as a vision of equal rights, balanced roles, respectful relationships, and a renewed theology of voluntary, not obligatory, suffering and sacrifice.[57]

It is worthwhile to note that pastors are able to be helpful when they are willing to take action to intervene in the violence, not just listen passively to the victims. In fact, battered women who rated their pastors helpful tended to be from churches that normally addressed social problems in general and that created an environment where women felt safe in coming forward with their stories.[58]

The Meaning of Forgiveness: Theological Shift from Obligation to Healing Relationship

For a battered woman, the issues of guilt, forgiveness, repentance, and reconciliation loom large. The battered woman experiences guilt when she says "if only" or "I could have . . ." She tends to be quick to accept responsibility for her batterer's behavior. She is told repeatedly by her pastor that she should forgive her abusive husband. However, if she desires to stay with her husband and work with him on their marriage, how does she forgive the beatings of several years, even though they may have stopped? What is the meaning of forgiveness in her case? What does it mean for her husband to repent? If there are possibilities to build a marriage on the basis of non-violence, what is the meaning of reconciliation?

Unfortunately, churches have had a tendency to urge the victim of violence—especially intimate violence—to forgive their abusers. They may encourage going back as if nothing ever happened. The victim may also be reminded of the model of forgiveness Jesus prayed from the cross: "Father, forgive them, for they do not know what they are doing" (Luke 23:34 NIV). This leads to the confusion of a desire and willingness to forgive with the reality of how forgiveness—and the necessary repentance—actually takes place. She may be reminded that Jesus told us to forgive "seventy times seven" (Matt 18:21–22), but an unconditional willingness to work out forgiveness is not the same as a masochistic surrender to chronic cyclical suffering.

57. Wood and McHugh, "Women Battering," 192.
58. Ibid., 191–92.

Because of the obligation to forgive that is taught in Christian formation, women who are victims of domestic violence often feel that they must forgive their offender immediately. This obligation is communicated through pastors, Christian family, and friends. Further, those who forgive the abuser are seen as better Christians, more spiritual, more mature, more holy.

However, Marie M. Fortune suggests that forgiveness should probably be the last step in the healing process rather than the first.[59] She states that "forgiveness before justice is 'cheap grace' and cannot contribute to authentic healing and restoration to wholeness of the victim or for the offender."[60] As a result, she believes that "premature" forgiveness cuts the healing process short and undercuts the redemption of abusers, by making them less fully accountable for their violent actions.[61] Seen from this perspective, forgiveness that is demanded of the victim too early in the healing journey by either pastors or by the perpetrator may actually slow the recovery process for the victim. "Premature" forgiveness, which of course isn't really forgiveness in a biblical sense (where it is called "regaining the sister or the brother"), can be dangerous to the victim, suppress the possibility of reform in the life of the abuser, and perpetuate the abusive cycle in the relationship. As Fortune points out, without justice, forgiveness is "an empty exercise."[62]

With this belief, Fortune proposes some prior steps that are necessary in order for a victim of violence and abuse to be freed to forgive.[63] In Luke's gospel, Jesus describes the process of forgiveness very clearly, that forgiving does not mean allowing oneself to be abused repeatedly: "So watch yourselves. If your brother sins, rebuke him, and if he repents, forgive him. If he sins against you seven times in a day, and seven times comes back to you and says, 'I repent,' forgive him" (Luke 17:3–4 NIV).[64] Jesus teaches that a person must be willing to confront the offense and be willing to forgive as many times as it takes. But it is also clear in this Scripture that a person's forgiveness is dependent on the offender's repentance.[65]

---

59. Marie M. Fortune, "Forgiveness: The Last Step," in *Abuse and Religion*, ed. Horton and Williamson, 215.
60. Ibid., 216.
61. Ibid.
62. Ibid.
63. Ibid., 216–17.
64. Fortune, *Sexual Violence*, 209.
65. Ibid.

Using a helpful exploration of the biblical understanding of forgiveness, Fortune finds three preliminary steps before forgiveness is considered: confession, repentance, and restitution.[66] The first step of the process is "confession." Making justice begins in the acknowledgement of what has been done to one person by another.[67] As noted above, in Luke's gospel, this is referred to as "rebuking," or confronting, the offender. To be confronted is to be called to accountability for unjust acts. Second, "repentance" is needed. Remorse may be easily forthcoming, but repentance is harder; repentance is derived from *metanoia*, or fundamental change.[68] Third, "restitution" is necessary for justice-making. It is the responsibility of the abuser to provide materially for the restoration of those harmed. Though restitution cannot remove the past for the victim, as if nothing ever happened, it can acknowledge the real cost to the victim and represent an effort to make right what was broken. This model of restitution is also seen in New Testament community where offenses were dealt with in the community of faith.

> If your brother sins against you, go and show him his fault, just between the two of you. If he listens to you, you have won your brother over. But if he will not listen, take one or two others along, so that "every matter may be established by the testimony of two or three witnesses." If he refuses to listen to them, tell it to the church; and if he refuses to listen even to the church, treat him as you would a pagan or a tax collector" (Matt 18:15–17 NIV).

Furthermore, Alan Richardson helps us understand the biblical meaning of repentance. He notes that "forgiveness is throughout conditional upon repentance, a word which quite clearly in its OT and NT equivalents involves a change of mind and intention."[69] He continues, "For Jesus Christ, and therefore for the Christian, there is no limit to forgiveness, assuming always that there is true repentance on the part of the forgiven one."[70]

It is necessary for the damage to be confronted and confessed for repentance to begin. Repentance means making the wrong right and doing whatever is necessary to change. Richardson also defines the meanings of the word "forgiveness" in both the Old and New Testaments. In the Old

---

66. Fortune, "Forgiveness: The Last Step," in *Abuse and Religion*, ed. Horton and Williamson, 216–17.

67. Ibid.

68. Ibid., 216.

69. Richardson, *Theological Word Book*, 86.

70. Ibid.

Self-Sacrifice and Marital Violence

Testament, the idea of repentance is expressed by the words *turn* or *return*. "Turning means much more than a mere change of mind, though it includes this; it represents a reorientation of one's whole life and personality, which includes the adoption of a new ethical line of conduct, a forsaking of sin and a turning to righteousness." The New Testament echoes this emphasis. "Repent in its NT usage implies much more than a mere 'change of mind'; it involves a whole reorientation of the personality, a 'conversion.'"[71] But change from a pattern of abuse in the family is not accomplished through only good intentions; it requires time, hard work, and even therapy.

According to Fortune, justice, forgiveness, and healing cannot be dependent on the wishes of the offender and his timetable.[72] Forgiveness should happen in its own time and cannot be rushed from the outside. These processes become part of the responsibility of the wider society, including the church and the legal system, as well as family and friends who want to support the victim. Fortune believes that the task of the helping professional is to provide the central ingredients necessary for justice, including truth telling and an acknowledgement of the harm done to the victim, breaking the silence of the reality of the abuse, hearing the whole story and thereby refusing to minimize its consequences, and offering protection of the vulnerable who might still be at risk.[73] David Augsburger also asserts that "the forgiver can offer forgiveness without sacrificing self-respect; the forgiven can receive forgiveness by affirming a self that is free to change, capable of transcending the past, worthy of being accepted in the future."[74] In the process of forgiving, there must be a genuine encounter with the offender and the offense. Augsburger, quoting Dietrich Bonheoffer, says, "Cheap grace is the preaching of forgiveness without requiring repentance."[75] So, forgiveness is the recognition that repentance is intended, embraced, pursued.

Augsburger points out that there may be no demands as conditions for seeing the others as worthful and precious, but people need to risk trust, open future, discern reality, and settle for the truly good rather than what

---

71. Ibid., 191–92.

72. Fortune, "Forgiveness: The Last Step," in *Abuse and Religion*, ed. Horton and Williamson, 217.

73. Ibid., 217–18.

74. Augsburger, *Helping People Forgive*, 16.

75. Ibid.

is right.[76] Forgiving does not necessarily mean automatically trusting or returning to the old relationship with the offender. Trust that has been so savagely broken can be regained only over time, if at all. The return to a relationship is the reconstruction of trust: Can the survivor genuinely trust this person not to abuse her again? How much are the victims willing to risk? This is the question that victims should ask before they go back to the relationship. For victims, trust and risk always go together.

Augsburger also helps us to understand forgiveness in the context of community.[77] He puts forgiveness in the context of community, where confrontation, confession, repentance, and reconciliation take place. He summarizes that

> forgiveness is a brother-brother, sister-sister process, a two-way mutual interaction of resolving differences and re-creating relationships between persons of equal worth. . . . Repentance is owning what was in full acknowledgement of the past and it is choosing what will be in open responsibility for one's behavior in the future. . . . In repentance past injuries are fully recognized, future intentions are truly genuine, and right relationships are now being expressed and experienced with each other.[78]

Forgiveness is a journey that we must take, an arduous journey into the self as well as forward into the relationship. Augsburger states that

> forgiveness is not an act—it is a process. It is not a single transaction—it is a series of steps. Beware of any view of instant, complete, once for all forgiveness. Instant solutions tend to be the ways of escape, of avoidance, or of denial, not of forgiveness. Forgiveness takes times—time to be aware of one's feelings, alert to one's pain and anger, open to understand the others' perspective, willing to resolve the pain the reopen the future.[79]

Within this paradigm, victims need to await the possibility of forgiveness and absolution of the offender until the conditions that arise from justice have been addressed. Forgiveness does not involve forgetting, nor does it mean that a victim return automatically to relationship with the abuser. Forgiveness deals with the issue of the past and its consequences;

---

76. Ibid.

77. Augsburger, *Caring Enough to Forgive*, 82–83; Augsburger, *Helping People Forgive*, 158–64.

78. Augsburger, *Caring Enough to Not Forgive*, 34, 72.

79. Augsburger, *Freedom of Forgiveness*, 42.

the decision to resume relating is a separate decision of wise choices for the future. Forgiveness encompasses setting new goals "where the memory of abuse is put into perspective so that it no longer dominates one's choices, one's limitations, or one's daily life."[80] In this sense, waiting patiently with victims until it is appropriate to forgive, until the issues involved have been addressed, until the victim is ready to forgive, until the perpetrator is prepared to suffer the insult of being forgiven, may be the most charitable and compassionate act the church and its pastors can offer. Forgiveness is a time-consuming and often emotionally difficult process for the victim, a humiliating and self-reconstructing process for the offender.

We as pastors and counselors should take seriously the power of forgiveness to bring people to healing in relationship. These challenges are helpful theological shifts that give us a way both to hold perpetrators of violence accountable and to help empower those who have been victims of violence.

Challenges to Pastors and Counselors: Theological/Practical Proposals

As we develop a pastoral counseling approach to help women victimized in intimate relationships, we must reverse centuries of neglectful processes and shameful abuse. Sadly, many pastors report that dealing with wife abuse in the church is one of the most difficult pastoral problems that they face. As noted earlier, pastors feel torn between their theological beliefs, their personal experiences with people accused of violence, and their sympathies with a victim.[81] Without challenging some of the "traditional" doctrines that support a patriarchal power system, pastoral care cannot appropriately provide a safe and healing environment for abused women. Nor can it appropriately call offenders to account. It is very regrettable to acknowledge that the church will continue to be known by its silence in the face of abuse and by its collusion with those who do harm.

How then can we, as pastors, address the violence that occurs in the family, especially in the faith community? What is the proper role of pastors in providing answers to the problems of family abuse? How can pastors help abused women promote an understanding of the sacredness of human life, as well as the importance of justice and human dignity? What

---

80. Nason-Clark, *Battered Wife*, 54.
81. Neuger, *Counseling Women*, 112.

are theological resources for pastors to help victims of domestic violence in the church?

Pastoral Intervention

The issue of domestic violence in the Christian family has been hidden in and by the church for a long time. Larry Kent Graham and Marie M. Fortune say that the church needs to be known as a place where "we hold perpetrators accountable and we are on record as religious communities that abuse is not tolerated. When offenders are held accountable, we can become a safe community to heal."[82]

Pastors should break the silence about wife abuse in the families of their churches. A good place to start is by advocating nonviolence in the home from the pulpit. The sin of abuse needs to be addressed as actively as any other sin within the body of Christ. Through sermons, prayer, and Bible study groups, both the abused and the abuser will have an opportunity to bring the abusive relationships into open, shared reality and to learn how to deal with the violence occurring in their homes without forcing suffering people to be silent and to suffer in isolation. John Wall suggests that religious leaders can take a "prophetic" stance toward wife abuse that removes its stigma from women and places it instead on the community that enters into complicity with violence against women by failing vigorously to decry it.[83] A prophetic voice can empower women by condemning battery as violence against the trust and covenanted love of the entire community, by sympathetically rediscovering stories of women from scripture in which women have made a positive contribution to the community, and by inviting women into full partnership and participation in the church community.

Domestic violence requires pastoral intervention that may be quite different from what a pastor is used to offering. In general, inquiring and insight-oriented counseling with either spouse will not break an established pattern of marital violence. I strongly believe that direct intervention is required, and pastors must take a clear stand against any continuing abuse.

Rassieur gives us guidelines that can help a counselor plan an effective pastoral strategy for intervention in marital violence.[84] First, he proposes

---

82. Graham and Fortune, "Empowering the Congregation," 340.
83. Anderson et al., *Family Handbook*, 168.
84. Rassieur, *Pastor, Our Marriage Is in Trouble*, 111–12.

Self-Sacrifice and Marital Violence

that the pastor should explore very carefully and seriously any reference by either spouse to physical intimidation or abuse. The pastor should assess exactly when, how often, and under what circumstances such abuse has happened in order not to attribute to one spouse more abusive behavior than has actually occurred. However, it must always be remembered that if one spouse feels at all intimated by the other, for whatever reason, such intimidation most likely plays a major disruptive role in the marital relationship.[85]

Second, the pastor should begin from the victim's position. For example, a pastor might want to talk with her husband about his abusive behavior. However, the wife may feel that such a conversation with her husband can only make things worse, and she would prefer to find reasons to leave home for a day or two when she senses her husband's mood becoming tense. Although a pastor might wish to deal directly with the husband and his threatening behavior, the wife's wishes and concerns must be the final guide. The pastor should not make any intervention that the victim does not approve. The victim, powerless in the marriage, must be permitted to have the power of knowledge and consent in the counseling process.[86]

Third, in most counseling situations, the pastors and counselors will remain neutral and not express any judgment about a counselee's behavior. However, in the case of marital violence, pastors and counselors should be willing to use more intense moral responses to protect vulnerable people from being harmed by others. It is essential that the pastor say clearly that there is no place for any physical abuse or violence in a marriage, except of course in the case of self-defense against physical attack.[87] The pastor should state clearly that both spouses are responsible for their own behavior, regardless of what the other person might say or do, and they need to add that nothing, no matter how outrageous, can justify an abusive response. In addition, pastors must understand their own belief on the issue of domestic violence under which they are able to give advice and counsel to the abused women. This self-examination or self-reflection helps pastors articulate the moral and spiritual dimensions of violence and their response to it.

Fourth, the victim should clearly understand every resource that is available for help. It is essential that the victim not continue to feel powerless and helpless. Knowing all one's options and having several plans for

---

85. Ibid., 111.
86. Ibid., 112.
87. Ibid.

action can give a victim greater confidence for handling the next step. Furthermore, if the women who come to a pastor for help are in danger of physical battery, it should be the first priority to provide for their physical safety. If the abuse continues, pastors need to send the women to a women's shelter. The pastors also should not release any information about her to her husband or relatives. More importantly, the church should be viewed as a safe place where abused women bring their concerns, where the women will be heard, where the women will be cared for, and where God's love and grace will be demonstrated. When the church is a supportive community for the abused woman, she can come to the church not only for emotional, physical, and spiritual support, but also for sharing her pain and suffering with the other members and even with God.

Pastoral Care for Batterers and Abusers

Generally speaking, battering is not a character defect or a sign of mental illness. Abusive men are found among all races, socioeconomic classes, and occupations. However, there is no universal cause of violence in intimate relationships. So the combination of the personality of the abuser and social influences should go together in predicting the likelihood of marital violence.

Characteristics of Batterers

First, pastors and counselors who work with men who batter have observed that "assaultive" men believe stereotypes about male-female roles and over-identify with the stereotypic male role.[88] Because of this over-identification they feel that they possess the right to exercise control over anyone with less power or status (women and children). In marital relationships, these husbands think that authority is their privilege and may expect male pastors and counselors to affirm their traditional ideas about sex roles. As we have seen above, the inflexible adherence to traditional expectations for men in relation to women is one of the forces that make wives "appropriate victims." Whether Christian or not, the abusive husband expects his wife to fulfill a traditional sex role. He wants her to be responsible for all household and mothering chores and to be submissive and subservient. For example,

---

88. Adams, *Woman-Battering*, 14.

he might consider it perfectly appropriate to hit his wife because the dinner is not ready to be served when he comes home from work.

Second, family also acts as a context for training men in the art of household violence, as it offers models for venting stress through violence and gives cues for when and how men may resort to practicing violence. An abusive family provides not only the initial setting for exposing its members to physical violence, but also provides the example that gives permission for the use of violence to resolve conflict. A man who sees violence as the primary method for settling differences as a child is not going to have available, as an adult, very many alternate ways to channel anger. Abusers often come from dysfunctional family environments where appropriate problem-solving was never observed.

Third, abusive men have serious deficiencies in expressing emotions, as well as in identifying and handling intense and threatening feelings when they occur. When frustrated, a man who batters has come to believe that he needs to discharge the unconscious store of anger onto either self or other, especially the under-privileged—women and children. This belief in a hydraulic view of anger is not true for the healthy population: belief in a hydraulic view of anger as pressure that must be ventilated or discharged is a dysfunctional way of thinking that must be relearned. This type of hydraulic mechanical man is rarely capable of true intimacy and may feel very threatened by the prospect of being open and vulnerable. It also has been suggested that "men use their inexpressiveness as a power strategy to maintain a position of dominance within the family."[89] Silence gives the father power, because the family never knows exactly what he is thinking. If this inexpressiveness proves to be ineffective in maintaining their authority, some men resort to physical violence as the only way they know to get what they want.[90]

Fourth, low self-esteem is a factor that is often associated with aggressive behavior, and not surprisingly has been implicated in wife abuse.[91] Abusive husbands are more likely to perceive their wives' behavior as threatening to their sense of self. Data on abusive men and low self-esteem support the idea that the probability of violence is increased when a man with low self-esteem perceives that his sense of self is being threatened.[92]

89. Martin, *Counseling for Family Violence and Abuse*, 33.
90. Ibid.
91. Nason-Clark, *Battered Wife*, 10.
92. Ibid.

Fifth, an abusive man lacks other supportive relationships and tends to maintain only superficial contact with persons outside his own family. Although he may identify a number of people as friends, the typical batterer tends to view these relationships as "non-gratifying."[93] Because of his fear of losing his spouse and his distrust of his family and friends, it is highly possible that the abusive man will perceive physical violence as his only recourse.

Sixth, men who abuse their partners have often been found to have a problem with substance abuse. It has been reported that 67% of batterers frequently abuse alcohol, and the abuse of alcohol is likely to result in more serious injuries to women.[94] Although some form of substance abuse is usually present in abusive relationships, this does not mean that drug or alcohol abuse is necessarily causing the violence, since more than half of abuse cases occur in the absence of drinking alcoholic beverages.[95] However, we should not underestimate the relationship between alcohol and violence, since there is a strong correlation between alcohol use and physical violence in the home. In addition, the use of alcohol and drugs often allow the abuser to avoid responsibility for his behavior ("I am sorry I misbehaved but I was drunk out of my mind and did not know what I was doing").

Ministry in Caring for Batterers

Claire Wolfteich suggests that religious groups may find important ministry in caring for those who have committed acts of violence.[96] In ministering to domestic violence, pastors need to realize that the abusive husband may be another victim of this society structured by sexism, classism, and racism. Especially in Korean society, they have learned from their society to exercise dominant power and control over women. Men who batter their wives are also victims in that they are victimized by their inability to channel their anger, their lack of communication skills, their fear of closeness, and their dependency on the women they abuse.[97] They may not know how

---

93. Martin, *Counseling for Family Violence and Abuse*, 33.
94. Ibid., 36.
95. Nason-Clark, *Battered Wife*, 11.
96. Anderson et al., *Family Handbook*, 185.
97. Martin, *Counseling for Family Violence and Abuse*, 98.

Self-Sacrifice and Marital Violence

to respect the opposite sex, to accept ambiguity and loss of control, and to control their own feelings of powerlessness.

For example, "Father's school" has become a very popular program provided by the Korean church today. A number of Christian fathers actively participate in this school to learn what the Bible teaches about true manhood and fatherhood, how their marriage relationship can be renewed, and how fathers should deal with marital problems. The school deals with many existing and potential marital problems through the lens of biblical and practical theology. This school is very successful and helpful by giving the husband a chance to restructure his beliefs of manhood, fatherhood, and marital relationships within a biblical perspective. In the light of the successful father's school, it is very important for the husband to be encouraged to construct for himself a new definition of manhood that includes valuing and respecting the female gender.

The majority of abusive husbands are not monsters. They are good fathers and husbands in situations where they do not feel threatened, helplessness, or out of control of anger and frustration. They may not know how to live with their families on the basis of equality, justice, and respect. There can be no intimacy without equal power, and a renewed balance of power in a marital relationship for many will reduce the danger of violence. Thus, pastors and counselors need to focus not only on the individual level, but also on the many social factors that have influenced abuse within marital relationship.

There are warning signs of violent behavior which both partners need to learn to recognize. When husbands catch these signs, they need to leave the potentially explosive situation and cool off until such a time that they can communicate nonviolently.[98] However, there are no certain predictors that signal when a person will become violent. One or more of the following warning signs may be displayed before a person becomes violent, but these do not invariably indicate that an individual will become violent. A display of these signs should trigger concern, as they are usually exhibited by people experiencing problems:

- Irrational beliefs and ideas
- Verbal, nonverbal, or written threats or intimidation
- Fascination with weaponry and/or acts of violence
- Expressions of a plan to hurt oneself or others

98. Anderson et al., *Family Handbook*, 167.

- Externalization of blame
- Unreciprocated romantic obsession
- Taking up much of a teacher's time with behavior or performance problems
- Fear reactions among family
- Drastic changes in belief systems
- Displays of unwarranted anger
- New or increased sources of stress at home or work
- Inability to take criticism
- Feelings of being victimized
- Intoxication from alcohol or other substances
- Expressions of hopelessness or heightened anxiety
- Violence toward inanimate objects
- Steals or sabotages projects or equipment
- Lack of concern for the safety of others.[99]

In addition, Lenore Walker has listed some characteristics that may help us identify a potential batterer:

1. Does a man report having been physically or psychologically abused as a child?
2. Was the man's mother battered by his father?
3. Has the man been known to display violence against other people?
4. Does he play with guns and use them to protect himself against other people?
5. Does he lose his temper frequently and more easily than seems necessary?
6. Does he commit acts of violence against objects and things rather than people?

---

99. Adapted from *Reducing School Violence: Building a Framework for School Safety*, written by Stephanie Kadel-Taras and produced by the Southeastern Regional Vision for Education (associated with the University of North Carolina-Greensboro) and the Florida Department of Education, with assistance from the Southeastern Regional Center fro Drug-Free Schools and Communities.

Self-Sacrifice and Marital Violence

7. Does he drink alcohol excessively?
8. Does he display an unusual amount of jealousy when his wife is not with him? Is he jealous of significant other people in her life?
9. Does he expect his wife to spend all her free time with him or keep him informed of her whereabouts?
10. Does he become enraged when his wife does not listen to his advice?
11. Does he appear to have a dual personality?
12. Is there a sense of overkill in his cruelty or in his kindness?
13. Does his wife get a sense of fear when he becomes angry with her? Does not making him angry become an important part of her behavior?
14. Does he have rigid ideas of what people should do that are determined by male or female sex-role stereotypes?
15. Does the woman think or feel she is being battered? If so, the probability is high that she is a battered woman and should seek help immediately.[100]

Men need to be conscious of and learn to express their feelings in ways that are not abusive. Support groups, men's retreats, and men's study groups where they can face these issues apart from women will help. Important subjects are intimacy, power, conflict management, role change, and awareness and management of feelings. If pastors or counselors are males, they can be role models to live out ways of relating to women other than by using power and coerciveness. Pastors or counselors should acknowledge their own sexism and cultural conditioning and invite men to join them on a journey to a new way of living. If pastors or counselors are females, they can also be role models of assertive women showing the way women can relate to men in their local church.

Conclusion

Today, families in the church are not exempt from domestic violence. Many women are suffering from abuse, and turn to the church and pastors for help. In the face of this painful reality of domestic violence, the church should break the silence and take responsibility to address the issue of domestic violence, to affirm the value of the woman as a person, and to

---

100. Adapted from Walker, *Battered Women Syndrome*, 128–31.

take action to help abused women by providing a safe place and supportive group. In addition, the church and pastor should recognize the destructive effects of their teaching in regard to (1) suffering as a required Christ-like means of redemption; (2) self-sacrifice, self-denial, and submission as the ideal of Christian love; (3) patriarchal systems, male headship, control, and domination over the female on family and church community.

It is the time for the church and its pastors to acknowledge that their failure to build strong families in the body of Christ encourages domestic violence in many ways. In the face of destructive violence in the family, it is an important task for the church and pastors to present a good model based on equality, mutual love, and respect in the marriage, and to offer renewed commitments and promises so that couples can experience new hope and trust in God as well as the family.

Now I will turn my focus to the reality of those situations where Korean people choose to make self-sacrifice. To explore the way in which Korean people experience self-sacrifice, I want to find the hidden motives, attitudes and beliefs, and definitions of self-sacrifice through a questionnaire. This empirical study will seek to establish a baseline for understanding Koreans' motivation in self-sacrifice in various interpersonal relationships, especially in family relationships. Through this study I will present a positive, working model of self-sacrifice for Koreans.

5

Empirical Study on Self-Sacrifice in Korean American Relationships

Reality and Motives

IN UNLOCKING AND EXPLORING the dynamics of theology and the practice of self-sacrifice for Korean Americans, we have explored cultural virtues, marital relationships, gender inequality, domestic violence, and their theological implications. In this final chapter, we will examine existing previous studies on the empirical and theoretical aspects of self-sacrifice. Then we will explore the actual attitudes, beliefs, and motives of self-sacrifice as reported by Korean Americans in a qualitative and quantitative research study. What are Korean Americans' definitions or understanding of self-sacrifice? In what relationships are they more likely to make a personal self-sacrifice? What motivates them to make self-sacrifice? The research design will be described, the methodology defined, and the resulting data interpreted.

Previous Studies on Self-Sacrifice: Pros and Cons

M. L. Clements and A. E. Mitchell suggest that all sacrifices, both large and small, share three important similarities.[1] First, the person is giving up *something of value* to the self in order to benefit the relationship or the relationship partner. If the gesture of giving something up is of little or no personal value, this is to say, if the person can be *indifferent* about the thing given up, the act is not sacrificial at all. Second, sacrifice is a *choice*. If a sacrifice is not voluntary but the behavior results from yielding to a social or familial obligation, this is not sacrifice but rather the consequence of yielding to coercion. Third, sacrifice is by definition for the good of the *other*, not for the good of the self. In other words, the person is giving up something out of genuine desire to help the other rather than out of any desire to induce guilt or to coerce future sacrifices. This sacrifice is something a person chooses to give up out of concern for the other, not out of the desire to be recognized for their selfless behavior.

When self-sacrifice comes out of coercion and obligation rather than from voluntary motives, then it truthfully cannot be called self-sacrifice. Let's then explore some empirical and theoretical studies regarding the beliefs and motives of both the positive and negative sides of self-sacrifice.

The Positive Side of Self-Sacrifice

The concept of self-sacrifice is so essential to both human love and Christian life that we can no longer ignore this issue en route to becoming mature persons. As Christians, we are called to love and serve each other. This is often demanded as part of Christian life: "Love your God and your neighbor as yourselves" is what Jesus commands us to do (Matthew 22:37–40). In fact, as Clements and Mitchell argue, some degree of sacrifice is necessary to ensure long-term human community.[2] Sacrifice is an essential component of family love. The unselfish love of husband and wife for each other, and for their parents, as well as the selfless love parents have for their children, has been seen as the heart and soul of morality. Moreover, especially, voluntary sacrifice is important for sustained harmonious interaction within a community. Paul A. M. Van Lange and his colleagues state that in the con-

---

1. Clements and Mitchell, "Noncoercion, Nonviolence, and Sacrifice," in *Why Psychology Needs Theology*, ed. Dueck and Lee, 93–94.

2. Ibid., 94.

text of ongoing, close relationships, willingness to sacrifice, defined as the propensity to forego immediate self-interest to promote the well-being of a partner or relationship, is basic to human relationship.[3] They also suggest that commitment is a central motive in ongoing relationships, and feelings of commitment promote pro-relationship transformation and willingness to sacrifice.[4] They found in their study that willingness to sacrifice is associated with strong commitment, high satisfaction, constructive search for alternatives, and high investment in relationship. Moreover, willingness to sacrifice is associated with superior couple functioning, operationalized in terms of level of dyadic adjustments and probability of couple persistence.[5]

Furthermore, Whitton and her colleagues, in their review of the broader psychological literature on sacrifice, note that the likelihood of sacrifice increases as the degree of intensity in relationship increases, and sacrifice is more likely to occur in relationships that are loving and committed, such as spousal or parent-child relationships, as compared to those that are transitory, such as casual dating or roommate relationships.[6] The sacrifices that we make for others form the glue that holds families and communities together. Without this glue, families and communities—and individuals—suffer problems such as irresponsible abortions, precipitous divorce, repetitious domestic violence, abandoned and overtaxed single parents, and so on. Lasting associations and stable societal order depend upon the willingness to sacrifice individual needs for the greater good at crucial times.

Kathleen S. Bahr criticizes that "today much literature designates self-sacrifice as defective and unhealthy. We are all too familiar with the language and needs of self. We talk of self-esteem and self-direction as if they were a basic right; we are all well schooled in a language of fairness and rights."[7] Bellah and his colleagues also point out that even conservative Christians are uncomfortable with the language of sacrifice.

> While they wanted to maintain enduring relationships, they resisted the notion that such relationships might involve obligations that went beyond the wishes of the partners . . . they were troubled

---

3. Van Lange et al., "Willingness to Sacrifice in Close Relationships," 1373–95.

4. Ibid., 1374.

5. Ibid., 1373.

6. Clements and Mitchell, "Noncoercion, Nonviolence, and Sacrifice," in *Why Psychology Needs Theology*, ed. Dueck and Lee, 94.

7. Bahr, "Families, Children, and Self-Sacrifice," 30–35.

by the ideal of self-denial the term sacrifice implied.... Since the only measure of the good is what is good for the self, something that is really a burden to the self cannot be part of love ... it was hard for people to find a way to say why genuine attachment to others might require the risk of hurt, loss, or sacrifice.[8]

Over the last decade, we have been swept away by a steady stream of ideas dominated by rational choice theory, market models of human relationships, and "therapeutic relationship," which emphasizes that relationships must be based on the autonomous needs of two separate individuals and are *incompatible* with self-sacrifice. In therapeutic relationships, obligation of any kind becomes problematic. Love has been reduced to an emotional state, feelings of affection, grounded in chemistry. In this sense, Bahr strongly argues that "the old morality grounded in selfless concern for the well being of others has been replaced with an ethic of duty to self."[9]

Bahr admits that there are some aspects of sacrifice that are pathological, but doubts that "their existence justifies the neglect of sacrifice as an essential social process, the basis of meaning in life, and a powerful source of human bonding and community solidarity."[10] Bahr concludes that criticisms directed at those who do *too much* sacrifice are actually critiques of persons who *lose themselves* by making wrong choices in the direction of sacrifice. Rather than sacrificing for the greater good of one's family, group, or society, they lose themselves to corporations, to the military, to the government, to the television set, to money, or to the internet.[11] No one would consider such as self-sacrifice, but it is these that deserve our critique. Instead, the sacrifices that one makes for the greater good are under attack.

Bellah, in his study of individualism and commitment in the American life, proposes that the evangelical Christian worries about how to reconcile the spontaneous, emotional, and obligatory sides of love.[12] In the Christian family's view on Christian love, free choice and obligation can be combined, but it is duty that comes first. Christians believe that love is not simply a matter of feelings, emotions, or lip service. For them love is a matter of will, decision, action, and commitment. Love is a willingness to sacrifice oneself for others. In the evangelical Christian view, love involves

8. Bellah et al., *Habits of the Heart*, 109.
9. Bahr, "Families, Children, and Self-Sacrifice," 30.
10. Ibid., 32.
11. Ibid., 35.
12. Bellah et al., *Habits of the Heart*, 93–97.

placing duty and obligation above the ebb and flow of feeling, and finding freedom in willing sacrifice of one's own interests to others. This view of love is used to define the distinctive commitment of Christians to permanence in marriage. Evangelical Christians often criticize modern society for the loss of any basis for permanent commitment in marriage, and question whether any exists apart from Christian faith itself. Christian love is a commitment to and an act of obedience to God. Love rests less on feelings than on decisions and actions. Real love may require emotional self-denial, pushing feelings to the back in order to live up to one's commitment. Of course, these Christians seek some of the same qualities of sharing, communication, and intimacy in family that define love for most individual Americans. But they are determined that these are to be sought within a framework of binding commitments and not as *reasons for* adhering to a commitment. By having an obligation to something higher than one's own preference or fulfillment, Christians insist that permanent loving relationships can be achieved. This is a commitment that is, at best, profoundly voluntary and based upon love of God; at its worst, it is obligatory, binding and compulsory, not an expression of grace and compassion.

The Negative Side of Self-Sacrifice

Despite these apparent benefits, the role of sacrifice in relationships is controversial. Criticisms of sacrifice have focused on the hazards of "asymmetrical" sacrifice.[13] Some forms of sacrifice could certainly be taken to "unhealthy" extremes. For example, in Korean American family relationships, parents' one-sided sacrifice for children can be unhealthy for whole family dynamics. Korean American parents frequently claim to give up everything for the children and sacrifice themselves for the sake of the child. But this is often colored by resentment and grief when children are ungrateful for their sacrifice. In a recent, more extreme case, there was a "goose father"[14] who raped his daughter after he felt he was betrayed by his family. He believed that he sacrificed himself to support both his wife and

---

13. Bahr, "Families, Children, and Self-Sacrifice," 94.

14. "Goose father" refers to a father who lives alone in Korea having sent his spouse and children to a foreign country to study. The term goose father derives from the Korean view of the goose as a traditional symbol of family loyalty. Like many other Korean men with family members in the United States, they stay behind in South Korea, working hard and getting paid in Korean won.

his daughter abroad. However, without acknowledgement of this sacrifice from his family, he felt both used and rejected. After the investigation, the police concluded that his expectations upon his daughter had crumbled and subsequently, he was motivated by vindictive rage for his wife and child. This type of sacrifice causes parents to feel upset; they compensate to hide their failure, form a sense of injustice against the child, deepen their own sense of depression and frustration, and ultimately this engenders revenge toward the very members of the family for whom they purport to have sacrificed so much.

On the other hand, children become utterly dependent upon the parent who does everything for the child. Furthermore, if the parent does not fulfill established expectations of the child, then the child may in turn develop feelings of hate and anger toward the parents. This one-sided parent-child relationship does not allow much room for trust and openness and buries the pain of failures and disappointment. It leaves little room for the grace of God to work in the midst of chaotic family relationships. In this family relationship, the role of the parents is understood as the one that makes self-sacrifice for the children, without expecting something in return. This idea implies that only those who give of themselves so selflessly may attain true virtue. They end up hiding their own limits, failures, and frustration under the name of self-sacrifice. At this point we may ask if this really *is* self-sacrifice.

In addition, several theoretical accounts of behavior in close relationships suggest that sacrifice may be a deterrent of healthy couple functioning.[15] Feminist theorists have held that women are socialized to sacrifice in relationships.[16] For women, growing up in relationship-oriented family, commitment is a central motive in family relationships. Harvard University psychologist Carol Gilligan and Wellesley College psychiatrist Jean Baker Miller have stated that "a guiding principle of women's lives is importance of establishing and maintaining close personal relationships."[17] If this is true, women would be willing to give up whatever it takes (such as their own goals and interests) to make a relationship successful. Women who question social norms as male-dominant can lose their sense of being "appropriately" feminine and be denied the social approval attendant on being a good wife and feminine woman, which is often the love or attachment

15. Van Lange et al., "Willingness to Sacrifice in Close Relationships," 1373–95.
16. Clements, 94.
17. Caplan, *Myth of Women's Masochism*, 10.

and economic support of their husbands. This leaves most women virtually no real choice. In fact, this socialization may lead women to sacrifice even when it is harmful to them to do so.

Paula Caplan, as well, argues that a misogynistic society has created a myriad of situations that make woman unhappy.[18] This society uses "the myth of women's masochism" to blame the woman herself for her misery. This is a common pattern for the woman: blaming herself rather than other people and the larger society, because this is the feminine thing to do. Women are far more likely than men to be held responsible if anything goes wrong in their relationships or if harm befalls their children. Caplan calls this tendency the characteristic of "scapegoating."[19] Although the woman's self-sacrificial role of being the scapegoat, to save or restore their family relationships now and in the future, has certain advantages, the price she pays with disconnectedness, isolation, rejection, shame, and guilt can be extremely costly. A woman could not begin to take care of herself if she feared that changes on her part might destabilize a marital arrangement that was for her not only a crucial emotional relationship, but also a matter of survival. Because of her financial dependence, it would become difficult or impossible for her to break that relationship. Her self-sacrifice must be maintained in the framework of that relationship. In this sense, women need to understand the "unquestioned" feelings, beliefs, and motives that lead them to play a self-sacrificial role in family relationships. We may then begin to understand the motives behind all the work that women do in order to salvage these relationships.

Harriet Goldnor Lerner points out the problem of women's excessive self-sacrifice, called "de-selfing."[20] She proposes that the de-selfing (excessive self-sacrifice) process begins in the family of origin and is continued most noticeably in women's relationship with men. Their most important relationships could survive only if they continued to maintain the status quo. To articulate thoughts with more clarity, to act stronger, and to be more assertive, separate, and self-directed were all considered destructive initiatives that would threaten a woman's partner.

Of course, emotional connectedness is a basic human need, as well as strength. Valuing relationship is not the problem. Rather, it is *what happens* to women in relationships that deserves our attention. The structuring of

---

18. Ibid., 9–10.
19. Ibid., 11.
20. Lerner, *Women in Therapy*, 227.

gender roles and the profound impact of women's subordinate and devalued status have far-reaching implications for a woman's vulnerable position in her family of origin and in marriage.[21] In this context, feelings of depression, low self-esteem, self-betrayal, and even self-hated are inevitable when women fight but continue to submit to unfair circumstances, when they have little choice but to participate in relationships that betray their own beliefs, values, and personal goals, or when they find themselves fulfilling society's stereotype of the bitchy, nagging, bitter, or destructive woman.[22] If Korean American women possess only a self-directed emotional reactivity, or "*Han*," then they are not able to identify their own problems and are unable to change their relationship patterns. The ways in which women have suffered from the traditional structures of family life are inseparable from the problems of dysfunctional forms of self-sacrifice.

Gill-Austern points out some of the negative effects on women and the institutional and systemic inequalities that give birth to such behavior.[23] First, women whose loving has consistent patterns of self-sacrifice commonly lose touch with their own needs and desires. Second, it often leads to a loss of a sense of self and a loss of voice. Third, the fall-out from self-sacrifice often accumulates as a reservoir of resentment, bitterness, and anger as women come more and more to feel victimized. Fourth, love as self-sacrifice frequently leads to over-functioning on behalf of others and under-functioning on behalf of self, which contributes to a loss of sense of self-esteem and a sense of one's own direction. Fifth, self-sacrificing love can undermine the capacity for genuine mutuality and intimacy. Sixth, love as self-sacrifice and self-denial creates great stress and strain. Seventh, love understood as self-sacrifice can lead women to abdicate their public responsibility to use their God-given gifts on behalf of the greater community and for the common good. Eighth, love understood as self-sacrifice can unwittingly contribute to exploitation and domination of relationship by the more powerful party.

As Gill-Austern notes, if love is understood as self-sacrifice, then the tendency is to not expect mutuality from the relationship. And if self-sacrifice is encouraged to become the most important virtue, along with a reinforced sense of responsibility, they feel used and abused and void of

21. Ibid., 250.
22. Ibid., 248.
23. Gill-Austern, "Love Understood as Self-Sacrifice and Self-Denial," in *Through the Eyes of Women*, ed. Moessner, 310–15.

self. Self-sacrificial love turns to resentment of those who demand self-sacrifice. And if this self-sacrifice continues, there will be detrimental effects on themselves and the relationship.

Others see a danger in the ethic of self-sacrifice in that *justice* is overlooked. Annemie Dillen argues that when love is only conceived of in the second person ("I-Thou" relation), it supposes a kind of never-ending love and devotion to the other.[24] She points out that

> this can be seen as a form of self-sacrifice in spite of myself. However, what is important is responsibility in third person. This is not only the responsibility for the concrete others, but also for all others, for "third persons." This requires justice. . . . This justice takes love seriously because love does not count for only one unique person, but is broaden to others and becomes more universal.[25]

As Dillen noted, sacrifice without justice, sacrifice that is routine is a self-sacrifice practiced *in spite of* oneself. If one ignores others' needs with an explicit focus upon the needs of his or her own direct family members, then this self-sacrifice loses social significance. The sacrifice that is directed only to the sphere of personal relationship, so that one cares for one's family member and friends but ignores the needs of anyone outside that limited sphere, is problematic, and is especially prevalent in Korean American families. Our perspective of self-sacrifice should widen from first person ("I-Thou") to the third person. Our sacrifice should not be limited in scope to our own nuclear family, but as needed, be broadened to a more universal perspective.

The critics of self-sacrifice see another danger in an *ethic of care*, in that one may care *too much* for others. Many people have been taught to be a "cheerful giver," to fight their own suffering by helping those who are worse off than themselves, to "lose" themselves in service through religious training, their families of origin, and society at large. But they have not been taught how to identify and express their own feelings. Many times they feel underappreciated or unappreciated. Other times it feels more like guilt when taking time for personal needs somehow means having to disappoint or neglect someone else. Carmen Renee Berry calls this as "Messiah trap," which means habitually putting everyone else first.[26] Those who are bound to fulfill this "Messiah trap" view love as merely being the sacrifice

---

24. Dillen, "Holy Families?," 269–70.
25. Ibid.
26. Berry, *When Helping You Is Hurting Me*, 13–21.

of one for another. This view partially misunderstands love. In this case, caring has become a *compulsion* that chains the self to a self-damaging, addictive way of life. In its totality, love is balanced and fair, non-exploitive, caring, strong, and resourceful. This is no competition between lovers, no choice between one or the other, because love is full and whole and large enough to encompass us all.

The problem for those who care too much for others is that the desire to please becomes a responsibility to be *always* pleasing. They feel responsible for other people's happiness, and when others are displeased they usually experience feelings of guilt and failure. They easily become "people pleasers" who try to make others feel comfortable, constantly doing little things for others. So they choose to suffer rather than disappoint anyone else. They dance to someone else's tune with feet tangled in frustration and in denial of their true feelings.

Sacrificing for another is a virtue, not a vice. However, when the giver feels compelled to sacrifice, and acts only out of obligation, it is no longer giving, it is paying a duty. Guilt, not giving or sacrificing for others, becomes the hidden motive. If a person has no choice but to sacrifice, he or she is no longer giving but is being exploited. When a person feels used in such a manner, the joy of giving is replaced by resentment and feelings of entrapment. Therefore one of the crucial preconditions for authentic self-sacrifice is a sense of empowerment, choice, and autonomous free will.

Some Theological Dimensions of Self-Sacrifice

Between Love and Justice: Agape

We have seen, so far, two aspects of self-sacrifice: one as a necessary ethical element in the smallest units of society with enduring benefits; the other as pathological, one-sided, obligatory, manipulative, and destructive to family relationships. It may be helpful to turn to theological insight for some mediating thoughts. How can we discuss self-sacrifice without a discussion of love and justice? Love is often seen as unconditional, unilateral giving and self-denying, whereas justice, on the contrary, is exacting, fair, balanced, calculated, and precise. When discussing self-sacrifice, on the one hand, we acknowledge that there is an intrinsic propensity to side on either extreme of love or justice; on the other hand, we recognize that love and justice are not mutually exclusive categories but rather a continuum. It is Gene

Outka who appropriates *agape* as the central focus as a practical mediating impetus between love and justice.

Outka discusses the relation of *agape* to self-love and to justice. He addresses what love is as a normative, ethical principle, or standard means. His concentration is upon how one's understanding of agape affects how one understands neighbor-love. Outka contends that crucial aspects of agape include the fact that agape is independent and unalterable. "Regard is for every person qua human existent, to be distinguished from those special traits, actions, etc., which distinguish particular personalities from each other."[27] Furthermore, Outka contends that agape entails a basic *equality* whereby the well being of one neighbor is as valuable as another neighbor's well-being.

However, Outka tries to understand "love language" in which many of the historic ethical concerns of the Judeo-Christian tradition have been encapsulated, so he tries to define more clearly just what has been meant by that language.[28] Outka criticized the Christian perfectionist who either claimed that these tasks could be accomplished more perfectly by the "love method" or who have sought to prove that their love was "perfect," even if they had to disavow responsibilities to preserve its perfection.[29] He argued that there is no sharp distinction between sacrificial love and mutual love—that is, between the love which is, and which is not, reciprocated and historically justified. He criticized the tendency to identify these two facets of love completely, so that the New Testament ethic is reduced to the limits of a prudential ethics, according to which we are counseled to forgive our foe because he will then cease to be our foe and are promised that if suffering love becomes sufficiently general it will cease to be suffering and change society into a harmony of life in which no one need suffer.[30] Upon reflecting on the matters that have arisen in his examination of love texts, Outka comes to a tentative suggestion for the meaning of agape as "an active concern for the neighbor's well-being, which is somehow independent of particular actions of the other."[31] This means in part that the human must not let disparities and inequalities determine his or her basic attitudes toward others among whom he or she interacts.

27. Outka, *Agape*, 9.
28. Ibid., 5.
29. Ibid., 28.
30. Ibid.
31. Ibid., 260.

Outka also notes that various problems arise when one understands self-sacrifice as the quintessence of agape. He states, "Generally, therefore, I am inclined to think that instead of appraising self-sacrifice as the purest and most perfect manifestation of agape, the difficulties I have considered are voided if one allows it only instrumental warrant. Self-sacrifice must always be purposive in promoting the welfare of others and never simply expressive of something resident in the agent."[32]

Regard of one's self ought to be based on the fact that he or she is a creature of God who is more than a means to some end. Outka also notes that agape involves certain social and personal relations thus entailing an overlap between regard of others and social cooperation. In this sense, self-sacrifice does not comprise the whole of agape, but perhaps a necessary aspect of it. It is a portion of agape but is not definitive.

From One-Sided Submission to Mutual Submission: Reflecting on Paul's Teaching

As Outka contends, we need to move away from a definition of agape that refers to one-way submission, absence of self-respect, and yielding to imposed obligations within a patriarchal culture, and approach a more mutual understanding of love. In fact, love with mutuality and equal regard is not uniquely Christian. Love with mutuality becomes *explicitly* Christian when it is grounded on the *imago Dei* in humans and renewed by the capacity for sacrificial love, a love that recapitulates the Christic drama and the passion of God.[33] "Love your neighbor as yourself" (Matt 22:39 NIV). In the New Testament, the love commandment is more universal and is frequently combined with Deuteronomy 6:5, on the love of God, and formulated as the double commandment to love both God and neighbor (Matt 22:37–39; Mark 12:30; Luke 10:27).[34]

In another Scripture passage, Ephesians 5:28–29 (NIV) says, "In this same way, husbands ought to love their wives as their own bodies. He who loves his wife loves himself. After all, no one ever hated his own body, but he feeds and cares for it, just as Christ does the church." The mutuality of the love commandment is visible even at the beginning of the passage when

---

32. Ibid., 278.
33. Ibid., 273.
34. Ibid.

it says, in ways we would not say today, "Be subject to one another out of reverence for Christ" (Ephesians 5:21 NIV).[35]

In interpreting Ephesians 5, Craig S. Keener states an interesting fact: "Paul is certainly among the minority of ancient writers in that he devotes more space to the exhortation of husbands to love in Ephesians 5 than to that of wives to submit."[36] Paul defines the husband's role quite differently from the culture of his time, even at the risk of raising the charge of subversion he had worked so carefully to avoid.[37] Paul does not address the husband's role in the wife's submission; he does not urge the husband to inculcate submission in his wife. Paul's only instructions to the husband are to serve their wives as Christ served the church, and since husband and wife are "one flesh" (Gen 2:24), to love her as he would his own body.[38]

With this, Paul presents the model that demonstrates how submission and love are to be expressed; Christ's relationship with his church is as a husband relates to his wife. As Christ's love is explicitly defined in the passage in terms of self-sacrificial service, not in terms of his authority (Eph 5:25–27), the husband should recognize his role in terms of loving and serving his wife as Christ did to his church. Furthermore, Keener calls us to pay careful attention to the meaning of "submit." He asserts that "to submit oneself could mean to 'give in' or 'cooperate,' and need not mean 'obey'; the closest thing Paul gives to a definition of the term in this context, in fact, is the word 'respect' in 5:33, where he plainly summarizes his whole exhortation to wives."[39] All Christians must submit to one another: if the wives are to submit to their husbands, then likewise, the husbands must submit to their wives. With this conclusion, Ephesians 5:22–33 advocates *mutual* submission, rather than women's one-sided submission or obedience based on authority and hierarchy.

In addition, S. Scott Bartchy concludes from an examination of 1 Corinthians 7:4–5 that Paul understood marriage between Christians as a matter of full mutuality. The term *homois*, translated "likewise," is the strongest word available in Greek to express the meaning "in the very same way."[40] Bartchy continues,

35. Ibid., 274.
36. Keener, *Paul, Women & Wives*, 167.
37. Ibid., 166.
38. Ibid., 167.
39. Ibid., 168.
40. 1 Cor 7:4–5 (NIV): "The wife's body does not belong to her alone but also to her

> Paul also calls for the most complete two-sidedness, which included the kind of communication and agreement mentioned in verse 5. The term translated by "agreement" is *symphonia*, from which our world "symphony" is derived, meaning "with one voice." For Paul to say, "There is neither male nor female in Christ" did not mean that human sexuality as such was to be rejected, nor did it mean that sexual differences were to be denied. It did mean that the traditional sexual roles in which males were given permission to give orders and females were expected to obey them had been discarded in favor of "mutual" decision-making based on sensitive communication.[41]

From this reading of these passages, we can conclude that it is not a one-sided, hierarchical view of submission that emanates from Scripture. Rather, the principle of mutual submission undergirds the Apostle Paul's view on Christian marriage and family (Eph 5:21; 1 Cor 7:3–4; 11:1–12; Gal 3:28). This model is for relationships between husbands and wives, parents and children, and families, ensuring that the qualities of mutual respect, protection, and kindness characterize marriage and family dynamics. It is a way of living that is both God-honoring and person-honoring. Such a biblical view of relationship, if actually endorsed by pastors, could provide a strongly needed support system for vulnerable members of a family, such women and children. Self-sacrifice does not *exclude* self-love, self-regard, or an ordinary concern with one's own self-fulfillment. It simply requires the other to give equal consideration to our fulfillment.

Breaking the Spiral of Violence: Girard and the Suffering of Jesus

Furthermore, the Christian narrative that surrounds equal regard—the narrative that God identifies with a suffering humanity through the life of Jesus—affirms human dignity even more.[42] In this sense, an important question is how to interpret the Christian tradition and the *suffering* of Jesus. Following Rene Girard's theory, Annemie Dillen and Water Wink's applica-

---

husband. In the same way, the husband's body does not belong to him alone but also to his wife. Do not deprive each other except by mutual consent and for a time, so that you may devote yourselves to prayer. Then come together again so that Satan will not tempt you because of your lack of self-control." See Bartchy, "Power, Submission, and Sexual Identity," 88.

41. Ibid.

42. Browning et al., *From Culture Wars to Common Ground*, 281.

tion of Girard's ground-breaking work deserves our serious consideration. First, Dillen states,

> The belief in the sacrifice of Jesus as a consequence of his devotion until the end is liberating, not because he is such a beautiful example, but because it liberates human persons from the task of being perfect themselves. The belief in the cross does not call people in the first place to activism, but enables to a deep spiritual experience of devotion arising from a belief in God. The human person can give him or herself without having to determine the whole future.[43]

When we reflect upon the cross, we often emphasize Christ's suffering and his perfect sacrifice, and become fixated on how to fulfill such example in our lives. *Theologia crucis*, understood exclusively as prescriptive and paradigmatic, will discount its critically descriptive features that expose the fallibility of human judicial systems. Dillen shows us that an obsession with a life of perfection and the perfect sacrifice that follows might actually be missing the point. Instead, we should be reminded that despite or *through* our shortcomings and failures, our true selves become closer to Christ in a process of authentic maturity through faith. As Dillen notes, this view of Christ's sacrifice gives us a path to liberation, hope, and freedom rather than demanding us to follow his example of perfect sacrifice. The goodness of the "Good News" is retained, and the reason for worship is not lost through some "messiah complex" that can strip the joy of submitting to God.

How might this other aspect of the theology of the cross prove to be good news to Korean American parents? Through the responsibility taken up by the parents for their children's future, one can gain an important insight into the tendencies of Korean American parents to live this life of perfect sacrifice. For example, Korean American parents place a greater weight on their role as caregivers. Most of their income is spent on their children's education, despite their concerns and worries about their future lives after retirement. However, they still see little or no conflict in sacrificing their careers to devote themselves to their children. According to Gallup research (1983), Korean parents are at the top in their willingness to pay off their children's debts and in paying their children's wedding expenses.[44]

---

43. Dillen, "Holy Families?," 270.

44. Kim and Choi, "Individualism, Collectivism, and Child Development," in *Cross-Cultural Roots*, ed. Greenfield and Cocking, 242–43.

Because the children take this sacrifice for granted, the children place blame, anger, and angst on parents who cannot guarantee their children's success despite all their best intentions. Parents likewise feel additional burdens and guilt because they are not able to sacrifice for their children more than they already have. This becomes, then, a self-destructive cycle that deteriorates the family relationship despite the sacrifices made and more that will be made.

With a holistic understanding of Jesus' sacrifice (and its meaning) Korean American parents can develop a relationship with their children without the unrealistic pressure of having to create their whole lives themselves. This is a very liberating model for Korean American families. With this perspective, Korean American parents can find new hope and courage. In difficult situations, parents may recognize the limits of their own capacity and leave the rest trustingly in the hands of God. In this way, families may more easily overcome crisis situations and develop a high degree of resiliency.

Further, Dillen points out that "the cross and faith in the resurrection cannot only liberate people from the often frenetic effort to realize a perfect intimate life, but also may motivate people to protest against suffering and evil."[45] The death of Jesus on the cross and the Christian faith signify a protest against the rhetoric of the necessity of sacrifice in the name of a higher goal.[46] Suffering, conflicts, and limitations are never beneficial in and of themselves.

Walter Wink agrees with Dillen that "God is revealed, not as demanding sacrifice, but as taking the part of the sacrificed. From Genesis to Revelation, the victims cry for justice and deliverance from the world of myth where they are made scapegoats. In the cross these cries find vindication."[47] Further, Wink points out that

> Jesus never succumbed to the perspective of the persecutors—neither in a positive way, by openly agreeing with his executioners, nor in a negative way, by yielding to vengeance in mimetic repetition of the executioners' crime. In Jesus there is a total absence of positive or negative complicity in violence. In his arraignment, trial, crucifixion, and death, the scapegoating mechanism is at last, categorically, revealed for all the world to see. Insofar as other

---

45. Dillen, "Holy Families?," 270.
46. Ibid.
47. Wink, *Engaging the Powers*, 147.

deaths reflect the truth revealed in his dying, they share its integrity and continue its revelations.[48]

Now, however, penal substitution theories of Christian atonement have argued, since Anselm, that God is the one who provides Jesus as a sacrificed lamb in our stead; that God is the angry and aggrieved party who must be placated by a blood sacrifice; that God is, finally, both sacrific*er* and sacrificed. Then, if God is unconditionally loving, forgiving, and nonviolent, why are all such bloody sacrifices necessary? Does God require his own son's death on our behalf? As Wink puts it, this false image of God changes suffering into violence.[49] In fact, it is *people* who require sacrifices of others in an abuse of power. "God needs no reparation, but human beings must be extracted from their own prison if they are to be capable of accepting the pure gift of freely offered love. . . . It is not God who must be appeased, but humans who must be delivered from their hated of God."[50]

Jesus' suffering on the cross disapproves of the sacrificial structure where violence reigns. "If you are the only one who does not use violence in a world that keeps using violence, then you become the victim of violence. Christ accepts the role of a scapegoat, not out of love for suffering or death, but exactly to denounce the phenomenon of the scapegoat, to make it unbearable and impossible."[51] Also, Walter Wink remarks,

> Jesus' crucifixion laid bare the true nature of the sacrificial system, which projected the need for substitutionary slaughter into the very Godhead. The violence that countless animal sacrifices were supposed to quench was never satisfied. The System required human lives as well. But *this* man was more than just one more innocent victim. This one gave his life voluntarily, freely, *deliberately*. The church understood his act as a sacrifice to end all sacrifice that exposed the scapegoating mechanism for all the world to see. In giving his body and blood he sealed a new covenant, irrevocable and everlasting. Into that covenant others could enter by undergoing a symbolic, spiritual death to the old order and rebirth to the new (Mark 14:22–25 par.; Rome. 6:1–11).[52]

---

48. Ibid., 148.
49. Ibid., 149.
50. Ibid., 151.
51. Dillen, "Holy Families?," 271.
52. Wink, *Engaging the Powers*, 126.

Jesus' death disrupts the traditional sacrificial structures: no new sacrifices are henceforth required on the part of God. Even while on the cross Jesus asks God for his forgiveness on behalf of the evildoers. The spiral of violence should end at that point; this taking into account the blood of the martyrs that followed through church history and new martyrs in their sacrifice even today. Through Jesus, the scapegoat mechanism is exposed and, at least conceptually, we are transferred from a realm ruled by a system of dominance into a realm of God's unconditional love and grace. It is now that we learn to stop the mimetic violence and scapegoating,[53] or to quote Jesus, "Now is the judgment of the world; now the ruler of this world will be driven out" (John 12:31 NRSV).

In another sense, Yoder contends that Christians are specifically called to imitate Jesus—in taking up the cross.[54] For Yoder, the Christian's cross is not any and every kind of suffering and affliction. It is the price of social nonconformity. Jesus' warning to expect persecution is "a normative statement about the relation of our social obedience to the messianity of Jesus. Representing as he did the divine order now at hand, accessible; renouncing as he did the legitimate use of violence and the accrediting of noninvolvement, his people will encounter in ways analogous to his own the hostility of the old order."[55] To place an inordinate emphasis of suffering, to place an exclusive emphasis on the sacrificial aspect on the *theologia crucis*, ends up legitimizing violence, perpetuating a system that warrants the continued cycle of dominance and scapegoating. In a familial context, non-coercive and non-domineering personal relations are essential and they contribute to happiness, success, and ultimate effectiveness. It is our challenge to see how Christian teachings on the family may be conducive to bringing an end to violence in families, rather than legitimizing it.

Proper Use of Power: Nonviolence and Coercion

In addition, we need to pay careful attention to the use of power in self-sacrifice. In Korean American family relationships, sacrifice usually comes out of power differentials. The use of power and coercion is especially important in parent-child and in elder-younger relationships. Even in Christian family, however, the husband is construed to have the right to control

---

53. Ibid., 152.
54. Yoder, *Politics of Jesus*, 95.
55. Ibid., 96.

the family simply because he is the *head* of the family, as in one metaphor (among many for the husband) through several passages in Paul's writings. If the husband is said to have the right and responsibility to control the family simply because he has a headship ordained by God, could not such a claim tempt him to employ all means available to him, including both physical and psychological violence, to maintain control?

Clements and Mitchell assert that sacrifice must represent an affirmative example of the respectful use of power in family relationships, especially parent-child relationships.

> Whereas non-coercion and non-violence represent the restraint of power, sacrifice reflects an active giving up of power. In sacrificing, the person chooses to give up something of value in order to improve the functioning of the relationship partner or the relationship itself. It is perhaps in sacrifice that parents best model for their children the respectful use of power. Both in their parents' sacrifice for each other and in their parents' sacrifices for them, children observe self-renunciation in action. Such sacrifices may play critical roles in enabling children to respectfully exercise their own power, both in sacrificing for others and in eschewing coercion and violence in their interactions with others.[56]

This is not advocating that there should not be any limitations or force within the parent-child relationship. There must be boundaries set for the roles of parents and children. And there may be cases where parents must exercise their authority to a certain degree. However, what I mean about the respectful use of parental power is that parents neither abuse nor abdicate their power. In parent-child relationship, effective child rearing involves exerting parental control in the context of a warm and loving relationship, establishing limits with both clear expectations for adherence and appropriate consequences for violation, and respecting the gift of the child with careful attention to the need for parental guidance and discipline.[57]

Also, it is Jesus himself who called us to examine the ways we use the power we have and any satisfaction we may feel with one-side submission. Bartchy cites Mark 10:42–43 as an example of how Jesus confronted the presupposition of male power and dominance.[58] Jesus rejected the concept

---

56. Clements and Mitchell, "Noncoercion, Nonviolence, and Sacrifice," in *Why Psychology Needs Theology*, ed. Dueck and Lee, 97.

57. Ibid., 97–98.

58. Bartchy, "Power, Submission, and Sexual Identity."

of power as control. In Mark's three-part discussion between Jesus and his followers we see: (1) Jesus' approaching suffering; (2) a naive request that is laden with irony, to be seated at Christ's right and left hand; (3) Jesus' clarification of "who is the greatest." In a Markan misunderstanding, James and John declare that they are ready to suffer anything if they can thereby be assured of being granted power-sharing seats at his right and his left hand when he comes into his "glory." That Jesus sees and rejects "power as control" at the heart of this disagreement is made clear in Mark 10:42–45 (NIV):

> You know that those who are recognized as rulers of the Gentiles lord it over them; and their great men exercise authority over them. But it is not so among you, but whoever wishes to becomes great among you shall be your servant; and whoever wishes to be first among you shall be slave of all.

Mark's Greek stresses the present tense of "not so with you," suggesting that he intended his reader to understand that when Jesus is present, the "power plays" typical of world-culture, characterized by exploitation, manipulation, and competition, are unnecessary and out of place.[59] In his life and ministry, Jesus chooses love, not coercive power; suffering, not vindictive triumph; mutual service, not mastery and domination. He leads us to question the values of our society, community, and age. In this context, Donald Kraybill insists that we should bring Scripture to bear on all areas of life—our value, stewardship of time and money, attitudes toward the outcast, and handling of violence.[60] He calls us to examine this notion: "The kingdom of God points to an inverted, or upside down, way of life that contrasts with the prevailing social order."[61] Kraybill poses difficult questions that we must grapple with. How do we refuse to participate in a system that enslaves? How can we *be* a neighbor to others, not merely ask, "Who is my neighbor?" How can we learn the art of nonviolent love in all relationships? How can we repent of our participation in and reliance on beliefs that support military solutions to human differences? What would it mean if we were willing to lose—not save—our lives in the decisions we make about success, about our life objectives, societal contributions, about security during advanced years, about our decisions in career and service right now?

59. Ibid.
60. Kraybill, *Upside-Down*, 9–10.
61. Ibid., 19.

Empirical Study on Self-Sacrifice in Korean American Relationships

Up to this point, we have examined previous material on empirical, theoretical, and theological studies on self-sacrifice. Then how do the Koreans living in the United States think of and commit to self-sacrifice in their lives? To answer this question, we must employ the methodology of an empirical study of Korean Americans' self-sacrifice to identify and appropriately name key motives that are the driving forces and key beliefs that reinforce Korean Americans' behavior of self-sacrifice.

Korean Americans believe that they find themselves committed to self-sacrifice for their family in their daily lives. However, it was noted in previous chapters that when self-sacrifice carries hidden motives—coercive responsibility, obligation, shame, guilt, or their own reputation—this "self-sacrifice" is neither self-giving nor serving nor of mutual benefit. Furthermore, being that giving is implicit to subordination, they have to tolerate this role in culturally defined situations (for example, son to father, wife to husband, employee to employer, parishioner to pastor, student to teacher). In this context, it is important to explore the *actual* attitudes and motives of self-sacrifice in Korean American families.

There is no prior research that has focused on the motives behind self-sacrifice in Korean American family relationships. This empirical study will seek to establish a baseline for understanding Korean Americans' motivation in self-sacrifice in various relationships, especially in family relationships. I hope the findings of this research will be viable data for counselors, pastors, and educators on the nature and function of attitudes in caring and inter-dependent relationships. By recognizing and identifying the attitudes, beliefs, and motives behind self-sacrifice by Korean Americans, I hope to help Korean Americans to shift the practices of self-sacrifice from unhealthy, obligatory motives to more voluntary, genuinely caring motives that are healthy and beneficial to both giver and receiver. Furthermore, by gathering this data, I hope to provide pastors and pastoral counselors with a valuable resource in counseling Korean Americans, especially in identifying and counseling victims of domestic violence who may be trapped by obligatory motives of self-sacrifice. I hope to contribute to a new vision of equality and mutuality for all Korean American families. Finally, I will provide a working model of self-sacrifice toward equality, mutuality and equal regard for all Korean American families.

Study

To investigate the motives, beliefs, and attitudes behind self-sacrifice, especially in a family setting, a survey was designed to specifically target Koreans living in America. This study will (1) inquire about the current self-definition or understanding of self-sacrifice held by Korean Americans; (2) identify diverse motives for self-sacrifice in a variety of six relationships, plus the likelihood of self-sacrifice for those outside of the family or close relationship in Korean Americans; (3) explore actual feelings held by those making sacrifices; and finally (4) provide preliminary evidence relevant for a new, healthier model of self-sacrifice that points more toward equality and mutuality for Korean Americans.

Specifically, we are hypothesizing that (1) there will be a significant difference in attitudes, motives, and beliefs about self-sacrifice between genders and the generations, particularly between first- and second-generation Korean American immigrants. More specifically, the older generation will have more negative attitudes than the younger generation and consider sacrifice more one-sided. The younger generation will have a more mutual approach to sacrifice. Women are more likely to practice actions of self-sacrifice than are men; (2) Korean American immigrants' attitudes and feelings toward self-sacrifice may be negative; (3) Korean Americans will be less willing to sacrifice for another's needs outside their family; (4) Korean Americans will be more likely to make personal self-sacrifice in parent-child relationship than in any other personal relationship (marital, friendship, workplace, and religious institution); (5) Korean Americans' motive for self-sacrifice will be deeply influenced by Confucian teaching (reputation or obligation rather than unconditional love or mutual benefit); (6) Korean Americans are more likely to commit self-sacrifice out of obligation or responsibility than out of mutual service, especially the older generation.

Participants

The participants of this study are exclusively Korean Americans currently living in the Unites States. Recruitment of the participants was open to both sexes of Korean Americans over the age of 18. The participants of this study were 41 men and 43 women (84 total participants) who were recruited from four local churches. Participants ranged in age from 20 to 67 years, with a median age of 38.63. There were 56 first-generation immigrants, 20

1.5-generation immigrants, and 8 second-generation immigrants, participating in the study.[62] Of the participants, 79 participants identified Korea as their birthplace and 5 participants identified the United States as their birthplace. A total of 63 participants chose Korean as their primary language, while 21 chose English as their primary language. Of the 84 questionnaires returned, 21 were completed in English, 63 were completed in Korean.

Four churches located in southern California were chosen randomly for this study: one from the Koreatown district in the city of Los Angeles, one from the city of San Diego, and two from the suburban area of Orange County. The four churches were chosen from these areas after considering the differences of immigrants residing in cities vs. suburban areas, factoring their social-economic diversity and backgrounds on residency. The constituency of these four churches is as follows. One church is exclusively composed of second-generation parishioners, speaking primarily English. Two are affiliated with Assemblies of God, one with Presbyterian, and one remains independent. While a future study with an explicit focus on the differences that denominational or theological orientation on present data may be useful, the purpose of this present study is limited and specific to: (1) Korean Americans and (2) general church membership from within that group.

Procedure

First, verbal agreements regarding dates and location for distribution of the questionnaires was obtained from the senior pastors of the four churches. Once having been obtained, the investigator visited the churches to distribute the questionnaires and answered any questions that the participants might have. Written agreements were collected at a later date.

The investigator first met with the senior pastor before meeting with the participants. After the senior pastor introduced the investigator to the prospective participants, the investigator then briefed them about the study and the questionnaire. The prospective participants were members of

62. First-generation Koreans refers to those who were born in Korea and came to the United States after about the age of twenty. 1.5-generation Koreans refers to those who were born in Korea and came to the United States after about the age of eight to twelve. Second-generation Koreans refers to those who were born in the United States or came to the United States at an early age. For the purpose of this study, the age cap was set at three.

various ministries within the local churches, such as teachers' meetings, Bible study meetings, and men's and women's fellowships, where there might be little pressure on the members to participate in the study. The meeting places for distributing the questionnaire were at the meeting place of these ministries, such as lounges, fellowship halls, and community centers (as applicable) within the church.

During the briefing session, the prospective participants were asked to give their general feelings, definitions, and beliefs about self-sacrifice. The participants were also asked to rate how hard or how easy they found certain personal goals, interests, and activities are to sacrifice in the following six relationships: parent-child, martial, workplace, church (pastor and parishioner), school (teacher and student), and friendship. Finally the participants were asked about their motives in self-sacrifice in those same six relationships. The participants also were informed that some background information, such as age and gender, would be collected for statistical analysis, the questionnaires would not collect any personally identifiable information. Finally, the participants were told that the time to complete the questionnaire would be approximately 15 to 20 minutes.

The prospective participants then received the informed consent form and the questionnaire. They were instructed to read the informed consent form. After reading the informed consent form, only those willing to participate were asked to complete the questionnaire. Should the participants have further questions regarding the study and the questionnaire, they were instructed to ask the investigator. Also, the phone number of the investigator was provided on the informed consent form if the participants had further questions after the session has concluded. Participants that finished the questionnaire immediately were asked to turn in the questionnaire to a designated collection box. Participants that required additional time or private space to complete the questionnaire were allowed to submit the questionnaire at a later time by mail. A self-addressed, stamped envelope was given to those participants who chose to finish the questionnaire at a later time. These steps would help to ensure that the participants were under no obligation from the church or the investigator to complete the questionnaire under a certain time and place, or under supervision.

This study design was reviewed and approved by the Human Subjects Review Committee at Fuller Theological Seminary and the Graduate School of Psychology. This study has been found to meet the criteria for the ethical treatment of human subjects in research.

Questionnaires

To measure their willingness to sacrifice in various relationships (such as parent-child, marital, workplace, church, academic, and friendship), I assessed priorities that were relatively central to the individual's goals and interests, such as time, money, labor, defending honor, giving up leadership, yielding conversation, and yielding one's own goals, and asked each participant to rate these on a scale of 1–5. To measure the motive of self-sacrifice in the same relationships, I assessed motives behind the importance of self-sacrifice by asking each participant to rate their motives on a scale between 1 (extremely unimportant) to 5 (extremely important) in 10 different categories.

To discover attitudes and beliefs about self-sacrifice, I asked a question regarding the participant's general feelings toward self-sacrifice. To further answer the definitions of self-sacrifice held by Korean American, I asked the participants to pick the top three definitions that they identified with. (For a sample, please refer to questionnaires 1 and 2 in the appendix).

Descriptive Analysis

General Feelings on Self-Sacrifice

The questionnaire asked respondents, "What are your general feeling toward the experience of self-sacrifice?" Respondents were instructed to rate their feeling toward self-sacrifice, from very positive to very negative.

Table 5.1 General feelings on self-sacrifice (total 84 respondents)

Total	N	Minimum	Maximum	Mean	Std. Deviation
General feelings	84	2	5	3.68	.763

Note: 1 = very negative; 2 = negative; 3 = somewhat; 4 = positive; 5 = very positive

The Motives of Self-Sacrifice in Korean American Culture, Family, & Marriage

Table 5.2 General feelings on self-sacrifice, by gender

Group Statistics

	gender	N	Mean	Std. Deviation	Std. Error Mean
general feelings	1	41	3.68	.722	.113
	2	43	3.67	.808	.123

Note: 1 = male; 2 = female
1 = very negative; 2 = negative; 3 = somewhat; 4 = positive; 5 = very positive

Table 5.3 General feelings on self-sacrifice, by primary language

Group Statistics

	gender	N	Mean	Std. Deviation	Std. Error Mean
general feelings	1	63	3.60	.794	.100
	2	21	3.90	.625	.136

1 = Korean; 2 = English
1 = very negative; 2 = negative; 3 = somewhat; 4 = positive; 5 = very positive

Table 5.4 General feelings on self-sacrifice, by generation

Group Statistics

	gender	N	Mean	Std. Deviation	Std. Error Mean
general feelings	1	57	3.56	.802	.106
	2	27	3.93	.616	.118

1 = 1st generation; 2 = 1.5 and 2nd generation
1 = very negative; 2 = negative; 3 = somewhat; 4 = positive; 5 = very positive

Overall, most participants (mean 3.68; std. dev. 0.763) held generally positive feelings about self-sacrifice. As indicated by table 5.2, male participants (3.68) had a positive feeling about self-sacrifice. Female participants (3.67) also had a generally positive feeling about self-sacrifice. Unexpectedly, both males and females have similar feelings toward self-sacrifice.

Primarily Korean-speaking participants also had generally positive feelings about self-sacrifice (mean 3.60). Comparatively, primarily English-speaking participants had slightly greater positive feelings toward

Empirical Study on Self-Sacrifice in Korean American Relationships

self-sacrifice (mean 3.90). Paralleling the language divide, first-generation Korean immigrants had (3.56), while the combined samples of 1.5- and second-generation immigrants had even stronger positive feelings toward self-sacrifice (3.96). The results suggest that those Korean Americans born in the United States or were raised in the United States since early childhood had more positive feelings regarding self-sacrifice (table 5.4, mean 3.96).

Definitions of Self-Sacrifice

Respondents were asked to select their top three in order (1–3) from five definitions of self-sacrifice. Table 5.5 presents the result.

Table 5.5 What is your definition or understanding of self-sacrifice?[63]

Gender	Definition 1	Definition 2	Definition 3	Definition 4	Definition 5
Male	8	10	4	1	5
Female	8	15	3	3	3

Primary language	Definition 1	Definition 2	Definition 3	Definition 4	Definition 5
Korean	6	23	5	2	7
English	10	2	2	2	1

Generation	Definition 1	Definition 2	Definition 3	Definition 4	Definition 5
First	6	18	3	2	5
Second	10	7	4	2	3

63. From the questionnaire:
"What is your definition or understanding of self-sacrifice?"
Definition 1: Delaying my own needs or gratifications temporarily in consideration of another's needs.
Definition 2: Self-giving actions are mutually beneficial in the give and take of family or community.
Definition 3: Caring kindness or love out of Christian obligation to others.
Definition 4: Surrender of my goals in order to gain some greater goal.
Definition 5: Another's' needs are greater than my own.

Both male and female participants identified most strongly with definition 2. Primarily Korean speaking participants identified most strongly with definition 2. Comparatively, primarily English speaking participants identified most strongly with definition 1.

Similarly to Korean speaking immigrants, first-generation Korean immigrants identified most strongly with definition 2. Like the English speaking immigrants, the combined samples of 1.5- and second-generation immigrants identified most strongly with definition 1.

Motives of Self-Sacrifice

Table 5.6 shows the average ratings for ten different motives for self-sacrifice, as it relates to six different relationships (parental-child, marital, workplace, church, academic, and friendship).[64] Table 5.6 shows the response of all 83 (out of 84) participants on motives for self-sacrifice in parent-child relationship. Table 5.7 shows the response of 53 (out of 84) participants on ten different motives for self-sacrifice in marital relationship. The sample size for marital relationship was smaller than expected due to the large number of singles participating in this study. The tables for the other four relationships (workplace, church, academic, and friendship) will be attached in the appendix.

---

64. From the questionnaire:
"Think about the last time where you felt you had to put aside your own needs in the following six relationships. As you reflect on that situation, rate your motives, or why you felt that sacrifice was necessary in the following six relationships. Select one from 1 to 5, with 1 being the extremely unimportant, 5 being the extremely important."
- Motive 1: Avoiding conflict and maintaining harmony.
- Motive 2: Yielding to obligation and duty to society, family, or other hierarchy.
- Motive 3: Holding to my sense of responsibility to family or others.
- Motive 4: Acting for the sake of others in unconditional love (agape).
- Motive 5: Expressing my high self-esteem, personal honor and dignity.
- Motive 6: Preserving my reputation as a generous and giving person.
- Motive 7: My willingness to yield is an expression of my loving personality.
- Motive 8: Strong commitment to the practice of mutual service and caring for others.
- Motive 9: Putting others first because it is central to my religious faith.
- Motive 10: Yielding appropriately as an expression of my traditional and cultural values, rooted in the historic traditions and teachings of Confucianism.

Table 5.6 Motives for self-sacrifice in parent-child relationship

	Avoiding Conflict	Obligation	Responsibility	Agape	Personal Honor	Reputation	Personality	Mutual	Religion	Tradition
N Valid / Missing	83 / 1	83 / 1	83 / 1	83 / 1	83 / 1	83 / 1	83 / 1	83 / 1	83 / 1	83 / 1
Mean	4.27	3.58	3.98	3.71	2.55	2.49	3.08	3.63	3.61	2.41
Std. Deviation	.717	.912	.869	.994	.978	1.097	1.118	1.090	1.102	1.093
Minimum	2	1	1	1	1	1	1	1	1	1
Maximum	5	5	5	5	5	5	5	5	5	5

1 = extremely unimportant; 2 = unimportant; 3 = somewhat; 4 = important; 5 = extremely important

Table 5.7 Motives for self-sacrifice in marital relationship

		Avoiding Conflict	Obligation	Responsibility	Agape	Personal Honor	Reputation	Personality	Mutual	Religion	Tradition
N	Valid	53	53	52	52	52	52	52	52	52	52
	Missing	31	31	32	32	32	32	32	32	32	32
Mean		4.36	3.64	4.13	3.67	2.88	2.56	2.96	3.58	3.58	2.58
Std. Deviation		.623	.922	.864	.985	1.114	1.092	1.137	1.073	1.177	1.258
Minimum		3	1	1	2	1	1	1	1	1	1
Maximum		5	5	5	5	5	5	5	5	5	5

1 = extremely unimportant; 2 = unimportant; 3 = somewhat; 4 = important; 5 = extremely important

Parent-Child Relationships

Of the 83 participants who answered this question, 89.2% of identified avoiding conflict as the most important motivation in committing to self-sacrifice in parent-child relationships (mean 4.36). One's sense of responsibility to family and others was the second most important motivating factor at 81.9% (mean 4.13), mutual service and caring was the third with 66.3%, unconditional love (*agape*) was the fourth with 65.1%, and parental obligation was ranked fifth at 62.6%. Traditional and cultural value (18.7%), personal honor (20.5%), and reputation (22.9%) were deemed unimportant by the study participants.

Marital Relationships

Of 84 participants, 52 participants answered questions in regards to motivations of self-sacrifice in marital relationships. The most important motivation among the participating participants was avoiding conflict and maintain harmony (92.5%), followed by one's sense of responsibility (86.5%), obligation and duty was third with 69.9%, unconditional love (*agape*) was fourth with 61.6%. Mutual sacrifice and caring was ranked fifth at 61.6%, personality (19%) and reputation (25%) seem to be unimportant motives for Korean American in marital relationship. The least important motivation among the participants was traditional and cultural value (17.9%).

The results clearly and unambiguously show that Korean American families place significant importance on avoiding conflicts and maintaining harmony in regards to self-sacrifice. One's sense of responsibility was also a driving motivation for self-sacrifice in parent-child and marital relationships. Due to their Christian faith, many respondents also placed some value on unconditional love (*agape*) as a motive for self-sacrifice (65.1%).

Workplace Relationships

A total of 76 participants answered questions in regards to motivations of self-sacrifice in workplace relationships. Again, the most important motivation among the participating participants was avoiding conflict and maintaining harmony (84%), followed by a sense of responsibility (73.3%), mutual service (69.7%), and obligation and duty (67.2%). Again, the least important motivation among the participants was traditional value (22.4%).

Unsurprisingly, avoiding conflict and a sense of responsibility were the most important motives for self-sacrifice in the work place. Interestingly, mutual service and caring (69.7%) ranked as the third most important motivation for self-sacrifice, followed by personal honor (63.2%) or reputation (46.1%).

Church Relationships

A total of 82 participants answered questions in regards to motivations of self-sacrifice in church relationship. Unsurprisingly, the most important motivation among the participating participants was avoiding conflict and maintaining harmony (90.2%), followed by the sense of responsibility (78.3%), unconditional love (*agape*) (73.2%), religion (69.5%), and obligation and duty (68.3%). The least important motivation among the participants was traditional and cultural value (19.5%).

In church relationship, predictably, unconditional love (*agape*) and religious faith were considered to be important motivations behind self-sacrifice in church relationships. Surprisingly, reputation (28.1%) was not an important motivation behind self-sacrifice in church relationship. Considering the fact that Korean Americans who strive to maintain their previous levels of compensation or reputation, value guarding one's reputation, this result is perhaps a reflection of this tendency of hiding their true feelings.

Academic Relationships

A total of 69 (out of 84) participants answered questions in regards to motivations of self-sacrifice in academic relationships. The most important motivation among the participating participants was avoiding conflict and maintaining harmony (85.7%), followed by responsibility (61.5%), mutual service (63.7%), religious faith (53.6%), unconditional love (*agape*) (50%), and personal honor (40%). Again, the least important motivation among the participants was traditional and cultural value (14.5%).

Personal honor (41.6%) was an important motivation behind self-sacrifice. Aside from the usual motives of avoiding conflict and maintaining harmony, no other motives were deemed important by the respondents, ranking around 20 to 30%. Interestingly, obligation and duty ranked sixth as an important motivation for self-sacrifice in academic relationships. Those in the academic environment placed higher value on responsibility than obligation.

FRIENDSHIPS

A total of 83 (out of 84) participants answered questions in regards to motivations of self-sacrifice in friendships. The most important motivation among the participating participants was avoiding conflict and maintaining harmony (94%), followed by responsibility (71.1%), mutual service (68.7%), religious faith (65.1%), obligation and duty (62.6%), and unconditional love (*agape*) (60.3%). The least important motivation among the participants was traditional value (19.3%).

Interestingly, in the friendship relationship, all motives were ranked as high as the motives within parent-child and marital relationships.

Group Comparisons

Since the participants represent a diverse set of individuals, varying in age, language, and culture (Korean, American, or both), it is reasonable to expect that scores averaged across the entire samples would mask differences within the sample set. The above ten motives of self-sacrifice were therefore also analyzed for evidence of group differences by gender, generation, and primary language (Korean and English).[65] Due to the comparatively small number of respondents identifying themselves as second generation, a future study on the views of self-sacrifice specifically in the second-generation Korean American immigrants may be worthwhile. Likewise, a specific study on the first generation of Korean Americans can yield in the future, yet another study on their *comparative* analysis.

GENERAL FEELINGS: GENDER, PRIMARY LANGUAGE, AND GENERATION

The results of general feelings toward sacrifice were analyzed by gender, primary language, and between generations. The results showed that there were no significant differences between genders and primary language. However, there was a statistically significant difference in general feeling between older and younger generations.[66]

---

65. Independent measures *t*-tests are used for differences by gender, generations, and languages.

66. The mean differences between older and younger generations were significant at $p < 0.5$. (1st generation, n = 57, mean = 3.56; 2nd generation, n = 27, mean 3.93;

The Motives of Self-Sacrifice in Korean American Culture, Family, & Marriage

Gender and Motives of Self-Sacrifice

Male and female respondents did not differ significantly on any of the ten motives of self-sacrifice. However, avoiding conflict and maintaining harmony were the most important motives for both sexes in all six relationships. Among the male participants, avoiding conflict and maintaining harmony in friendship was the most important motivation for self-sacrifice (n = 40, mean = 4.30), followed by a sense of responsibility in marital relationship (n = 40, mean = 4.26). Among the female participants, avoiding conflict was the most important motivation for self-sacrifice for nearly all participants. This was especially true for both parent-child and martial relationships, where the mean was near 4.5 (in parent-child relationship, mean = 4.42; in marital relationship, mean = 4.48).

Primary Language and Motives of Self-Sacrifice

Primary language—whether Korean or English—proved to be a significant factor in the two motives of self-sacrifice: personal honor and reputation.[67] Avoiding conflict and agape showed the most difference of mean values on motives behind self-sacrifice.[68] For Korean speakers, avoiding conflict ranked higher, while agape was ranked higher for English speakers. Also, primary Korean speakers ranked maintaining harmony highly, while primary English speakers ranked responsibility, personal honor, and reputation higher.

Generations and Motives of Self-Sacrifice

Surprisingly, there were no significant differences between the generations on the motives of self-sacrifice. The only notable difference between the

---

$t(84) = -2.291$).

67. For motives of personal honor, primary Korean speakers, n = 50, mean = 14.24; primary English speakers, n = 16, mean = 16.75; $t(66) = -2.609$, $p < 0.5$; for motive of reputation, primary Korean speakers, n = 50, mean = 13.18; primary English speakers, n = 16, mean = 16.12; $t(66) = -2.416$, $p < .05$.

68. For motive of avoiding conflict, primary Korean speakers, n = 49, mean = 21.12; primary English speakers, n = 16, mean = 19.68; for motive of agape, primary Korean speakers, n = 50, mean = 17.36; primary English speakers, n = 16, mean = 19.37.

Empirical Study on Self-Sacrifice in Korean American Relationships

groups on self-sacrifice was regarding tradition, where the means differed by nearly 2.0 points.[69]

For first-generation immigrants, avoiding conflict (mean = 4.40) ranked highly in parent-child relationships. Personal honor (mean = 2.60), reputation (mean = 2.46), and traditional value (mean = 2.46) were deemed unimportant. Mutual service (3.54) was considered somewhat important by the respondents.

In marital relationship, avoiding conflict (mean = 4.45) and sense of responsibility (mean = 4.07) were deemed important. Personal honor (2.84), reputation (2.47), and traditional value (2.53) ranked last.

In workplace relationship, avoiding conflict (4.06) again ranked high, while traditional value (2.60) and reputation (2.74) ranked lowest.

In church relationship, avoiding conflict (4.28) was once again the most important motive for self-sacrifice. Personal honor (2.75), reputation (2.47), and traditional value (2.33) were ranked lowest.

Similar results were observed in both the academic relationship and friendship.[70] For 1.5- and second-generation immigrants, sense of responsibility (4.35) ranked the highest for self-sacrifice in parent-child relationship, followed by avoiding conflict (3.96), unconditional love (*agape*) (3.81), and mutual service (3.81). Traditional and cultural value (2.29) ranked as the least important motives among 1.5- and second-generation immigrants.

In marital relationship, again, sense of responsibility (4.44) was the most important motivation, followed by unconditional love (*agape*) (4.00) and mutual service (3.78). Compared to the first-generation immigrants, mutual service (3.53) ranked fairly high.

In workplace relationship, avoiding conflict (4.15) was the most important motivation for self-sacrifice, followed by the sense of responsibility (3.69). Traditional and cultural value (2.35) and personality (3.04) were the least important.

In church relationship, avoiding conflict (4.20) once again ranked first, followed by responsibility (4.12), unconditional love (*agape*) (3.92), religious faith (3.96), and mutual caring and service (3.80). Reputation (2.88), personal honor (2.96), and traditional value (2.24) were ranked lowest.

69. For motive of tradition, 1st generation, n = 43, mean = 12.6; 2nd generation, n = 22, mean = 10.7.

70. In academic relationships, avoiding conflict (4.24); tradition (2.47); reputation (2.72). In friendship, avoiding conflict (4.44); personal honor (2.88); reputation (2.67); tradition (2.44).

Interestingly, in academic relationship, there were no motives considered important by the respondents (that is, rated higher than 4). Avoiding conflict (3.71) ranked the highest, and once again, traditional value (2.04) is the lowest.

In friendship, avoiding conflict (4.12) was ranked highest, though not many other motives were deemed important. Reputation (2.73) and personal honor (2.92) were ranked lowest.

Implications

The purpose of this study has been to identify attitudes, beliefs, and motives of self-sacrifice. I have made predictions that: (1) there will be a significant difference in attitudes, beliefs, and motives about self-sacrifice between genders and the generations, particularly between first- and second-generation Korean American immigrants. Specifically, the older generation will have more negative attitudes than the younger generation and consider sacrifice more one-sided. The younger generation will have a more mutual approach to self-sacrifice; (2) Korean American immigrants' attitudes and feelings toward self-sacrifice will be clearly negative; (3) Korean Americans will be less willing to sacrifice for another's needs outside their family; (4) Koreans Americans' motives for self-sacrifice will be deeply influenced by Confucian teaching (reputation or obligation rather than unconditional love or mutual benefit); (5) Korean Americans are more likely to commit self-sacrifice out of obligation or responsibility than out of mutual service, especially the older generation.

Through this survey, there were seven interesting, crucial, and occasionally unexpected findings about self-sacrifice among Korean Americans. Here is the summary of my findings.

First, I predicted that responsibility would be the most important motives behind self-sacrifice among Koreans living in the United States. Surprisingly, respondents showed that in all of the six relationships, avoiding conflicts and maintaining harmony were the most important motives for self-sacrifice. However, responsibility was still an important motive for self-sacrifice as predicted, ranked by the respondents as the second most important motive.

On the other hand, mutual service and unconditional love (*agape*) were considered not important. Not surprisingly, 1.5- and second-generation immigrants placed mutual service and caring as more important motives behind self-sacrifice than the first-generation immigrants. Most likely, this is the result of the younger immigrants interacting with American individualistic culture.

I now want to examine the results of the survey within the context of Korean American immigrants' lives. Korean immigrants experience major cultural and intergenerational conflict in the course of their lives. The process of immigration and adaption to the new country is nothing short of a revolutionary process for the family involved. Within a short period of time, families must adapt themselves to their new environments, necessitating the adoption of a new culture and significant changes in even the simplest things. Concurrently, they also cling to the culture and traditions from home. The family relationship that was previously established is now under pressure from dual forces of adaptation and tradition. Traditional family and gender roles are challenged by the adaptation to a new environment as all members of the family now must take more responsibility. All of these sources of stress become points for conflict within the family. Korean immigrants, as shown by the respondents in the survey, may use avoidance of conflict as a way to evade this source of conflict. They choose rather to give in, to commit to one-sided sacrifice to avoid conflict in order to maintain a harmonious relationship in the family. However, as I have noted in chapter 4, this passive avoidance can lead to domestic violence and many other family relationship problems. The issue of domestic violence is becoming ever more serious in the Korean American community. And as I have shown in chapter 1, this also conforms to the mindset of the hermit culture and the concept of *Han*: a deeply rooted grief as characterized in hiding, avoiding conflict, and passive surrender.

Particularity, in parent-child relationships in traditional Korean family dynamics, it is a child's primary responsibility to avoid conflict no matter what the parent's behavior. Children are expected not to act against their parents' wishes, even when the parents' behavior is inappropriate. The only acceptable responses on the part of the children are acceptance, forbearance, and avoidance. This pattern can easily be found in the typical Korean American family. Korean American children are still expected to avoid the conflict and will not cause their parents' to lose face or take on more burdens. They try hard to focus on maintaining harmonious interpersonal relationships with close relations even at their own expense. The children then are more likely to sacrifice their own goals and desire to conform to their parents' wishes and expectations.

If self-sacrifice, however, is simply motivated by conflict avoidance and maintaining harmony, this can easily become an unhealthy, one-sided sacrifice. Instead of confrontation, sacrificing to avoid conflicts or just giving up creates its own set of problems. Through the result of this study and reflecting on what motivates Korean American immigrants to commit to self-sacrifice, Korean Americans can learn sacrifices that are mutually beneficial and build healthy families.

Second, I predicted that there will be a significant difference in attitudes, beliefs, and motives about self-sacrifice between genders, especially that women are more prone to self-sacrifice than men. I also predicted that women will have more negative attitude toward self-sacrifice than men. The reasoning for the above prediction is due to the Confucian conditioning that is deeply embedded into the fiber of Korean traditional gender roles. However, in this survey result, there are no significant differences reported between men and women, indicating conflict avoidance as the most important motive behind self-sacrifice. This may indicate that as men and women work as equal partners, traditional gender roles that demand greater sacrifice on women became less influential. Even though traditional Korean culture is at the core of the Korean American familial experience, Western cultural influence may have effectively bridged the gap in the former gender roles and expected differences in self-sacrifice. Finally, it is possible that Korean American men are expected to be the main source of income for their families, more so than women, in which case the self-sacrifice of men becomes more evident, resulting in the obvious lack of difference in the data between male and female.

Third, sense of responsibility was considered to be the most important motive of self-sacrifice in parent-child and marital relationships for second-generation immigrants. This is explained in that many Korean immigrants came to America to fulfill the typical American Dream. Therefore, Korean immigrant parents place significant importance on education of the children. The children of these immigrants grew up with the responsibility of fulfilling the high expectations of success placed by their parents, the responsibility to take care of their family and to fulfill the debt owed to their parents and their sacrifice. Parental expectations clearly impose a kind of family discipline that some of the children could identify but few were willing to challenge, having been inculcated from the earliest ages that the ultimate success of their families would depend on their education and economic achievement. Therefore, Korean American children often developed commitments to repaying their parents both by surpassing them in educational and economic achievement and by buying them goods that would make their sacrifices appear worthwhile. They feel such a strong obligation to repay their parents that they sacrifice their own dreams and desires. Many Korean American young people, though not all, have either gone into medicine, law, and business or are preparing to do so; these are the professions they assume will have the greatest possible earning power and are therefore the only options open to them. Following their own interests at the expense of economic potential would disappoint their parents and inhibit their ability to repay them with either cultural or economic success. In this context, Korean American children tend to resolve the conflict caused by American social imperatives and Korean American families' cultural values and economic structure, and they attempt to secure their relationship with their family to study hard, to parlay advanced education into economic security, and to purchase markers of upward mobility that can be publicly displayed, such as luxury cars and homes. They believe that only this kind of outcome may be appropriate recompense for their parents' many sacrifices. With this background, we can begin to see why responsibility ranks so high among second-generation immigrants.

Fourth, many immigrants have generally positive views on self-sacrifice. This was especially true for immigrants that lived longer here in the United States. The younger immigrants likely view self-sacrifice more positively. After seeing their parents sacrifice for their family, after being taught about the previous generation (the WWII generation, e.g.) who have sacrificed much in the name of their country, the younger immigrants have received a positive picture of self-sacrifice during their formative years. Another indication is that self-giving and self-sacrifice are valued virtues within the Christian church, these respondents would have likely had more positive views of self-sacrifice than those without these teachings.

Furthermore, Korean American parishioners find their identity and personal value in sacrificing for family, children, and even church and are forced to fit into the church community (and by extension the Korean American community) by sacrificing themselves. Their personal narratives picture such sacrifice positively. However, in reality, they feel burned out from the churches they serve without rest. In some cases, these parishioners are volunteering their time after working seventy hours during the work week. They are expected to attend all church activities—early morning prayer services, Wednesday and Friday evening services, Sunday worship and activities, and numerous Bible studies, small group gatherings, committee meetings, and seasonal revival meetings. Ironically, the children are left on their own without family time and supervision due to their parent's devotion to their church. It is highly possible that most participants answer positively to their view on self-sacrifice in that they have not been exposed to constructive, alternative, and counter-narratives in regard to self-sacrifice which is out of equal regard and mutual service.

In this context, I strongly suggest that it is the Korean immigrant churches' responsibility that they should offer alternative narratives to their parishioners' stories and contexts. This is not to avoid all burden or responsibility from family and church, but to broaden their view of sacrifice with balance. The parishioners need to be taught that not all sacrifice is positive or negative, that the individual parishioners must paint their own canvas with a mutually beneficial view of self-sacrifice. For example, some Korean immigrant churches encourage their parishioners to have family time after Sunday worship service by not holding any meetings after Sunday worship. These churches provide an excellent counter-narrative by allowing parishioners to balance church and family life. If Korean American churches would provide these constructive alternatives or counter-narratives, then the general Korean American population may understand self-sacrifice in a more constructive manner.

Fifth, traditional and cultural value was the least important motivation for self-sacrifice. There is a tendency for some immigrants living in the United States to disregard or ignore traditions set by their home country. Also, there is the tendency to highlight the negative aspects of one's old culture while adapting to the new. Though these immigrants think that they may not be as strongly influenced by Confucian teachings, nonetheless, I still strongly believe they are influenced by Confucian teachings and traditions.

Unexpectedly, according to this study, reputation was another motive that was considered unimportant. For Korean Americans, "saving face" is very important aspect in their social life because "face" has to do with the image of credibility of the person they are dealing with. If someone experiences insults, embarrassment, or shame in public and personal relationship, they will lose "face." Korean Americans are driven to maintain a positive reputation while secretly living in fear of what others may think. However, through the results of this survey, the Korean American immigrants place more value on responsibility, care for their family, and avoiding conflict than maintaining one's own reputation.

Finally, I predicted that Korean Americans are less willing to sacrifice for another's needs outside their family. This study shows that although Korean Americans have a strong willingness to sacrifice for their own family members, they are also willing to sacrifice for their friends, as well. Generally, for Korean Americans, friendships or other social relationships are considered to be secondary to the needs of the family. However, for most immigrants, their extended family is still in Korea, and their friends have, in essence, become a part of their extended family in the United States.

Limitations of This Study

Due to the limitation of this study, we were warned to be careful in interpreting and applying the results directly.

First, self-sacrifice in the context of relationship can be different from situation to situation. Though there were efforts to define the motives of self-sacrifice in six specific interpersonal relationships, the motives behind self-sacrifice can be different from situation to situation, even in the same type of interpersonal relationship. Second, there was difficulty in gauging the amount of sacrifice. Just how much sacrifice is too much sacrifice? Third, there are many compound variables in measuring the motives of self-sacrifice. Unless there were stark and distinct differences, it is difficult to generalize the motives behind self-sacrifice. Fourth, despite the anonymity of the survey, there may be distinct tendencies by the respondents to want to be seen as generous or good people. This can bias the result toward the positive. Fifth, many respondents may already have a positive impression or value of self-sacrifice since the survey was directed toward Korean American Christians. Sixth, despite one's thoughts or intentions of self-sacrifice, this does not necessarily show in action. Seventh, Korean Americans have a tendency to be agreeable to everyone. There are ways to test the distributions in such tables for significance, but the interpretation is complicated. Eighth, as noted earlier, due to the comparatively small number of respondents identifying themselves as second generation, it is suggested that the views of self-sacrifice in second-generation Korean American immigrants would be clarified and expanded by future study.

Indications for Further Research

Due to these limitations, I suggest some indications for further research arising from this first exploration into Korean American motives of self-sacrifice.

First, it is very difficult to generalize these results to a greater Korean population. With these limitations in mind, further study comparing the views of self-sacrifice between Koreans (living in Korea) and Korean American immigrants is necessary. Despite their core similarities, Korean American immigrants possess unique values not shared by their native Korean counterparts, as shown by the results of the survey. To truly distinguish the unique values held by the immigrants, the study should be expanded to encompass not only Korean American immigrants, but the general Korean population.

Second, as noted earlier in the implication section, more study is needed on the motives of sacrifice among men, especially immigrants. As we have seen in an earlier chapter (goose fathers), men have their own unique values that contribute to their overall motives of sacrifice. However, as this study focused on the general motives of sacrifice, I was not able to explore deeply why certain men tend to sacrifice more than others, to the point of self-denial and, ultimately, self-destruction. A future study would greatly help to explore why certain men are willing to sacrifice so much for their family.

Finally, being that we now have preliminary data in the present study with initial impressions of the idea of self-sacrifice as it is expressed in the Korean American context, it would be interesting to see diachronic follow-up studies. The scope of this survey has been limited to the interest of actual motives in the attitude of Korean Americans in regards to self-sacrifice, but it would be likewise interesting to see future studies with more variables, such as the impact of Christian faith, or other religious faiths, for that matter.

6

Toward a More Authentic Approach to Self-Sacrifice

UP TO THIS POINT, we have examined previously existing studies on the empirical, theoretical, and theological aspects of self-sacrifice. Then we have explored the actual attitudes, beliefs, and motives of self-sacrifice as reported by Korean Americans in a qualitative and quantitative research study. In chapter 5, from the results of the survey, we found out that (1) avoiding conflicts and maintaining harmony are the most important motives of self-sacrifice of Korean Americans; (2) responsibility is still an important motive for self-sacrifice as predicted. Especially, in parent-child relationships, second-generation children feel such a strong obligation to repay their parent that they sacrifice themselves at all cost. Also, it is common for parents to give up everything for their children. Parents place a high value on their children's educational and economic success; (3) Korean Americans find their identity and personal value in sacrificing for family, children, and even church and are forced to fit in to the church community (and by extension the Korean American community) by sacrificing themselves. Unfortunately, they often develop wrong conceptions of self-sacrifice and suffer such consequences as unhappy and unfulfilled family lives; (4) traditional values have an insignificant influence on Korean American family; (5) there is no significant difference on gender in regard to self-sacrifice; (6) friendship plays an important role in replacing extended family; (7) Korean Americans have not been exposed to constructive alternatives in regards to self-sacrifice, such as equal regard and mutual service.

In this final chapter, I will attempt to answer a significant question that is relevant to many Korean American pastors and pastoral counselors: "How will we bridge the gap between the deficiencies of Confucian understanding of self-sacrifice and mutual love as prescribed by a Christian perspective?" I will follow this with a new approach that incorporates a healthier and broader understanding of self- sacrifice in Korean American family relationships.

How Will We Bridge the Gap between Confucian Understanding of Self-Sacrifice and Christian Understanding of Self-Sacrifice?

On the surface, there are shared similarities between Confucian and Christian ethics, which emphasize father-son relationships and sacred family relationships. However, this overlooks the fact that there are some critical differences in the Confucian notion of family and that of Christianity. Nam-Soon Kang argues that there is a crucial difference in the understanding of human beings, on which the idea of human rights and equality are based.[1] The idea of human rights requires "a certain level of individualism, wherein the individual person would be valued for his/her own sake, and not just as a relationship to others."[2] In Confucianism, there is no sense of individuality because family as a group overrides any individual person. In Confucian tradition, the concept of individuality exists but is deliberately muted or denied. The underlying idea is

> not individual liberty or equality but order and harmony, not individual independence but selflessness and cooperation, not freedom of individual conscience but conformity to orthodox truth. . . . The purpose of society was not to preserve and promote individual liberty but to maintain the harmony or the hierarchical order.[3]

---

1. Kang, "Confucian Familism," 177.
2. Kung and Moltmann,*Ethics of World Religions*, 12.
3. Louis Henkin, "Human Rights Idea in Contemporary China," in *Human Rights in Contemporary China*, by Edwards et al., 21.

So, in Confucian tradition, the relationship between family members is more important than the individual, which is not problematic alone in itself. The problem here arises from the fact that the relationship is hierarchical according to gender, age, and social status. In this hierarchical relationship, "the human being in Confucianism has rights only if he/she has a certain position in a family."[4] The individual person in the family has rights not as an individual person per se, but as a father, son, or brother. In other words, there is no place for a woman to claim her human rights as an individual, especially in the public sphere—not even as wife, daughter, or mother.[5]

On the other hand, in Christianity, there is a strong sense of ethical individualism in its understanding of the human being as created in God's image, giving rise to the idea that all humans are to be treated with the same reverence and respect because they are equally created by God in God's image.[6] All human beings are to have dignity and rights as created of equal worth, regardless of their sex, class, or race. Christian love primarily means equal regard, which includes elements of both sacrifice and fulfillment.

Confucianism in Korea is not the *only* force for promoting the patriarchal reality in Christianity, but it justifies, reinforces, and finally perpetuates a strong patriarchal ethos in Christianity.[7] Kang argues that

> Confucianism has tended to be extremely conservative, supporting the ruling elite and the status quo, providing theoretical justification for authoritarianism, and justifying inequality between the sexes and age groups. It strives to maintain the existing social hierarchical structure, and it reinforces and justifies women's subordination to men in family, society, and church in the name of harmony. It has strongly influenced the contemporary patriarchal construction of Christianity in Korea.[8]

In reality, Christianity in Korea is ethically "Confucianized" in many ways. The patriarchal elements in Christianity is conflated with the patriarchal value system of Confucianism. This combination of Confucianism with Christianity in Korea has primarily contributed to the misunderstanding of the concept of self-sacrifice. For example, emphasizing respect for

4. Kang, "Confucian Familism," 178.
5. Ibid.
6. Ibid., 180.
7. Ibid., 184.
8. Ibid.

authority and elders often serves as a road to underpinning established social and political hierarchies and a ground on which people—especially women, minors, and the lower social class—are forced to endure an authoritarian community (i.e., in family, school, and even church).[9] Even in church, being duty-oriented is so foundational that the relation to their church and communities come first, rather than individual or family. Being deeply rooted in the notion of human interconnectedness often has led to injustice and dominance of those in the weaker position.

Furthermore, the combination of Christian and Confucian patriarchy seems to be one of the major reasons the leadership of Korean Christian women has not been well developed.[10] Although women comprise more than 70% of Korean Christians, they have largely been excluded from church leadership. Even after completion of rigorous seminary training, many women have a difficult time getting situated in a ministry leadership position. Even if they are fortunate enough to find a location where they can serve, because of a continued bias against women's service in the clergy, their roles are limited to Sunday school or care for the elderly in the church. Whatever positions are deemed important, these are reserved for the men, while the more "menial" positions are automatically relegated to the women. There is also a gross difference between the salaries of male and female leadership. Even though we see an increase of women's movement in the church, and a steady reduction in the gap between men and women, this progressivism is well within the minority. The public at large is requiring more time to grow to get used to the idea of female leadership, and both the Korean churches and the Korean American churches are in need of reform for the most part, from the historical disregard of women and their leadership roles in the church.

Considering the aforementioned anticipations for change, we need new approaches and ethics that not only put great importance on harmony, cooperation, consensus, and social solidarity among members of an organization, but also respect individuals' value and worth. As mentioned in chapter 1, B. S. Oh called this "new Confucian ethics." This is in sharp contrast with a Western emphasis on competition, "having it all" individualism, or self-interest. Today, the harmonious integration of values stressing cooperation and competition appears increasingly crucial for Korean society's continued development. When a culture validates not only interconnected

---

9. Ibid., 185.
10. Kang, "Creating Dangerous Memory," 26.

relationship, cooperation, and harmony, but also personal cultivation and self-achievement, we may overcome any residual tendencies toward one-sided, obligatory, or imposed self-sacrifice. In this way, mutual love and sacrifice in Korean American family relationships, community, and society at large may be fostered and my flourish in the ages to come.

New Approach toward Equality and Mutual Service

Then, we need a new approach that provides the most adequate understanding of the motivation of self-sacrifice in Korean American family relationships. In *Dissident Discipleship*, David Augsburger describes six types of motivations for service. This scale offers important components missing in Korean Americans' self-awareness in the motivation for self-sacrifice. Augsburger's scale is presented below.

Figure 6.1 Motivations for service[11]

"It's really about me"						"It's truly about you"
← self-serving other-using					other-serving self-forgetting	→
1	2	3	4	5		6
Exploitive	Egocentric	Egalitarian	Obedient	Benevolent		Sacrificial
Eros		Philea		Agape		
(self-satisfaction, self-pleasing)		(fellow-feeling friendship)		(care and concern for the others as other)		

According to this scale, *exploitive* service is done solely for self-advancement achieved, profit gained, righteousness demonstrated, moral superiority proved, power seized, or political clout claimed. *Egocentric* service fulfills ego needs, inflates self-esteem, justifies the giver's pride, raises the giver above others, or claims virtue. *Egalitarian* service is of equal benefit to both parties, a quid-pro-quo exchange of help and of the benefits of reward or repayment. *Obedient* service fulfills a moral imperative to care for the neighbor, help the needy, even aid the enemy out of a committed, willing obedience to a core of internalized values. *Benevolent* service is freely given, offered as a gift that goes beyond mere payment. It is primarily offered out

---

11. Augsburger, *Dissident Discipleship*, 147–70.

of caring, mercy, or compassion. *Sacrificial* service is self-forgetting concern for the other's needs that helps even though the cost is real sacrifice and voluntary self-investment.

As we look at both sides of the continuum, each have their own strengths and weaknesses, advantages and disadvantages. There are too many circumstantial variables to categorize an individual to one side or another. Also, from different phases of our lives we may find ourselves at different places on this continuum. In other words, a person may commit an act that is egocentric followed by another that is benevolent. Depending on relationships and situations, the level of sacrifice may oscillate from person to person, and with the same person, from one level of motivation to another. For instance, parents who are very committed to sacrificing for their children may not show any sacrifice when it comes to their work life or friendship. Also, depending on the character or family background of the person, what may be a great act of self-sacrifice for one person, can be seen as a simple gesture of service to another. Even though human personality and relationships are incredibly complex, the above continuum is a helpful instrument to gauge our own motivation for service or sacrifice ourselves. Ultimately, however, the scale alone is not sufficient; cultivation of introspection and self-reflection in regards to the motives behind each of our actions are required in order to determine our orientation.

The concept of service and self-sacrifice is highly important to Korean Americans. They are raised within the construct of interconnected family and society—the importance of family and community overrides that of the individual. With age, social status, and gender-defined roles and hierarchy (rather than equality and justice), self-sacrifice and service become instrumental in maintaining family and social relationships. So, as defined by the Augsburger scale of motivation, their sacrifice leans more toward obligatory, exploitive, or unilaterally sacrificial. The survey results validate this tendency, showing that the most important motive for Korean American to sacrifice in various relationships is conflict avoidance. And this motivation for self-sacrifice can be seen ironically enough, as self-serving and the motives of avoiding conflict can be passive obedience or sacrificial service, which is far from benevolent or mutual sacrifice. Of course, avoiding conflict may be a form of beneficial sacrifice for the self and a way of obtaining peace and maintaining a harmonious relationship with others. However, even through this sacrifice, if that peace and harmony is not achieved, the relationship is likely to deteriorate, resulting in frustration and potentially ending up in violence. When hidden motives of self-sacrifice are out of conflict avoidance, responsibility, obligation, shame, and guilt, then this self-sacrifice is neither self-giving nor serving. They simply tolerate this sacrificial role in culturally and socially constrained situations, not offering themselves freely as gift.

Based on Augsburger's scale, unfortunately and disappointingly, "love as equal regard," such as benevolent service, is culturally the least conceived and developed aspect in most Korean Americans. As the survey results shows, with the exception of second-generation immigrants, mutual service ranked consistently as an unimportant motive for self-sacrifice. Confucianism, and even Christianity, in Korea teach that the highest virtue of love and service is self-sacrifice and self-denial; especially sacrificial love toward parents, children, and family is considered natural. So, Korean Americans are not readily adept at developing mutuality and equal-regard as integral components of love and sacrifice.

In conclusion, Augsburger points out that serving others means voluntary, inner-directed, sometimes naive, and truly collaborative.[12] However, he calls *benevolent service* and *sacrificial service* "a higher call," which means both arise from a deep commitment to act in love toward the neighbor, to serve out of concern or compassion for the other's needs, and to offer help even at one's own expense, because love is something one does.[13] He also emphasizes the importance of mutuality in relationships, saying that

> mature service leans toward the collaborative. . . . It is the nature of true maturity to learn to love the work one does for the work's sake, to value the service one can provide for the worth of the service itself, not for the acclaim or esteem it may earn. Competition is a useful motivation, but not our highest calling.[14]

Also, Browning et al. assert that love as mutuality or equal regard, rather than love as self-sacrifice, is at the core of Christian love, in both families and life in general.[15] Love as "equal regard" is central a meaning of *agape*, as the word is used in the New Testament, and that love as equal regard is the most adequate view of love for families.[16] Equal regard features

12. Augsburger, *Dissident Discipleship*, 147.
13. Ibid., 152.
14. Ibid., 161.
15. Browning et al., *From Culture Wars to Common Ground*, 273.
16. Ibid., 101–2.

mutuality and *benevolence*, which include elements of both sacrifice and fulfillment. It is a view of Christian love that makes sacrifice transitional to the restoration of equal regard that makes sacrifice primarily a matter of self-giving, sometimes even self-assertion, in the name of restoring mutuality.[17]

In spite of this benefit, it is important to consider that sacrificial or self-giving love in the service of mutuality *has its limits*, especially for vulnerable women and children. Sacrificial and self-giving love as an ideal can be abused. Christian love can be identified too completely with the symbolism of sacrifice or the cross of Christ.[18] Unfortunately, even in family relationships, sacrifice has more to do with submission and endurance than it does with a sacrificial leadership that is redemptive. In this sense, Bellah et al. propose that love creates a dilemma for Christians.[19] Like loving someone, sacrifice is the quintessential expression of individuality and freedom. At the same time, it offers intimacy, mutuality, and sharing. In the ideal love relationship, these two aspects of love are perfectly joined—love is both absolutely free and completely shared. However, such moments of perfect harmony among free individuals are rare or exceptional. The sharing and commitment in a love relationship can sometimes seem to swallow up the individual, making her lose sight of her own interests, opinions, and desires.[20] One loses oneself when one passively adapts to others' needs and goals. Love and sacrifice are understood to be a spontaneous choice by free individuals, but someone who has lost one's individuality cannot really love others nor contribute to one's personal relationships. Losing a sense of oneself may also lead to becoming exploited, or even abandoned by the person one loves.

When reviewing self-sacrifice in patriarchal and hierarchical Korean society, those who are in a vulnerable or weakened position, especially women and children, are seen to be encouraged to offer love for their family through obligatory, one-sided self-sacrifice. Christianity has seemed to reinforce the notion that such one-way self-sacrifice was a virtue most divine. However, we have seen that this obligatory, one-way self-sacrifice is conducive to destroying, not transforming, family relationships. We need to

17. Ibid., 127.
18. Ibid.
19. Bellah et al., *Habits of the Heart*, 93.
20. Ibid.

realize and acknowledge the human limitations of sacrificial love, especially for those in a position in which this one-way self-sacrifice is demanded.

Even so, self-sacrifice or sacrificial love cannot be eliminated from Christian understandings of love.[21] Sacrificial love has a central role in the Christian life and in Christian families. Indeed, Christian love, *agape*, is the sacrifice of self in the service of another. *Agape* cannot be directed toward oneself; if it is, it ceases to be *agape*. It ceases to be self-sacrifice, and becomes self-service. John Stott argues that self-love, directing one's concern and service toward oneself, is the biblical concept not of virtue but of sin.[22] It is precisely because of this that we need to preserve a high doctrine of *agape*, portraying the love of God and love of others. While we should resist the current idea of self-love based on self-centered need fulfillment, we need to learn to affirm our true self, be free to love ourselves *and* our neighbor, and be free to lose ourselves in the selfless loving of God and neighbor—then we will find the true nature of self-sacrifice.

Conclusion

I believe that the element of "equal regard" as pertaining to self-sacrifice offers Korean Americans a refreshing hope in the perspective of familial relationships and a liberating casting-off of culturally and religiously imposed burdens. The Korean American family ought to be grounded on a love ethic of equal regard, and place its value on mutuality, self-sacrifice, and individual fulfillment. When this is done, sacrificial love can be understood as justly appropriated for both husbands and wives, males and female, parents and children. This way, Christian teaching and theology may deliver a more transparent message of true *agape* and its liberating effects to the marginalized, especially women and children.[23]

Korean Americans will benefit much from reflecting on the motives of their self-sacrifice; rather than sacrificing out of coercion or out of obligation and duty, the true motives should be mutually beneficial for all of those involved. Sacrificial service *is* good in itself. This sacrifice is freely given as a gift of compassion and mercy. The model of self-sacrifice carefully balances the obligations of regard for others with a legitimate regard for oneself and recognizes the social, cultural, and theological elements required to

21. Ibid., 127.
22. Stott, "Must I Really Love Myself?," 34.
23. Ibid., 58–59.

maintain it. It is my hope that Korean Americans depart from their tendencies of one-sided submission, giving up of self-respect, and wholesale yielding to imposed obligations within its patriarchal culture and venture into a realm of service seasoned with mutuality and authentic self-sacrifice.

Appendix

Questionnaire

English Form

Personal Information

1. Gender: male female (check one)
2. Age:
3. Where were you born?
   Korea USA Other (if other, please name country)

   If you were born in Korea, how long have been in USA? year(s) month(s)

   Which language do you feel is your primary language? English Korean other

My Attitudes and Beliefs about Self-Sacrifice

(Please answer the following questions as truthfully and honestly as possible)

1. What is your general feeling towards the experience of self-sacrifice? Rate your feeling towards self-sacrifice. Select one from 1 to 5, with 1 being very negatively towards self-sacrifice and 5 being very positively towards self-sacrifice.

1	2	3	4	5
Very Negatively	Negatively	Ambivalently	Positively	Very Positively

Appendix

2. What is your definition or understanding of self-sacrifice? (Please select top three in order (1–3) from the following)

   Delaying my own needs or gratifications temporarily in consideration of another's needs.

   Self-giving actions are mutually beneficial in the give and take of family or community.

   Caring kindness or love out of Christian obligation to others.

   Surrender of my goals in order to gain some greater goal.

   Another's' needs are greater than my own

3. How easy or how hard do you find yourself sacrificing certain activities, goals, or aspects of your life in the following six personal relationships? Rate how easy and how hard it is to sacrifice your activities, goals, and interests. Select one from 1 to 5, with 1 being extremely easy and 5 being extremely hard.

   A. Parent-Child Relationship

	1	2	3	4	5
Personal time (such as time for hobbies, rest, vacation, activities, etc.).	Extremely Easy	Easy		Hard	Extremely Hard
Money (where significant financial investment maybe necessary).	Extremely Easy	Easy	3	Hard	Extremely Hard
Labor (where significant physical work maybe required).	Extremely Easy	Easy	3	Hard	Extremely Hard
Defending one's honor and/or pride.	Extremely Easy	Easy	3	Hard	Extremely Hard
Giving up position of leadership to another.	Extremely Easy	Easy	3	Hard	Extremely Hard

Appendix

| Letting another talk or dominate a conversation. | 1 Extremely Easy | 2 Easy | 3 | 4 Hard | 5 Extremely Hard |

| Yielding your own goals (position of power, ambition, etc.) for your own ego/benefit. | 1 Extremely Easy | 2 Easy | 3 | 4 Hard | 5 Extremely Hard |

B. Marital Relationship (If you are not married, please skip this question)

| Personal Time (such as time for hobbies, rest, vacation, activities, etc.). | 1 Extremely Easy | 2 Easy | 3 | 4 Hard | 5 Extremely Hard |

| Money (where significant financial investment maybe necessary). | 1 Extremely Easy | 2 Easy | 3 | 4 Hard | 5 Extremely Hard |

| Labor (where significant physical work maybe required). | 1 Extremely Easy | 2 Easy | 3 | 4 Hard | 5 Extremely Hard |

| Defending one's honor and/or pride. | 1 Extremely Easy | 2 Easy | 3 | 4 Hard | 5 Extremely Hard |

| Giving up position of leadership to another. | 1 Extremely Easy | 2 Easy | 3 | 4 Hard | 5 Extremely Hard |

| Letting another talk or dominate a conversation. | 1 Extremely Easy | 2 Easy | 3 | 4 Hard | 5 Extremely Hard |

Appendix

Yielding your own goals (position of power, ambition, etc.) for your own ego/benefit.	1 Extremely Easy	2 Easy	3	4 Hard	5 Extremely Hard

C. Workplace Relationship

Personal Time (such as time for hobbies, rest, vacation, activities, etc.).	1 Extremely Easy	2 Easy	3	4 Hard	5 Extremely Hard
Money (where significant financial investment maybe necessary).	1 Extremely Easy	2 Easy	3	4 Hard	5 Extremely Hard
Labor (where significant physical work maybe required).	1 Extremely Easy	2 Easy	3	4 Hard	5 Extremely Hard
Defending one's honor and/or pride.	1 Extremely Easy	2 Easy	3	4 Hard	5 Extremely Hard
Giving up position of leadership to another.	1 Extremely Easy	2 Easy	3	4 Hard	5 Extremely Hard
Letting another talk or dominate a conversation.	1 Extremely Easy	2 Easy	3	4 Hard	5 Extremely Hard
Yielding your own goals (position of power, ambition, etc.) for your own ego/benefit.	1 Extremely Easy	2 Easy	3	4 Hard	5 Extremely Hard

Appendix

D. Church Relationship (between a pastor and a parishioner)

	1	2	3	4	5
Personal time (such as time for hobbies, rest, vacation, activities, etc.).	Extremely Easy	Easy		Hard	Extremely Hard
Money (where significant financial investment maybe necessary).	Extremely Easy	Easy		Hard	Extremely Hard
Labor (where significant physical work maybe required).	Extremely Easy	Easy		Hard	Extremely Hard
Defending one's honor and/or pride.	Extremely Easy	Easy		Hard	Extremely Hard
Giving up position of leadership to another.	Extremely Easy	Easy		Hard	Extremely Hard
Letting another talk or dominate a conversation.	Extremely Easy	Easy		Hard	Extremely Hard
Yielding your own goals (position of power, ambition, etc.) for your own ego/benefit.	Extremely Easy	Easy		Hard	Extremely Hard

Appendix

E. Academic Relationship (between a teacher and a student)

	1	2	3	4	5
Personal time (such as time for hobbies, rest, vacation, activities, etc.).	Extremely Easy	Easy		Hard	Extremely Hard
Money (where significant financial investment maybe necessary).	Extremely Easy	Easy	3	Hard	Extremely Hard
Labor (where significant physical work maybe required).	Extremely Easy	Easy	3	Hard	Extremely Hard
Defending one's honor and/or pride.	Extremely Easy	Easy	3	Hard	Extremely Hard
Giving up position of leadership to another.	Extremely Easy	Easy	3	Hard	Extremely Hard
Letting another talk or dominate a conversation.	Extremely Easy	Easy	3	Hard	Extremely Hard
Yielding your own goals (position of power, ambition, etc.) for your own ego/benefit.	Extremely Easy	Easy	3	Hard	Extremely Hard

Appendix

F. Friendship

Personal time (such as time for hobbies, rest, vacation, activities, etc.).	1 Extremely Easy	2 Easy	3	4 Hard	5 Extremely Hard
Money (where significant financial investment maybe necessary).	1 Extremely Easy	2 Easy	3	4 Hard	5 Extremely Hard
Labor (where significant physical work maybe required).	1 Extremely Easy	2 Easy	3	4 Hard	5 Extremely Hard
Defending one's honor and/or pride.	1 Extremely Easy	2 Easy	3	4 Hard	5 Extremely Hard
Giving up position of leadership to another.	1 Extremely Easy	2 Easy	3	4 Hard	5 Extremely Hard
Letting another talk or dominate a conversation.	1 Extremely Easy	2 Easy	3	4 Hard	5 Extremely Hard
Yielding your own goals (position of power, ambition, etc.) for your own ego/benefit.	1 Extremely Easy	2 Easy	3	4 Hard	5 Extremely Hard

Appendix

7. Think about the last time where you felt you had to put aside your own needs in the following six relationships. As you reflect on that situation, rate your motives, or why you felt that sacrifice was necessary in the following six relationships. Select one from 1 to 5, with 1 being the extremely unimportant, 5 being the extremely important.

H. Parent-Child Relationship

	1	2	3	4	5
Avoiding conflict and maintaining harmony.	Extremely Unimportant	Not Important		Important	Extremely Important
Yielding to obligation and duty to society, family, or other hierarchy.	Extremely Unimportant	Not Important		Important	Extremely Important
Holding to my sense of responsibility to family or others.	Extremely Unimportant	Not Important		Important	Extremely Important
Acting for the sake of others in unconditional love (*agape*).	Extremely Unimportant	Not Important		Important	Extremely Important
Expressing my high self-esteem, personal honor and dignity.	Extremely Unimportant	Not Important		Important	Extremely Important
Preserving my reputation as a generous and giving person.	Extremely Unimportant	Not Important		Important	Extremely Important

Appendix

My willingness to yield is an expression of my loving personality.	1 Extremely Unimportant	2 Not Important	3	4 Important	5 Extremely Important
Strong commitment to the practice of mutual service and caring for others.	1 Extremely Unimportant	2 Not Important	3	4 Important	5 Extremely Important
Putting others first because it is central to my religious faith.	1 Extremely Unimportant	2 Not Important	3	4 Important	5 Extremely Important
Yielding appropriately as an expression of my traditional and cultural values, rooted in the historic traditions and teachings of Confucianism.	1 Extremely Unimportant	2 Not Important	3	4 Important	5 Extremely Important

I. Marital Relationship (If you are not married, please skip this question)

Avoiding conflict and maintaining harmony.	1 Extremely Unimportant	2 Not Important	3	4 Important	5 Extremely Important
Yielding to obligation and duty to society, family, or other hierarchy.	1 Extremely Unimportant	2 Not Important	3	4 Important	5 Extremely Important
Holding to my sense of responsibility to family or others.	1 Extremely Unimportant	2 Not Important	3	4 Important	5 Extremely Important

Appendix

Acting for the sake of others in unconditional love (*agape*).	1 Extremely Unimportant	2 Not Important	3	4 Important	5 Extremely Important
Expressing my high self-esteem, personal honor and dignity.	1 Extremely Unimportant	2 Not Important	3	4 Important	5 Extremely Important
Preserving my reputation as a generous and giving person.	1 Extremely Unimportant	2 Not Important	3	4 Important	5 Extremely Important
My willingness to yield is an expression of my loving personality.	1 Extremely Unimportant	2 Not Important	3	4 Important	5 Extremely Important
Strong commitment to the practice of mutual service and caring for others.	1 Extremely Unimportant	2 Not Important	3	4 Important	5 Extremely Important
Putting others first because it is central to my religious faith.	1 Extremely Unimportant	2 Not Important	3	4 Important	5 Extremely Important
Yielding appropriately as an expression of my traditional and cultural values, rooted in the historic traditions and teachings of Confucianism.	1 Extremely Unimportant	2 Not Important	3	4 Important	5 Extremely Important

J. Workplace Relationship

Avoiding conflict and maintaining harmony.	1 Extremely Unimportant	2 Not Important	3	4 Important	5 Extremely Important

Appendix

Yielding to obligation and duty to society, family, or other hierarchy.	1 Extremely Unimportant	2 Not Important	3	4 Important	5 Extremely Important
Holding to my sense of responsibility to family or others.	1 Extremely Unimportant	2 Not Important	3	4 Important	5 Extremely Important
Acting for the sake of others in unconditional love (*agape*).	1 Extremely Unimportant	2 Not Important	3	4 Important	5 Extremely Important
Expressing my high self-esteem, personal honor and dignity.	1 Extremely Unimportant	2 Not Important	3	4 Important	5 Extremely Important
Preserving my reputation as a generous and giving person.	1 Extremely Unimportant	2 Not Important	3	4 Important	5 Extremely Important
My willingness to yield is an expression of my loving personality.	1 Extremely Unimportant	2 Not Important	3	4 Important	5 Extremely Important
Strong commitment to the practice of mutual service and caring for others.	1 Extremely Unimportant	2 Not Important	3	4 Important	5 Extremely Important
Putting others first because it is central to my religious faith.	1 Extremely Unimportant	2 Not Important	3	4 Important	5 Extremely Important

Appendix

Yielding appropriately as an expression of my traditional and cultural values, rooted in the historic traditions and teachings of Confucianism.	1 Extremely Unimportant	2 Not Important	3	4 Important	5 Extremely Important

K. Church Relationship (between pastor and parishioner)

Avoiding conflict and maintaining harmony.	1 Extremely Unimportant	2 Not Important	3	4 Important	5 Extremely Important
Yielding to obligation and duty to society, family, or other hierarchy.	1 Extremely Unimportant	2 Not Important	3	4 Important	5 Extremely Important
Holding to my sense of responsibility to family or others.	1 Extremely Unimportant	2 Not Important	3	4 Important	5 Extremely Important
Acting for the sake of others in unconditional love (*agape*).	1 Extremely Unimportant	2 Not Important	3	4 Important	5 Extremely Important
Expressing my high self-esteem, personal honor and dignity.	1 Extremely Unimportant	2 Not Important	3	4 Important	5 Extremely Important
Preserving my reputation as a generous and giving person.	1 Extremely Unimportant	2 Not Important	3	4 Important	5 Extremely Important
My willingness to yield is an expression of my loving personality.	1 Extremely Unimportant	2 Not Important	3	4 Important	5 Extremely Important
Strong commitment to the practice of mutual service and caring for others.	1 Extremely Unimportant	2 Not Important	3	4 Important	5 Extremely Important

Appendix

Putting others first because it is central to my religious faith.	1 Extremely Unimportant	2 Not Important	3	4 Important	5 Extremely Important
Yielding appropriately as an expression of my traditional and cultural values, rooted in the historic traditions and teachings of Confucianism.	1 Extremely Unimportant	2 Not Important	3	4 Important	5 Extremely Important

L. Academic Relationship (between a teacher and student)

Avoiding conflict and maintaining harmony.	1 Extremely Unimportant	2 Not Important	3	4 Important	5 Extremely Important
Yielding to obligation and duty to society, family, or other hierarchy.	1 Extremely Unimportant	2 Not Important	3	4 Important	5 Extremely Important
Holding to my sense of responsibility to family or others.	1 Extremely Unimportant	2 Not Important	3	4 Important	5 Extremely Important
Acting for the sake of others in unconditional love (*agape*).	1 Extremely Unimportant	2 Not Important	3	4 Important	5 Extremely Important
Expressing my high self-esteem, personal honor and dignity.	1 Extremely Unimportant	2 Not Important	3	4 Important	5 Extremely Important
Preserving my reputation as a generous and giving person.	1 Extremely Unimportant	2 Not Important	3	4 Important	5 Extremely Important

Appendix

	1	2	3	4	5
My willingness to yield is an expression of my loving personality.	Extremely Unimportant	Not Important		Important	Extremely Important
Strong commitment to the practice of mutual service and caring for others.	Extremely Unimportant	Not Important		Important	Extremely Important
Putting others first because it is central to my religious faith.	Extremely Unimportant	Not Important		Important	Extremely Important
Yielding appropriately as an expression of my traditional and cultural values, rooted in the historic traditions and teachings of Confucianism.	Extremely Unimportant	Not Important		Important	Extremely Important

M. Friendship

	1	2	3	4	5
Avoiding conflict and maintaining harmony.	Extremely Unimportant	Not Important		Important	Extremely Important
Yielding to obligation and duty to society, family, or other hierarchy.	Extremely Unimportant	Not Important		Important	Extremely Important
Holding to my sense of responsibility to family or others.	Extremely Unimportant	Not Important		Important	Extremely Important
Acting for the sake of others in unconditional love (*agape*).	Extremely Unimportant	Not Important		Important	Extremely Important

Expressing my high self-esteem, personal honor and dignity.	1 Extremely Unimportant	2 Not Important	3	4 Important	5 Extremely Important
Preserving my reputation as a generous and giving person.	1 Extremely Unimportant	2 Not Important	3	4 Important	5 Extremely Important
My willingness to yield is an expression of my loving personality.	1 Extremely Unimportant	2 Not Important	3	4 Important	5 Extremely Important
Strong commitment to the practice of mutual service and caring for others.	1 Extremely Unimportant	2 Not Important	3	4 Important	5 Extremely Important
Putting others first because it is central to my religious faith.	1 Extremely Unimportant	2 Not Important	3	4 Important	5 Extremely Important
Yielding appropriately as an expression of my traditional and cultural values, rooted in the historic traditions and teachings of Confucianism.	1 Extremely Unimportant	2 Not Important	3	4 Important	5 Extremely Important

Appendix

Korean Form

개인 정보

1. 성별: 남 여
2. 나이: 세
3. 당신이 태어난 곳은 어디입니까?

   한국 미국 그 외 (나라 이름은?)

   만약에 한국에서 태어나셨다면, 미국 거주하신 기간은? 년 개월

   한국어와 영어 중 어떤 언어가 더 편하신가요? 한국어 영어

자기 희생(self-sacrifice)에 관한 나의 태도와 동기
(다음 질문들에 가능한 정직하고 성실하게 대답해 주십시오)

4. "자기 희생"이라는 말을 들을 때, 여러분이 가지고 있는 일반적인 느낌은 무엇입니까? 여러분의 일반적인 느낌을 1점에서 5점으로 점수를 매겨 주세요 (1점은 아주 부정적인 느낌이고, 5점은 아주 기분 좋고 긍정적인 느낌입니다)

1	2	3	4	5
아주 부정적	부정적		긍정적	아주 긍정적

5. "자기 희생"은 어떤 것이라고 생각하십니까? (아래의 보기들 중에 자신이 가장 중요하다고 생각되는 개념을 1에서 3으로 체크해 주세요. 단 1이 가장 중요한 개념이고, 그 다음으로 2, 3을 체크해 주세요)

   다른 사람의 필요를 고려해서, 내가 하고 싶은 것을 잠시 나중으로 미루는 것

   서로 상호적인 유익을 위해 하는 자기 희생적인 행동 (self-giving)

   기독교인이라는 의무 때문에, 다른 사람에게 베푸는 사랑과 친절

   더 큰 목적을 성취하기 위해서, 지금 나의 목표를 다른 사람에게 양보하는 것

   나 자신보다 다른 사람의 더 커 보여서 하는 행동

6. 아래에는 여러분이 주로 속해 있는 여섯 가지 다른 관계들이 있습니다. 각각의 관계 속에서, 여러분이 하고 싶은 활동이나 목

Appendix

표, 삶의 특정한 부분들을 희생하는 것이 얼마나 쉽습니까? 또는 얼마나 어렵습니까? 각각의 관계 속에서, 여러분 자신의 삶의 어떤 부분 (예를 들면, 돈, 시간, 육체적 노동 등)을 희생하기가 얼마나 쉬운지, 혹은 어려운지 점수를 매겨주세요 (희생하기가 너무 쉽다고 생각하면 1점을, 희생하기가 굉장히 힘들다고 생각하면 5점을 매겨 주세요).

A. 부모와 자녀 관계

개인적인 시간 (예를 들면, 취미, 휴식, 휴가, 내가 하고 싶은 활동, 기타 등등)	1 아주 쉽다	2 쉽다	3	4 어렵다	5 아주 어렵다
돈 (부담이 되는 지출이 요구될 때)	1 아주 쉽다	2 쉽다	3	4 어렵다	5 아주 어렵다
일이나 노동 (육체적으로 힘든 일이 요구될 때)	1 아주 쉽다	2 쉽다	3	4 어렵다	5 아주 어렵다
나의 명예와 자존심을 지키는 것	1 아주 쉽다	2 쉽다	3	4 어렵다	5 아주 어렵다
나의 리더십 자리를 넘겨 주는 것	1 아주 쉽다	2 쉽다	3	4 어렵다	5 아주 어렵다
의견을 말할 기회를 주거나 아예 대화의 주도권을 가지게 하는 것	1 아주 쉽다	2 쉽다	3	4 어렵다	5 아주 어렵다
나 자신의 이익(체면)을 위해서 내 자신의 목표나 야심을 내려놓는 것	1 아주 쉽다	2 쉽다	3	4 어렵다	5 아주 어렵다

Appendix

B. 배우자와의 관계
(만약 결혼한 상태가 아니라면 이 문항은 뛰어 넘으십시오)

	1	2	3	4	5
개인적인 시간 (예를 들면, 취미, 휴식, 휴가, 내가 하고 싶은 활동, 기타 등등)	아주 쉽다	쉽다		어렵다	아주 어렵다
돈 (부담이 되는 지출이 요구될 때)	아주 쉽다	쉽다		어렵다	아주 어렵다
일이나 노동 (육체적으로 힘든 일이 요구될 때)	아주 쉽다	쉽다		어렵다	아주 어렵다
나의 명예와 자존심을 지키는 것	아주 쉽다	쉽다		어렵다	아주 어렵다
나의 리더십 자리를 넘겨 주는 것	아주 쉽다	쉽다		어렵다	아주 어렵다
의견을 말할 기회를 주거나 아예 대화의 주도권을 가지게 하는 것	아주 쉽다	쉽다		어렵다	아주 어렵다
나 자신의 이익(체면)을 위해서 내 자신의 목표나 야심을 내려놓는 것	아주 쉽다	쉽다		어렵다	아주 어렵다

C. 직장에서 상사와의 관계

	1	2	3	4	5
개인적인 시간 (예를 들면, 취미, 휴식, 휴가, 내가 하고 싶은 활동, 기타 등등)	아주 쉽다	쉽다		어렵다	아주 어렵다

Appendix

돈 (부담이 되는 지출이 요구될 때)	1 아주 쉽다	2 쉽다	3	4 어렵다	5 아주 어렵다
일이나 노동 (육체적으로 힘든 일이 요구될 때)	1 아주 쉽다	2 쉽다	3	4 어렵다	5 아주 어렵다
나의 명예와 자존심을 지키는 것	1 아주 쉽다	2 쉽다	3	4 어렵다	5 아주 어렵다
나의 리더십 자리를 넘겨 주는 것	1 아주 쉽다	2 쉽다	3	4 어렵다	5 아주 어렵다
의견을 말할 기회를 주거나 아예 대화의 주도권을 가지게 하는 것	1 아주 쉽다	2 쉽다	3	4 어렵다	5 아주 어렵다
나 자신의 이익(체면)을 위해서 내 자신의 목표나 야심을 내려놓는 것	1 아주 쉽다	2 쉽다	3	4 어렵다	5 아주 어렵다

D. 교회에서 교역자와 성도와의 관계

개인적인 시간 (예를 들면, 취미, 휴식, 휴가, 내가 하고 싶은 활동, 기타 등등)	1 아주 쉽다	2 쉽다	3	4 어렵다	5 아주 어렵다
돈 (부담이 되는 지출이 요구될 때)	1 아주 쉽다	2 쉽다	3	4 어렵다	5 아주 어렵다

Appendix

일이나 노동 (육체적으로 힘든 일이 요구될 때)	1 아주 쉽다	2 쉽다	3	4 어렵다	5 아주 어렵다
나의 명예와 자존심을 지키는 것	1 아주 쉽다	2 쉽다	3	4 어렵다	5 아주 어렵다
나의 리더십 자리를 넘겨 주는 것	1 아주 쉽다	2 쉽다	3	4 어렵다	5 아주 어렵다
의견을 말할 기회를 주거나 아예 대화의 주도권을 가지게 하는 것	1 아주 쉽다	2 쉽다	3	4 어렵다	5 아주 어렵다
나 자신의 이익(체면)을 위해서 내 자신의 목표나 야심을 내려놓는 것	1 아주 쉽다	2 쉽다	3	4 어렵다	5 아주 어렵다

E. 학교에서 교사와 학생과의 관계

개인적인 시간 (예를 들면, 취미, 휴식, 휴가, 내가 하고 싶은 활동, 기타 등등)	1 아주 쉽다	2 쉽다	3	4 어렵다	5 아주 어렵다
돈 (부담이 되는 지출이 요구될 때)	1 아주 쉽다	2 쉽다	3	4 어렵다	5 아주 어렵다
일이나 노동 (육체적으로 힘든 일이 요구될 때)	1 아주 쉽다	2 쉽다	3	4 어렵다	5 아주 어렵다

Appendix

나의 명예와 자존심을 지키는 것	1 아주 쉽다	2 쉽다	3	4 어렵다	5 아주 어렵다
나의 리더십 자리를 넘겨 주는 것	1 아주 쉽다	2 쉽다	3	4 어렵다	5 아주 어렵다
의견을 말할 기회를 주거나 아예 대화의 주도권을 가지게 하는 것	1 아주 쉽다	2 쉽다	3	4 어렵다	5 아주 어렵다
나 자신의 이익(체면)을 위해서 내 자신의 목표나 야심을 내려놓는 것	1 아주 쉽다	2 쉽다	3	4 어렵다	5 아주 어렵다

F. 친구나 동료와의 관계

개인적인 시간 (예를 들면, 취미, 휴식, 휴가, 내가 하고 싶은 활동, 기타 등등)	1 아주 쉽다	2 쉽다	3	4 어렵다	5 아주 어렵다
돈 (부담이 되는 지출이 요구될 때)	1 아주 쉽다	2 쉽다	3	4 어렵다	5 아주 어렵다
일이나 노동 (육체적으로 힘든 일이 요구될 때)	1 아주 쉽다	2 쉽다	3	4 어렵다	5 아주 어렵다
나의 명예와 자존심을 지키는 것	1 아주 쉽다	2 쉽다	3	4 어렵다	5 아주 어렵다

Appendix

	1	2	3	4	5
나의 리더십 자리를 넘겨 주는 것	아주 쉽다	쉽다		어렵다	아주 어렵다
의견을 말할 기회를 주거나 아예 대화의 주도권을 가지게 하는 것	아주 쉽다	쉽다		어렵다	아주 어렵다
나 자신의 이익(체면)을 위해서 내 자신의 목표나 야심을 내려놓는 것	아주 쉽다	쉽다		어렵다	아주 어렵다

7. 아래에는 여러분이 주로 속해 있는 여섯 가지 다른 관계들이 있습니다. 각각의 관계 속에서, 여러분이 가장 최근에 여러분 자신의 필요를 포기해야 했던 상황을 떠올려 보십시오. 아래에는 각 관계 속에서, 여러분이 희생을 해야겠다고 생각했을 것 같은 동기나 이유를 10가지로 나누어 놓았습니다. 아래의 각 문항에 점수를 매겨 주세요. 각각의 문항을 보고, 여러분 자신이 희생을 선택한 가장 중요하지 않는 이유라고 생각되면 1점을, 가장 중요한 이유라고 생각되면, 5점을 매겨 주십시오.

A. 부모와 자녀 관계

	1	2	3	4	5
갈등을 피하고, 화목을 유지하고 싶어서	전혀 중요하지 않다	중요하지 않다		중요하다	아주 중요하다
가족이나 사회를 위해 해야 하는 어쩔 수 없는 의무감 때문에	전혀 중요하지 않다	중요하지 않다		중요하다	아주 중요하다
가족이나 다른 사람들에 대한 책임감 때문에	전혀 중요하지 않다	중요하지 않다		중요하다	아주 중요하다

Appendix

다른 사람에게 무조건적인 사랑을 베푸는 것이 중요하기 때문에	1 전혀 중요하지 않다	2 중요하지 않다	3	4 중요하다	5 아주 중요하다
나의 개인적인 자존심과 품위를 지키고 싶어서	1 전혀 중요하지 않다	2 중요하지 않다	3	4 중요하다	5 아주 중요하다
다른 사람에게 관대하고 나누어 주는 사람으로 보여지고 싶어서	1 전혀 중요하지 않다	2 중요하지 않다	3	4 중요하다	5 아주 중요하다
나는 원래 다른 사람에게 잘 양보하는 성격을 가지고 있어서	1 전혀 중요하지 않다	2 중요하지 않다	3	4 중요하다	5 아주 중요하다
나는 희생이 일방적인 것이 아니라 서로 상호적이고, 서로 섬기는 것이라는 것이라고 생각하기 때문에	1 전혀 중요하지 않다	2 중요하지 않다	3	4 중요하다	5 아주 중요하다
나의 종교적인 믿음 때문에, 다른 사람의 필요를 늘 먼저 생각해야 하기 때문에	1 전혀 중요하지 않다	2 중요하지 않다	3	4 중요하다	5 아주 중요하다
나는 유교적인 문화에서 자라와서, 그 영향으로 잘 양보하는 편이기 때문에	1 전혀 중요하지 않다	2 중요하지 않다	3	4 중요하다	5 아주 중요하다

B. 배우자와의 관계
(만약 결혼한 상태가 아니라면 이 문항은 뛰어 넘으십시오)

Appendix

	1	2	3	4	5
갈등을 피하고, 화목을 유지하고 싶어서	전혀 중요하지 않다	중요 하지 않다		중요하다	아주 중요 하다
가족이나 사회를 위해 해야 하는 어쩔 수 없는 의무감 때문에	전혀 중요하지 않다	중요 하지 않다		중요하다	아주 중요 하다
가족이나 다른 사람들에 대한 책임감 때문에	전혀 중요하지 않다	중요 하지 않다		중요하다	아주 중요 하다
다른 사람에게 무조건적인 사랑을 베푸는 것이 중요하기 때문에	전혀 중요하지 않다	중요 하지 않다		중요하다	아주 중요 하다
나의 개인적인 자존심과 품위를 지키고 싶어서	전혀 중요하지 않다	중요 하지 않다		중요하다	아주 중요 하다
다른 사람에게 관대하고 나누어 주는 사람으로 보여지고 싶어서	전혀 중요하지 않다	중요 하지 않다		중요하다	아주 중요 하다
나는 원래 다른 사람에게 잘 양보하는 성격을 가지고 있어서	전혀 중요하지 않다	중요 하지 않다		중요하다	아주 중요 하다
나는 희생이 일방적인 것이 아니라 서로 상호적이고, 서로 섬기는 것이라는 것이라고 생각하기 때문에	전혀 중요하지 않다	중요 하지 않다		중요하다	아주 중요 하다
나의 종교적인 믿음 때문에, 다른 사람의 필요를 늘 먼저 생각해야 하기 때문에	전혀 중요하지 않다	중요 하지 않다		중요하다	아주 중요 하다

Appendix

나는 유교적인 문화에서 자라와서, 그 영향으로 잘 양보하는 편이기 때문에	1 전혀 중요하지 않다	2 중요 하지 않다	3	4 중요하다	5 아주 중요 하다

C. 직장에서 상사와의 관계

	1	2	3	4	5
갈등을 피하고, 화목을 유지하고 싶어서	전혀 중요하지 않다	중요 하지 않다		중요하다	아주 중요 하다
가족이나 사회를 위해 해야 하는 어쩔 수 없는 의무감 때문에	전혀 중요하지 않다	중요 하지 않다		중요하다	아주 중요 하다
가족이나 다른 사람들에 대한 책임감 때문에	전혀 중요하지 않다	중요 하지 않다		중요하다	아주 중요 하다
다른 사람에게 무조건적인 사랑을 베푸는 것이 중요하기 때문에	전혀 중요하지 않다	중요 하지 않다		중요하다	아주 중요 하다
나의 개인적인 자존심과 품위를 지키고 싶어서	전혀 중요하지 않다	중요 하지 않다		중요하다	아주 중요 하다
다른 사람에게 관대하고 나누어 주는 사람으로 보여지고 싶어서	전혀 중요하지 않다	중요 하지 않다		중요하다	아주 중요 하다
나는 원래 다른 사람에게 잘 양보하는 성격을 가지고 있어서	전혀 중요하지 않다	중요 하지 않다		중요하다	아주 중요 하다

Appendix

나는 희생이 일방적인 것이 아니라 서로 상호적이고, 서로 섬기는 것이라는 것이라고 생각하기 때문에	1 전혀 중요하지 않다	2 중요 하지 않다	3	4 중요하다	5 아주 중요 하다
나의 종교적인 믿음 때문에, 다른 사람의 필요를 늘 먼저 생각해야 하기 때문에	1 전혀 중요하지 않다	2 중요 하지 않다	3	4 중요하다	5 아주 중요 하다
나는 유교적인 문화에서 자라와서, 그 영향으로 잘 양보하는 편이기 때문에	1 전혀 중요하지 않다	2 중요 하지 않다	3	4 중요하다	5 아주 중요 하다

D. 교회에서 교역자와 성도와의 관계

갈등을 피하고, 화목을 유지하고 싶어서	1 전혀 중요하지 않다	2 중요 하지 않다	3	4 중요하다	5 아주 중요 하다
가족이나 사회를 위해 해야 하는 어쩔 수 없는 의무감 때문에	1 전혀 중요하지 않다	2 중요 하지 않다	3	4 중요하다	5 아주 중요 하다
가족이나 다른 사람들에 대한 책임감 때문에	1 전혀 중요하지 않다	2 중요 하지 않다	3	4 중요하다	5 아주 중요 하다
다른 사람에게 무조건적인 사랑을 베푸는 것이 중요하기 때문에	1 전혀 중요하지 않다	2 중요 하지 않다	3	4 중요하다	5 아주 중요 하다
나의 개인적인 자존심과 품위를 지키고 싶어서	1 전혀 중요하지 않다	2 중요 하지 않다	3	4 중요하다	5 아주 중요 하다

Appendix

다른 사람에게 관대하고 나누어 주는 사람으로 보여지고 싶어서	1 전혀 중요하지 않다	2 중요 하지 않다	3	4 중요하다	5 아주 중요 하다
나는 원래 다른 사람에게 잘 양보하는 성격을 가지고 있어서	1 전혀 중요하지 않다	2 중요 하지 않다	3	4 중요하다	5 아주 중요 하다
나는 희생이 일방적인 것이 아니라 서로 상호적이고, 서로 섬기는 것이라는 것이라고 생각하기 때문에	1 전혀 중요하지 않다	2 중요 하지 않다	3	4 중요하다	5 아주 중요 하다
나의 종교적인 믿음 때문에, 다른 사람의 필요를 늘 먼저 생각해야 하기 때문에	1 전혀 중요하지 않다	2 중요 하지 않다	3	4 중요하다	5 아주 중요 하다
나는 유교적인 문화에서 자라와서, 그 영향으로 잘 양보하는 편이기 때문에	1 전혀 중요하지 않다	2 중요 하지 않다	3	4 중요하다	5 아주 중요 하다

E. 학교에서 교사와 학생과의 관계

갈등을 피하고, 화목을 유지하고 싶어서	1 전혀 중요하지 않다	2 중요 하지 않다	3	4 중요하다	5 아주 중요 하다
가족이나 사회를 위해 해야 하는 어쩔 수 없는 의무감 때문에	1 전혀 중요하지 않다	2 중요 하지 않다	3	4 중요하다	5 아주 중요 하다
가족이나 다른 사람들에 대한 책임감 때문에	1 전혀 중요하지 않다	2 중요 하지 않다	3	4 중요하다	5 아주 중요 하다

Appendix

다른 사람에게 무조건적인 사랑을 베푸는 것이 중요하기 때문에	1 전혀 중요하지 않다	2 중요 하지 않다	3	4 중요하다	5 아주 중요하다
나의 개인적인 자존심과 품위를 지키고 싶어서	1 전혀 중요하지 않다	2 중요 하지 않다	3	4 중요하다	5 아주 중요하다
다른 사람에게 관대하고 나누어 주는 사람으로 보여지고 싶어서	1 전혀 중요하지 않다	2 중요 하지 않다	3	4 중요하다	5 아주 중요하다
나는 원래 다른 사람에게 잘 양보하는 성격을 가지고 있어서	1 전혀 중요하지 않다	2 중요 하지 않다	3	4 중요하다	5 아주 중요하다
나는 희생이 일방적인 것이 아니라 서로 상호적이고, 서로 섬기는 것이라는 것이라고 생각하기 때문에	1 전혀 중요하지 않다	2 중요 하지 않다	3	4 중요하다	5 아주 중요하다
나의 종교적인 믿음 때문에, 다른 사람의 필요를 늘 먼저 생각해야 하기 때문에	1 전혀 중요하지 않다	2 중요 하지 않다	3	4 중요하다	5 아주 중요하다
나는 유교적인 문화에서 자라와서, 그 영향으로 잘 양보하는 편이기 때문에	1 전혀 중요하지 않다	2 중요 하지 않다	3	4 중요하다	5 아주 중요하다

F. 친구나 동료와의 관계

갈등을 피하고, 화목을 유지하고 싶어서	1 전혀 중요하지 않다	2 중요 하지 않다	3	4 중요하다	5 아주 중요하다

Appendix

| 가족이나 사회를 위해 해야 하는 어쩔 수 없는 의무감 때문에 | 1
전혀 중요하지 않다 | 2
중요 하지 않다 | 3 | 4
중요하다 | 5
아주 중요 하다 |

| 가족이나 다른 사람들에 대한 책임감 때문에 | 1
전혀 중요하지 않다 | 2
중요 하지 않다 | 3 | 4
중요하다 | 5
아주 중요 하다 |

| 다른 사람에게 무조건적인 사랑을 베푸는 것이 중요하기 때문에 | 1
전혀 중요하지 않다 | 2
중요 하지 않다 | 3 | 4
중요하다 | 5
아주 중요 하다 |

| 나의 개인적인 자존심과 품위를 지키고 싶어서 | 1
전혀 중요하지 않다 | 2
중요 하지 않다 | 3 | 4
중요하다 | 5
아주 중요 하다 |

| 다른 사람에게 관대하고 나누어 주는 사람으로 보여지고 싶어서 | 1
전혀 중요하지 않다 | 2
중요 하지 않다 | 3 | 4
중요하다 | 5
아주 중요 하다 |

| 나는 원래 다른 사람에게 잘 양보하는 성격을 가지고 있어서 | 1
전혀 중요하지 않다 | 2
중요 하지 않다 | 3 | 4
중요하다 | 5
아주 중요 하다 |

| 나는 희생이 일방적인 것이 아니라 서로 상호적이고, 서로 섬기는 것이라는 것이라고 생각하기 때문에 | 1
전혀 중요하지 않다 | 2
중요 하지 않다 | 3 | 4
중요하다 | 5
아주 중요 하다 |

| 나의 종교적인 믿음 때문에, 다른 사람의 필요를 늘 먼저 생각해야 하기 때문에 | 1
전혀 중요하지 않다 | 2
중요 하지 않다 | 3 | 4
중요하다 | 5
아주 중요 하다 |

| 나는 유교적인 문화에서 자라와서, 그 영향으로 잘 양보하는 편이기 때문에 | 1
전혀 중요하지 않다 | 2
중요 하지 않다 | 3 | 4
중요하다 | 5
아주 중요 하다 |

Bibliography

Adams, Carol J. *Woman-Battering*. Creative Pastoral Care and Counseling Series. Minneapolis: Fortress, 1994.
Anderson, Herbert, Don S. Browning, Ian S. Evison, and Mary Stewart Van Leeuwen, editors. *The Family Handbook*. Louisville: Westminster John Knox, 1998.
Anderson, Herbert, David Hogue, and Marie McCarthy. *Promising Again*. Louisville: Westminster John Knox, 1995.
Anderson, Ray S. *The Shape of Practical Theology: Empowering Ministry with Theological Praxis*. Downers Grove: InterVarsity, 2001.
———. *The Soul of Ministry: Forming Leaders for God's People*. Louisville: Westminster John Knox, 1997.
———. *On Being Human: Essays in Theological Anthropology*. Pasadena, CA: Fuller Seminary Press, 1982.
Anderson, Ray S., and Dennis B. Guernsey. *On Being Family: A Social Theology of the Family*. Grand Rapids: Eerdmans, 1985.
Asian Women United of California, editors. *Making Waves: An Anthology of Writings by and about Asian American Women*. Boston: Beacon, 1989.
Atkinson, David. *To Have and to Hold: The Marriage Covenant and the Discipline of Divorce*. Grand Rapids: Eerdmans, 1979.
Augsburger, David W. *Caring Enough to Forgive: True Forgiveness*. Venture, CA: Regal, 1981.
———. *Caring Enough to Not Forgive: False Forgiveness*. Ventura, CA: Regal, 1983.
———. *Conflict Mediation across Cultures: Pathways and Patterns*. Louisville: Westminster John Knox, 1992.
———. *Dissident Discipleship: A Spirituality of Self-Surrender, Love of God, and Love of Neighbor*. Grand Rapids: Brazos, 2006.
———. *The Freedom of Forgiveness*. Chicago: Moody, 1988.
———. *Hate-Work: Working through the Pain and Pleasures of Hate*. Louisville: Westminster John Knox, 2004.
———. *Helping People Forgive*. Louisville: Westminster John Knox, 1996.
———. *Pastoral Counseling across Cultures*. Philadelphia: Westminster, 1986.
———. *Sustaining Love: Healing & Growth in the Passages of Marriage*. Ventura, CA: Regal, 1988.
Bahr, Howard M., and Kathleen S. Bahr. "Families and Self-Sacrifice: Alternative Models and Meanings for Family Theory." *Social Forces* 79 (2001) 1231–58.

Bibliography

Bahr, Kathleen S. "Families, Children, and Self-Sacrifice." *World Family Policy Forum,* 2001, 30–35. http://www.law2.byu.edu/wfpc/forum/2001/bahr.pdf.

Balswick, Jack O., and Judith K. Balswick. *The Family: A Christian Perspective on the Contemporary Home.* Grand Rapids: Baker, 1999.

Barnett, Ola W., et al. *Family Violence across the Lifespan: An Introduction.* Thousand Oaks, CA: Sage, 1997.

Bartchy, S. Scott. "Power, Submission, and Sexual Identity among the Early Christians." In *Essays on New Testament Christianity,* edited by C. Robert Wetzel, 50–80. Cincinnati: Standard, 1978.

Barton, Stephen C., editor. *The Family in Theological Perspective.* Edinburgh: T. & T. Clark, 1996.

Beek, Aart M. van. *Cross-Cultural Counseling.* Creative Pastoral Care and Counseling Series. Minneapolis: Fortress, 1996.

Beels, C. Christian, and Margaret Newmark. "Sacrifice: A Clinical View." *Family Process* 45 (2006) 305–9.

Bell, Norman W., and Ezra F. Vogel, editors. *A Modern Introduction to the Family.* New York: Free Press, 1968.

Bellah, Robert N., et al. *Habits of the Heart: Individualism and Commitment in American Life.* New York: Harper & Row, 1985.

Benner, David G., and Peter C. Hill, editors. *Baker Encyclopedia of Psychology & Counseling.* Grand Rapids: Baker, 1985.

Berry, Carmen Renee. *When Helping You Is Hurting Me: Escape the Messiah Trap.* New York: Crossroad, 2003.

Bilezikian, Gilbert G. *Beyond Sex Roles: What the Bible Says about a Woman's Place in Church and Family.* Grand Rapids: Baker, 1986.

Bowen, Murray. *Family Therapy in Clinical Practice.* New York: Aronson, 1978.

Brownback, Paul. *The Danger of Self-Love: Re-examining a Popular Myth.* Chicago: Moody, 1982.

Browning, Don S. *A Fundamental Practical Theology: Descriptive and Strategic Proposals.* Minneapolis: Fortress, 1991.

———. *Religious Thought and the Modern Psychology: A Critical Conversation in the Theology of Culture.* Philadelphia: Fortress, 1987.

Browning, Don S., et al. *From Culture Wars to Common Ground: Religion and the American Family Debate.* 2nd ed. Louisville: Westminster John Knox, 2000.

Buswell, Roberts E., Jr., editor. *Religions of Korea in Practice.* Princeton: Princeton University Press, 2007.

Buzawa, Eva S., and Carl G. Buzawa. *Domestic Violence: The Criminal Justice Response.* 2nd ed. Thousand Oak, CA: Sage, 1996.

Caplan, Paula J. *The Myth of Women's Masochism.* New York: Dutton, 1985.

Carse, James P. "Interracial Marriage: A Christian View." *Christian Century* 84 (1967) 779–82.

Cazenave, N. A., and Murray A. Straus. "Race, Class, Network Embeddedness and Family Violence: A Search for Parent Support System." *Journal of Comparative Family Studies* 10 (1979) 281–300.

Chantry, Walter J. *The Shadow of the Cross: Studies in Self-Denial.* Edinburgh: Banner of Truth, 1981.

Ching, Julia. *Confucianism and Christianity: A Comparative Study.* Tokyo: Kodansha International, 1977.

Bibliography

Cho, Kung-ho. *Maengja e Nat'anan Simnihakjok Hamui*. Vol. 5, part 1, *Insungnon ul Chungsim uro*. Seoul: Han'guk Simnihakjihoe: Sahoe, 1991.

Ch'oe, Chun-sik. *Han'guk Chonggyo Munhwa ro Ilnunda*. Vol. 1, *Mugyo, Yugyo, Bulgyo*. Kyonggi-do P'aju-si: Sagyejol Ch'ulp'ansa, 2004.

Ch'ae, Mu-song. *T'oegye Yulgok Ch'olhak ui Pigyo Yon'gu*. Seoul: Songgyungwan Taehakgyo Ch'ulp'anbu, 1985.

Cheung, Maria. "A Cross-Cultural Comparison of Gender Factors Contributing to Long-Term Marital Satisfaction: A Narrative Analysis." *Journal of Couple & Relationship Therapy* 4 (2005) 51–78.

Chong, Tong-sop. "Yugyo ui Sujik Yulli ka Han'gukin ui Kyolhon e Mich'in Yonghyang e taehan Kidokkyojok Pyongkka: Chedojok Kyolhon eso Tongbanjajok Kyolhon uro." In *Christian Counseling and Family Therapy*, vol. 3, by Bruce Litchfield and Nellie Litchfield, 77–91. Translated by Chong Tong-sop and Chong Sung-jun. Seoul: Yesujungdodan, 2002.

Christ, Carol P., and Judith Plaskow, editors. *Womanspirit Rising: A Feminist Reader in Religion*. New York: Harper & Row, 1979.

Chun, Shin-Yong. *Korean Society*. Korean Cultural Series 6. Seoul: International Cultural Foundation, 1982.

Clarke, Rita-Lou. *Pastoral Care of Battered Women*. Philadelphia: Westminster, 1986.

Cloud, Henry, and John Townsend. *Boundaries in Marriage*. Grand Rapids: Zondervan, 1999.

Cormack, Margaret, editor. *Sacrificing the Self: Perspectives on Martyrdom and Religion*. New York: Oxford University Press, 2001.

Couture, Pamela D., and Rodney J. Hunter, editors. *Pastoral Care and Social Conflict*. Nashville: Abingdon, 1995.

Crohn, Joel. "Asian Intermarriage: Love versus Tradition." In *Working with Asian Americans: A Guide for Clinicians*, edited by Evelyn Lee., 428–38. New York: Guilford, 1997.

———. "Intercultural Couples." In *Re-visioning Family Therapy: Race, Culture, and Gender in Clinical Practice*, edited by Monica McGoldrick, 295–308. New York: Guilford, 1998.

Crowell, Nancy A., and Ann W. Burgess, editors. *Understanding Violence against Women*. Washington, DC: National Academy, 1996.

David, James R. "The Theology of Murray Bowen or the Marital Triangle." *Journal of Psychology and Theology* 7 (1979) 259–62.

Deuchler, Martina, and Sandra Mattielli. *Virtues in Conflict: Tradition and the Korean Women Today*. Seoul: Samhaw, 1977.

Dillen, Annemie. "Holy Families? Religion, Sacrifice and Family Violence." *Irish Theological Quarterly* 71 (2006) 260–71.

Dobash, R. Emerson, and Russell Dobash. *Violence against Wives: A Case against Patriarchy*. New York: Free Press, 1979.

Driskill, Lawrence J. *Cross-Cultural Marriages and the Church: Living the Global Neighborhood*. Pasadena, CA: Hope, 1995.

Dueck, Alvin, and Cameron Lee, editors. *Why Psychology Needs Theology: A Radical-Reformation Perspective*. Grand Rapids: Eerdmans, 2005.

Dutton, Donald G. *The Domestic Assault of Women: Psychological and Criminal Justice Perspectives*. Boston: Allyn & Bacon, 1988.

Bibliography

Edwards, R. Randle, et al. *Human Rights in Contemporary China.* Studies of the East India Institute. New York: Columbia University Press, 1986.
Ferguson, Susan J. "Challenging Traditional Marriage: Never Married Chinese American and Japanese American Women." *Gender & Society* 14 (2000) 136–59.
Finkelhor, David, et al., editors. *The Dark Side of Families: Current Family Violence Research.* Beverly Hills, CA: Sage, 1983.
Fisher, Roger, and Scott Brown. *Getting Together: Building Relationships as We Negotiate.* New York: Penguin, 1988.
Fisher, Roger, William Ury, and Bruce Patton. *Getting to Yes: Negotiating Agreement without Giving In.* 2nd ed. New York: Penguin, 1991.
Forrester, Duncan B. *Truthful Action: Explorations in Practical Theology.* Edinburgh: T. & T. Clark, 2000.
Fortune, Marie Marshall. *Sexual Violence; The Unmentionable Sin.* New York: Pilgrim, 1983.
Friedman, Edwin H. *Generation to Generation: Family Process in Church and Synagogue.* New York: Guilford, 1985.
Frieze, Irene Hanson, et al. *Women and Sex Roles: A Social Psychological Perspective.* New York: Norton, 1978.
Gale, James S. "A History of the Korean People." *Korean Mission Field*, September 1926.
Gilligan, Carol, et al., editors. *Making Connections: The Relational Worlds of Adolescent Girls at Emma Willard School.* Cambridge: Harvard University Press, 1990.
Girard, René. *Violence and the Sacred.* Baltimore: Johns Hopkins University Press, 1977.
———. *The Scapegoat.* Baltimore: Johns Hopkins University Press, 1986.
Glaz, Maxine, and Jeanne Stevenson Moessner, editors. *Women in Travail and Transition: A New Pastoral Care.* Minneapolis: Fortress, 1991.
Glucklich, Ariel. *Sacred Pain: Hurting the Body for the Sake of the Soul.* New York: Oxford University Press, 2001.
Gordon, Albert Isaac. *Intermarriage: Interfaith, Interracial, Interethnic.* Boston: Beacon, 1964.
Graham, Larry Kent, and Marie M. Fortune. "Empowering the Congregation to Respond to Sexual Abuse and Domestic Violence." *Pastoral Psychology* 41 (1993) 337–45.
Greenfield, Patricia M., and Rodney R. Cocking, editors. *Cross-Cultural Roots of Minority Child Development.* Hillsdale, NJ: Erlbaum, 1994.
Groothuis, Rebecca Merrill. *Good News for Women: A Biblical Picture of Gender Equality.* Grand Rapids: Baker, 1997.
Ha, Tae Hung. *Folk Customs and Family Life.* Korean Cultural Series 3. Seoul: Korea Information Service, 1958.
Hall, C. Margaret. *The Bowen Family Theory and Its Uses.* New York: Aronson, 1981.
Hall, Douglas John. *Thinking the Faith: Christian Theology in a North American Context.* Minneapolis: Augsburg, 1989.
Harris, Joseph. "Interracial Counseling: A Pastoral Approach." *Journal of Pastoral Counseling* 22 (1987) 105–16.
Haugk, Kenneth C. *Christian Caregiving: A Way of Life.* Minneapolis: Augsburg, 1984.
Hess, Carol Lakey. *Caretakers of Our Common House: Women's Development in Communities of Faith.* Nashville: Abingdon, 1997.
Hestenes, Roberta, compiler. *Women and Men in Ministry: Collected Readings.* Pasadena, CA: Fuller Theological Seminary, 1988.
Ho, Man Keung. *Family Therapy with Ethnic Minorities.* Newbury Park, CA: Sage, 1987.

———. *Intermarried Couples in Therapy.* Springfield, IL: Thomas, 1990.
Hoekema, Anthony A. *The Christian Looks at Himself.* Grand Rapids: Eerdmans, 1975.
Hoffman, Lynn. *Family Therapy: An Intimate History.* New York: Norton, 2002.
Hong, Suk-ki. *Il kwa Simnihak.* Seoul: Nanam Ch'ulp'ansa, 1994.
Horton, Anne L., and Judith A Williamson, editors. *Abuse and Religion: When Praying Isn't Enough.* Lexington, MA: Lexington, 1988.
Huang, Wei-Jen. "An Asian Perspective on Relationship and Marriage Education." *Family Process* 44 (2005) 161–73.
Huisman, Kimberly A. "Wife Battering in Asian American Communities: Identifying the Service Needs of an Overlooked Segment of the U.S. Population." *Violence Against Women* 2 (1996) 260–83.
Hunter, Rodney J., editor. *Dictionary of Pastoral Care and Counseling.* Nashville: Abingdon, 1990.
Hwang, Kwang-Kuo. "Filial Piety and Loyalty: Two Types of Social Identification in Confucianism." *Asian Journal of Social Psychology* 2 (1999) 163–83.
Hyon, Sang-yun. *Chosun Yuhaksa.* Seoul: Minjungsogwan, 1960.
Ingoldsby, Bron B., and Suzanna Smith, editors. *Families in Multicultural Perspective.* New York: Guilford, 1995.
Jewett, Paul K. *Man as Male and Female: A Study in Sexual Relationships from a Theological Point of View.* Grand Rapids: Eerdmans, 1975.
Johnson, Michael P. "Patriarchal Terrorism and Common Couple Violence: Two Forms of Violence against Women." *Journal of Marriage and the Family* 57 (1996) 283–93.
Johnson, Walton R., and D. Michael Warren, editors. *Inside the Mixed Marriage: Accounts of Changing Attitudes, Patterns, and Perceptions of Cross-Cultural and Interracial Marriage.* Lanham, MD: University Press of America, 1994.
Jones, L. Gregory. *Embodying Forgiveness: A Theological Analysis.* Grand Rapids: Eerdmans, 1995.
Kang, K. Connie. *Home Was the Land of Morning Calm: A Saga of a Korean-American Family.* Cambridge, MA: Da Capo, 1995.
Kang, Nam-Soon. "Confucian Familism and Its Social/Religious Embodiment in Christianity: Reconsidering the Family Discourse from a Feminist Perspective." *Asia Journal of Theology* 18 (2004) 168–89.
———. "Creating Dangerous Memory: Challenges for Asian and Korean Feminist Theology." *Ecumenical Review* 47 (1995) 21–31.
Keener, Craig S. *Paul, Women & Wives: Marriage and Women's Ministry in the Letters of Paul.* Peabody, MA: Hendrickson, 1992.
Kendall, Laurel, and Mark Peterson, editors. *Korean Women: View from the Inner Room.* New Haven, CT: East Rock, 1983.
Kenneson, Phillip D. *Life on the Vine: Cultivating the Fruit of the Spirit in Christian Community.* Downers Grove: InterVarsity, 1999.
Kim, Dong-soo. "The Healing of Han in Korean Pentecostalism." *Journal of Pentecostal Theology* 15 (1999) 123–39.
Kim, Grace. "Oppression and Han: Korean Women's Historical Context." *Journal of Asian and Asian American Theology* (1999) 55–70.
Kim, Kyong-il. *Kongja ka Chugoya Nara ka Sanda.* Seoul: Pada Ch'ulp'ansa, 1999.
Kim, Myung-hye. "Transformation on Family Ideology in Upper-Middle-Class Families in Urban South Korea." *Ethnology* 32 (1993) 69–85.

Bibliography

Kim, Yon-tak. *Han'guk Chonggyo wa Kyohoe Songjang*. Seoul: Taehan Sinhak Taehakwon Ch'ulp'anbu, 1998.

Ko, Dorothy, et al., editors. *Women and Confucian Cultures in Premodern China, Korea, and Japan*. Berkeley: University of California Press, 2003.

Kostenberger, Andreas J. *God, Marriage, and Family: Rebuilding the Biblical Foundation*. Wheaton, IL: Crossway, 2004.

Kraybill, Donald B. *The Upside-Down Kingdom*. Scottdale, PA: Herald, 1990.

Kroeger, Catherine Clark, and James R. Beck, editors. *Healing the Hurting: Giving Hope and Help to Abused Women*. Grand Rapids: Baker, 1998.

Kum, Chang-tae. *Han'guk Yuhaksa ui Ihae*. Minjok Munhwasa: Soul T'ukp'yol-si, 1994.

Kung, Hans, and Jürgen Moltmann, editors. *The Ethics of World Religions and Human Rights*. London: SCM, 1990.

Law, Eric H. F. *Inclusion: Making Room for Grace*. St. Louis: Chalice, 2000.

Lee, Evelyn, editor. *Working with Asian Americans: A Guide for Clinicians*. New York: Guilford, 1997.

Lerner, Harriet Goldhor. *The Dance of Anger: A Woman's Guide to Changing the Patterns of Intimate Relationships*. New York: Harper & Row, 1985.

———. *Women in Therapy*. Northvale, NJ: Aronson, 1988.

Lewinsohn, Mark A., and Paul D. Werner. "Factors in Chinese Marital Process: Relationship to Marital Adjustment." *Family Process* 36 (1997) 43–61.

Litonjua, M. D. "Global Capitalism: The New Context of Christian Social Ethics." *Theology Today* 56 (1999) 210–28.

Luepnitz, Deborah Anna. *The Family Interpreted: Feminist Theory in Clinical Practice*. New York: Basic Books, 1988.

Macquarrie, John. *Principles of Christian Theology*. New York: Scribner, 1977.

Magli, Ida. *Women and Self-Sacrifice in the Christian Church: A Cultural History from the First to the Nineteenth Century*. Translated by Janet Sethre. Jefferson, NC: McFarland, 2003.

Martin, Grant L. *Counseling for Family Violence and Abuse*. Edited by Gary R. Collins, translated by Yeon Kim. Seoul: Tyrannus, 1995.

Mason, Mike. *The Mystery of Marriage*. Sisters, OR: Multnomah, 1985.

McAdoo, Harriette Pipes, editor. *Family Ethnicity: Strength in Diversity*. Newbury Park, CA: Sage, 1993.

McCullough, Michael E., et al. *To Forgive Is Human: How to Put Your Past in the Past*. Downers Grove: InterVarsity, 1997.

McFadden, Thomas M., editor. *Liberation, Revolution, and Freedom: Theological Perspectives*. New York: Seabury, 1975.

McGoldrick, Monica, editor. *Re-visioning Family Therapy: Race, Culture, and Gender in Clinical Practice*. New York: Guilford, 1998.

Mickelsen, Alvera, editor. *Women, Authority & the Bible*. Downers Grove: InterVarsity, 1986.

Miller, Alice. *For Your Own Good: Hidden Cruelty in Child-Rearing and the Roots of Violence*. New York: Noonday, 1990.

Miller, Melissa A. *Family Violence: The Compassionate Church Responds*. Scottdale, PA: Herald, 1994.

Min, Pyong Gap. "The Korean-American Family." In *Ethnic Families in America: Patterns and Variations*, edited by Charles H. Mindel et al., 174–198. New York: Elsevier, 1981.

Mindel, Charles H., and Robert W. Habenstein, editors. *Ethnic Families in America: Patterns and Variations*. 2nd ed. New York: Elsevier, 1981.

Bibliography

Moessner, Jeanne Stevenson, editor. *Through the Eyes of Women: Insights for Pastoral Care.* Minneapolis: Fortress, 1996.

Moltmann, Jürgen. *The Crucified God: The Cross of Christ as the Foundation and Criticism of Christian Theology.* New York: Harper & Row, 1974.

———. *Theology of Hope: On the Ground and the Implications of a Christian Eschatology.* New York: Harper & Row, 1967.

Monfalcone, Wesley R. *Coping with Abuse in the Family.* Philadelphia: Westminster, 1980.

Mortenson, Steven T. "Sex, Communication Values, and Cultural Values: Individualism-Collectivism as a Mediator of Sex Differences in Communication Values in Two Cultures." *Communication Report* 12 (2002) 57–70.

Mouton, Jane Srygley, and Robert R. Blake. *The Marriage Grid.* New York: McGraw-Hill, 1971.

Narramore, Bruce. *You're Someone Special.* Grand Rapids: Zondervan, 1978.

Nason-Clark, Nancy. *The Battered Wife: How Christians Confront Family Violence.* Louisville: Westminster John Knox, 1997.

Neuger, Christie Cozad. *Counseling Women: A Narrative Pastoral Approach.* Minneapolis: Fortress, 2001.

Neuger, Christie Cozad, and James Newton Poling, editors. *The Care of Men.* Nashville: Abingdon, 1997.

Nichols, Michael P. *Inside Family Therapy: A Case Study in Family Healing.* Boston: Allyn & Bacon, 1999.

Nichols, Michael P., and Richard C. Schwarts. *Family Therapy: Concepts and Methods.* Boston: Allyn & Bacon, 1998.

Noddings, Nel. *Caring: A Feminine Approach to Ethics & Moral Education.* Los Angeles: University of California Press, 1984.

Oh, Byung-sun. "Cultural Values and Human Rights: The Korean Perspective." *Focus* 11 (1998) no pages. http://www.hurights.or.jp/asia-pacific/no_11/no11_korean.htm. This article is a short version of the research paper included in *Human Rights in Asian Cultures, Continuity, and Change.* Edited by Jefferson R. Plantilla et al. Osaka: Hurights Osaka, 1997.

Oh, Jung Sun. *A Korean Theology of Human Nature: With Special Attention to the Works of Robert Cummings Neville and Tu Wei-ming.* Lanham, MD: University Press of America, 2005.

Olsen, V. Norskov. *The New Relatedness for Man and Woman in Christ: A Mirror of the Divine.* Loma Linda, CA: Loma Linda University, Center for Christian Bioethics, 1993.

Outka, Gene. *Agape: An Ethical Analysis.* New Haven: Yale University Press, 1972.

Pak, Min-ja. *Kajok kwa Han'guk Sahoe: Pyonhwahanun Han'guk Kajok ui Sam Ilkki.* Soul T'ukp'yolsi: Kyongmunsa, 1995.

Palmer, George Herbert. *The Nature of Goodness.* Boston: Houghton, Mifflin, 1903.

Park, Andrew S. *The Wounded Heart of God: The Asian Concept of Han and the Christian Doctrine of Sin.* Nashville: Abingdon, 1993.

Park, Insook Han, and Lee-Jay Cho. "Confucianism and the Korean Family." *Journal of Comparative Family Studies* 26 (1995) 117–34.

Park, Lisa Sun-Hee. *Consuming Citizenship: Children of Asian Immigrant Entrepreneurs.* Stanford: Stanford University Press, 2005.

Patton, John. *Is Human Forgiveness Possible? A Pastoral Care Perspective.* Nashville: Abingdon, 1985.

Bibliography

Patton, John., and Brian H. Childs. *Christian Marriage & Family: Caring for Our Generations.* Nashville: Abingdon, 1988.

Piper, John, "Is Self-Love Biblical?" *Christianity Today,* August 12, 1977.

Prinzing, Fred, and Anita Prinzing. *Mixed Messages: Responding to Interracial Marriage.* Chicago: Moody, 1991.

Rassieur, Charles L. *Pastor, Our Marriage Is in Trouble: A Guide to Short-Term Counseling.* Philadelphia: Westminster, 1988.

Remele, Kurt. "Self-Denial or Self-Actualization? Therapeutic Culture and Christian Ethics." *Theology* 99 (1997) 18–25.

Richardson, Alan, editor. *A Theological Word Book of the Bible.* New York: Macmillan, 1950.

Richardson, Ronald W. *Creating a Healthier Church: Family Systems Theory, Leadership, and Congregational Life.* Minneapolis: Fortress, 1996.

Romano, Dugan. *Intercultural Marriage: Promises & Pitfalls.* 2nd ed. Yarmouth, ME: Intercultural, 2001.

Root, Maria P. P. *Love's Revolution: Interracial Marriage.* Philadelphia: Temple University Press, 2001.

Rosenlee, Li-Hsiang Lisa. *Confucianism and Women: A Philosophical Interpretation.* New York: State University of New York Press, 2006.

Rozman, Gilbert, editor. *The East Asian Region: Confucian Heritage and Its Modern Adaptation.* Princeton: Princeton University Press, 1991.

Sarnoff, Irving, and Suzanne Sarnoff. *Love-Centered Marriage in a Self-Centered World.* New York: Hemisphere, 1989.

Satir, Virginia. *People Making.* Palo Alto, CA: Science & Behavior, 1972.

Scanzoni, John. *Love and Negotiate: Creative Conflict in Marriage.* Waco, TX: Word, 1979.

Schewe, Paul A., editor. *Preventing Violence in Relationships: Interventions across the Life Span.* Washington, DC: American Psychological Association, 2002.

Shults, F. LeRon, and Steven J. Sandage. *The Faces of Forgiveness: Searching for Wholeness and Salvation.* Grand Rapids: Baker Academic, 2003.

Shupe, Anson D., et al. *Violent Men, Violent Couples: The Dynamics of Domestic Violence.* Lexington, MA: Lexington, 1987.

Smoke, Jim. *Growing through Divorce.* Eugene, OR: Harvest House, 1976.

Sölle, Dorothee. *Beyond Mere Obedience.* Translated by Lawrence W. Denef. New York: Pilgrim, 1982.

———. *Suffering.* Translated by Everett R. Kalin. Philadelphia: Fortress, 1975.

Song, Young-Bae. "Crisis of Cultural Identity in East Asia: On the Meaning of Confucian Ethic in the Age of Globalization." *Asian Philosophy* 12 (2002) 109–25.

SteinhoffSmith, Roy Herndon. *The Mutuality of Care.* St. Louis: Chalice, 1999.

Steinmetz, Suzanne K. *The Cycle of Violence: Assertive, Aggressive, and Abusive Family Interaction.* New York: Praeger, 1977.

———. "The Battered Husband Syndrome." *Victimology* 2 (1977/78) 499–509.

Stets, Jan E., and Murray A. Straus. "The Marriage License as a Hitting License: A Comparison of Assaults in Dating, Cohabiting, and Married Couples." *Journal of Family Violence* 41 (1989) 33–52.

Stone, Howard W. *Theological Context for Pastoral Caregiving: Word in Deed.* New York: Haworth Pastoral, 1996.

Stott, John R. W. "Must I Really Love Myself?" *Christianity Today,* May 5, 1978.

Straus, Murray A. "Wife Beating: How Common and Why?" *Victimology* 2 (1977) 443–58.

Bibliography

Straus, Murray A., et al. *Behind Closed Doors: Violence in the American Family*. Garden City, NY: Anchor, 1981.
Sung, Kyu-t'ak. *Hyondae Han'gukin ui Hyo: Chont'ong ui Chisok kwa P'yohyon ui Pyonhwa*. Chipmundang: Kyonggi-do, P'aju-si, 2005.
Taylor, Ronald L., editor. *Minority Families in the United States: A Multicultural Perspective*. Upper Saddle River, NJ: Prentice Hall, 1994.
Travis, Carol. *Anger: The Misunderstood Emotion*. New York: Touchstone, 1989.
Trobisch, Walter. *Love Yourself: Self-Acceptance & Depression*. Downers Grove: InterVarsity, 1976.
Tu, Wei-ming. *Confucian Thought: Selfhood as Creative Transformation*. Albany: State University of New York Press, 1985.
Turpin, Jennifer, and Lester R. Kurtz, editors. *The Web of Violence: From Interpersonal to Global*. Chicago: University of Illinois Press, 1997.
Van Lange, Paul A. M., et al. "Willingness to Sacrifice in Close Relationships." *Journal of Personality and Social Psychology* 72 (1997) 1373–95.
Viano, Emilio C., editor. *Intimate Violence: Interdisciplinary Perspectives*. Washington: Hemisphere, 1992.
Vitz, Paul C. *Psychology as Religion: The Cult of Self-Worship*. Grand Rapids: Eerdmans, 1977.
Waanders, David D. "Ethical Reflections on the Differentiation of Self in Marriage." *Journal of Pastoral Care* 41 (1987): 100–110.
Walker, Lenore E. *The Battered Woman Syndrome*. Focus on Women 6. New York: Springer, 1984.
Wehrly, Bea, et al. *Counseling Multiracial Families*. Multicultural Aspects of Counseling Series 12. Thousand Oaks, CA: Sage, 1999.
West, Traci C. *Wounds of the Spirit: Black Women, Violence, and Resistance Ethics*. New York: New York University Press, 1999.
Wilmot, William W., and Joyce L. Hocker. *Interpersonal Conflict*. 6th ed. New York: McGraw-Hill, 2001.
Wink, Walter. *Engaging the Powers: Discernment and Resistance in a World of Domination*. Minneapolis: Fortress, 1992.
———. *The Powers That Be: Theology for a New Millennium*. New York: Galilee, 1998.
Winter, Gibson. *Love and Conflict: New Patterns in Family Life*. Garden City, NY: Dolphin, 1958.
Wood, Alberta D., and Maureen C. McHugh. "Women Battering: The Response of the Clergy." *Pastoral Psychology* 42 (1994) 185–96.
Yang, Jang-ae, and Kyoung-ho Shin. "Vulnerability, Resilience and Well-Being of Intermarriage: An Ethnographic Approach to Korean Women." *Journal of International Women's Studies* 10 (2008) 46–63.
Yeh, Kuang-Hui, and Olwen Bedford. "Filial Belief and Parent-Child Conflict." *International Journal of Psychology* 39 (2004) 132–44.
Yi, Kyu-tae. *Han'gukin ui Uisik Kujo*. Vol. 1. Seoul: Mullisa, 1977.
———. *Han'gukin ui Uisik Kujo*. Vol. 2. Seoul: Sinwon Munhwasa, 1983.
Yi, U-jung. *Han'guk Sokt'am e nat'anan Yosong ui Piinganhwa*. Sinhak kwa Yosong: Han'guk Yosinhakja Hyopuihoe, 1987.
Yoder, John Howard. *The Politics of Jesus: Vicit Agnus Noster*. Grand Rapids: Eerdmans, 1994.

www.ingramcontent.com/pod-product-compliance
Lightning Source LLC
Chambersburg PA
CBHW062017220426
43662CB00010B/1367